Socio-Ecological and Adaptation Challenges to Climate Change Mitigation

Mohinder Slariya, Ph.D.

ISBN-13: 978-1523648184
ISBN-10:152364818X

Preface and Acknowledgement

In modern time, climate change is one of the all-encompassing global environmental changes likely to have deleterious impacts on almost all spheres of life starting from natural, human systems, economies to all sorts of infrastructures. The risks associated with it needs a broad spectrum of policy responses and strategies at the local, regional, national and global level. The UNFCCC (United Nations Framework Convention on Climate Change) highlights two fundamental response strategies: *mitigation and adaptation*. While *mitigation* seeks to limit climate change by reducing the emissions of GHG (greenhouse gases) and by enhancing 'sink' opportunities, *adaptation* aims to alleviate the adverse impacts through a wide-range of system-specific actions (Fussel and Klein, 2002). Sensitivity to the issue of adaptation has grown over the last couple of years, particularly after the IPCC (Intergovernmental Panel on Climate Change) TAR (Third Assessment Report). Adaptation has now emerged as an urgent policy priority, prompting action both within and outside the climate change negotiations (Parry et al. 2005).

Conventional approaches to understanding climate change were limited *to identifying and quantifying* the potential long-term climate impacts on different ecosystems and economic sectors. While useful in depicting general trends and dynamic interactions between the atmosphere, biosphere, land, oceans and ice, this top–down, science driven approach failed to address the regional and local impacts of climate change and the local abilities to adapt to climate-induced changes.

The international community is continuing to grapple with the likely socio-economic and environmental impacts that shall result from climate change. The question that needs to be address is how adaptation to climate variability and change can be more fully integrated into development policies and what are the funding instruments for adaptation? IPCC 2001, has defined term adaptation as "adjustments in ecological, social or economic systems in response to actual or expected stimuli and their effects or impacts. While mitigation can be defined as the act of mitigating, or lessening the force or intensity of something unpleasant, as wrath, pain, grief, or extreme circumstances, which further can be simplified as the act of making a condition or consequence less severe.

Keeping in view of need of hour to raise issues related to climate change, an international conference on, *"Development, Biodiversity and Climate Change: Issues and Challenges"* populalrly known as *"Chamba Climate Meet-2014"* has been organised in the month of October, 2014. This volume entitled, *"Socio-Ecological and Adaptation Challenges to Climate Change Mitigation"* is an outcome of the papers contributed by different scholars coming from different parts of the world.

This volume has been divided in 19 chapters contributed by different scholars coming from different countries. The first chapter entitled, understanding physical dimension of natural springs in draught prone area of Sikkim Himalayas, contributed by Basanti Rai et.al is a case study while second chapter contributed by a scholar from Nepal, Dhanej Thapa, is climate risk affecting cropping pattern of Nepal? is a study of Hattibangai VDC of Rupandehi District and added a new dimension to existing cropping patterns related studies in Himalayas. Shifting from Himalayas, next chapater has been contributed by Gulab Singh on the title, eutrophication: a major issue and chapter is a case study of rohtak district of Haryana state in India. The fourth chapter contributed by Kiran Lata Damle based on the primary data based study conducted by her on migration in house dust mites: a review. Environmental problems due to land use changes in the coastal areas of Bangladesh, contributed by Md. A Mannan & Bidita Beg is a fine illustration to mitigate the problem of climate change.

Sixth chapter contributed by three scholars i.e. Meenal Jain, Meenakshi Mital & Matt Syal is a review of existing solar energy policies and rural electrification in schemes in India is an attempt of the scholars to highlight policies of the govt. An attempt of Pusp Komor & Jayasree Borah in form of chapter entitled, adjusting to livelihood and environment by using traditional dairy farming practice among Nepali community is based on primary data based study conducted in lower dibang valley in Arunachal Pradesh, India. The eighth chapter focuses on plant diversity of mangroves in estuarine ecosystem of Kali River in Uttrakannda district in India, is contributed by Puttaraju, K. & S. P. Bhanusri. Rakesh Vyas has presented conservation value of ruralscape in south-east Rajasthan on the one hand and on the other Ratna and Miyo Tyaeng has put local perspective in the hydropower development.

Dr. PB Reddy and GR Gangle has done post-mortem of IPCC on climate change and put their research based perspective. Migration because of climate change is a big issue and critically reviewed the climate induce environment and Demographic situation of Assam documented by Sailajananda Saikia Bishmita Medhi from mitigation perspective. Evolving framework for sustainable development in India from sustainable development point of view, expressed by Dr. Sandhya Gihar & Sanjeev Bhardwaj. Catastrophic decline in the census of vulture has been noticed in context of climate change, emphatically stressed by Dr. Sanjay Narang, Kiran Chauhan and ML Thakur in next chapter and the title of the chapter is important aspects associated with catastrophic decline of vultures in the Indian subcontinent.

The XVth chapter entitled, riparian zone of Kulsi river in form of landscape is an ecological study in pre-monsoon season by Shah Nawaz Jelill, Mridul Boral & Prasanta Saikia. Shailesh Yadav in next chapte has presented an appraisal of environmental legislations in India which will help to smothen the process of adaption and mitigation. Sustainable use of medicinal plants to control meloidogyne incognita as a strategy to fight root knot disease of crops in Rajasthan, India has been contributed by botanist Prof. Soumana Datta, Trivedi, Lily & P. C. Trivedi. The second last chapter has been contributed by a young scholar from Panjab University, Chandigarh Miss Sachna and title of her contribution is securitization of climate change highlighting issues, concerns and implications. The last chapter has been contributed by Dr. Kewal Krishan, young professor aiming to presenting another aspect of hydropower development in context of climate change and the title of his work is resettlement and rehabilitation policy: issues and challenges faced by executors in context of climate change.

Sometimes it seems very difficult to put on record gratitude to many people who had made remarkable contribution in such academic ventures. First of all I would like to thank all sponsors of the conference in general and Asia Climate Change Education Centre,

Jeju, South Korea and it's director, Prof. Jeong without whose collaboration it would never be a reality. I would like to thank all contributors/presenters/attendees of the conference who made the conference happened in general and contributors of this volume in specific.

I am thankful to Ministry of External Affairs/Home Affairs, Govt. of India for permission to organise such big event in chamba. My thanks is due to Department of Higher Education, Govt. of Himachal Pradesh for permitting me and Principal of my college, who gave me free hand and cooperation to organise the conference.

My thanks to due to all my teachers who teach me at all level, particular Dr. Kaistha, Prof. SK Sharma, Prof. OP Monga are few to count and also to all my friends for their emotional and academic support. I am also thankful to my students who extend their cooperation during whole project.

Last, but not least I am thankful to my mother for her blessings and my wife and daughter to their emotional support and my son for formatting and computer related assistance and discussion before finalising any part of the book.

I am feeling thrilled to present this volume in the hands of readers with a hope that this attempt will prove an academic feast to all. For any quarry please feel free to contact me at mkslariya@gmail.com.

Place: Chamba, Himachal Pradesh, India

Date: 23rd of January, 2016

Dr. Mohinder K. Slariya

Table of Content

Chapter-I

Understanding Physical Dimension of Natural Springs in Draught Prone Area of Sikkim Himalayas

Basanti Rai, S. Tambe, U.K Sinha, U. Lal and Amit Manger*

Abstract

Springs in forms of natural seepage of gravity flow groundwater are the main source of water for inhabitants of Sikkim Himalaya. More than 80 percent of rural population is primarily dependent on natural springs for drinking, household and agricultural purposes. Yet, this resource has got few attention in academic researches due to its scattered and uneven nature. The change in climatic conditions leading to erratic precipitation pattern, land use and land cover change, anthropogenic factors such as developmental activities (roads, buildings, tunneling etc.) have further impacted on recharge- discharge regime of springs which is leading to seasonal flow or permanently drying up.

This study has been carried out in the draught prone area of Sikkim with an objective to understand spring's dynamics; with regard to spring discharge relationship with rainfall pattern and spring catchment area characteristics. Thirteen springs of Duga block has been studied. An average dependency of 38 household per springs has been found. Spring discharge was measured on a bi-monthly basis. The spring discharge and rainfall are found to be highly correlated which means local precipitation is the main source for spring recharge. Analyzing the hydrogeological aspects of springs, paper suggests developing spring sanctuaries with artificial measures which helps to rejuvenate and augment the spring discharge in a sustainable way.

Key words: Natural Springs, Draught, Physical Dimension,

         Developmental Activities

---

*Research scholar, Assistant Professor, Sikkim University, Sikkim and Special Secretary Rural Management and Development Department Government of Sikkim, Gangtok

Introduction

Water is indispensable for sustaining life and it is significant for socio- economic and environmental sustainability. The three quarters of the world is covered by water, but most of it is saline. Of all the water on the Earth, the saline water present in the earth is 92 percent, 2 percent is locked in ice and only 1 percent is potable water. AS per ICIMOD report (2010), mountain areas cover 24 percent of the world's land surfaces and are home to 12 percent of the global human population with a further 14 percent living in their immediate vicinity. Most of the world's major rivers have their origin in the Mountains and more than half of the world's mountain areas play a vital role in supplying water to downstream region. Mountain has often been regarded as world's water tower which provides essential freshwater to people in the mountain and downstream through snow-fed rivers. However, the people living there are primarily dependent on scattered water resources in forms of springs and streams. A spring is places where water issues from the ground and flows or where it lies in pools that are continually replenished from below [10]. Likewise, Larry W. Mays defines spring as a concentrated discharge of groundwater appearing at the ground surface as a current of flowing water [8]. Therefore, springs are points on ground surface from where water gets discharged and replenished from underlying aquifers under some pressure. Aquifers are defined as a saturated geological formation which can yield sufficient quantities of water to wells and springs [9]. These sources are often reported being seasonal or permanently drying out. Various studies on springs in Western Himalaya shows the probable factors for the marked decline of spring discharge and incidence of springs becoming seasonal are due to change in climatic condition as well as anthropogenic factor. The anthropogenic factor includes the developmental activities such as construction of road, bridges, buildings and other project work.

In Sikkim, 80 percent of rural population is primarily dependent on natural springs for domestic and agricultural purpose [1]. Most of the springs are rain fed and precipitation pattern of the region usually gets influenced by local orographic features. The lower part of South and West district of Sikkim receives comparatively less amount of rainfall due to its location in rain shadow zone of Darjeeling Hills. The scarcity of water in Sikkim is becoming a major concern for local people and a challenge for government.

Some attempts have been made at policy making levels to improve the water security. Rural Management and Development Department, Government of Sikkim under the programme 'Dhara Vikas' for rural area water security have identified eight blocks of Sikkim as drought prone area viz. Duga, Namthang, Melli, Jorethang, Namchi, Sikkip, Soreng and Kaluk. Therefore, it is important to have systematic study on natural springs to emphasis on water security so as to make local community resilient with regard to changing environment.

The present study is an attempt to understand the characteristics of natural springs of drought prone area, the Duga block with regard to changing resource utilization and land use practices. The growing populations, changing land use pattern and changes in climatic condition have brought new challenges in the area. It has high impact on the scattered water resource. The results are seen especially in marked decline in spring discharge; in some cases springs have become seasonal. Thus, scarcity of water has impacted on physical as well as socio- economic and physical landscape leaving tremendous impact on micro environment.

Study Area

The study has been carried out in the thirteen springs of Duga block in Eastern part of Sikkim Himalaya, which is located between 27.19 to 88.52 E and altitude ranges from 711 to 1830 meters. The total geographical area of study site is 65 km2. Duga has been considered as among the driest part of Sikkim by RMDD, Government of Sikkim under [5].

Climatic conditions

Precipitation

The local climatic condition and orographic features plays an important role in rainfall distribution. Duga receives highest mean rainfall in the month of August (1466±233) and diminishing trend starts from onset of September to February. Though the Eastern Himalayas receive abundant rainfall, but a large proportion of it is restricted to the monsoon season. Further study on climate data available from Gangtok indicates that winters are becoming increasingly warmer and drier with October to February being the exceptionally dry period [4].

Temperature

Duga exhibits a temperate climate condition with temperature ranging between 4-30oC at lower altitude (around 700 m) and at 1-25oC at moderate altitude (around 1750 m). The maximum temperature is observed during the month of July and minimum during the month of January. The weather of Sikkim can be divided into four seasons, namely winter (November- February); spring (March-April); Monsoon (May – mid September); and autumn (Mid-September- October).

Geology

Duga watershed is characterized by granite gneiss (mylonltic) lingtse gneiss in patches and interbedded chlorate- sericite schist/ phyllite and quartzite and blotetit quartzite of Gorubathan formation of Dailing Group. The Daling group (sensu lato) of Darjeeling- Sikkim Himalaya is characterized by distinct tectono- stratigraphic position being placed below high grade gneiss rocks limited by the sheared belt of mylonite granite gneiss. The formation consists of mappable, monotonous sequence of inter banded chlorite sericite schist / phyllite, quartzite, metagreywacke, pyritiferrous black slate/ carbon phyllite, basic metavolcanic. Chlorite phyllite is dark green to light green whereas the quartz chlorite phyllite is only light green in color. Intercalation of quartzite and chlorite schist is observed in Rongpo, Duga, Pandem, Singtam area. Quartzites are mainly white to light green in color depending upon the percentage of chlorite in them. They are also observed as grey to buff at places. Mostly these are fine grains in size and massive in nature [3].

Map 1.1: Block map of Sikkim showing study area- Duga, along with natural springs.

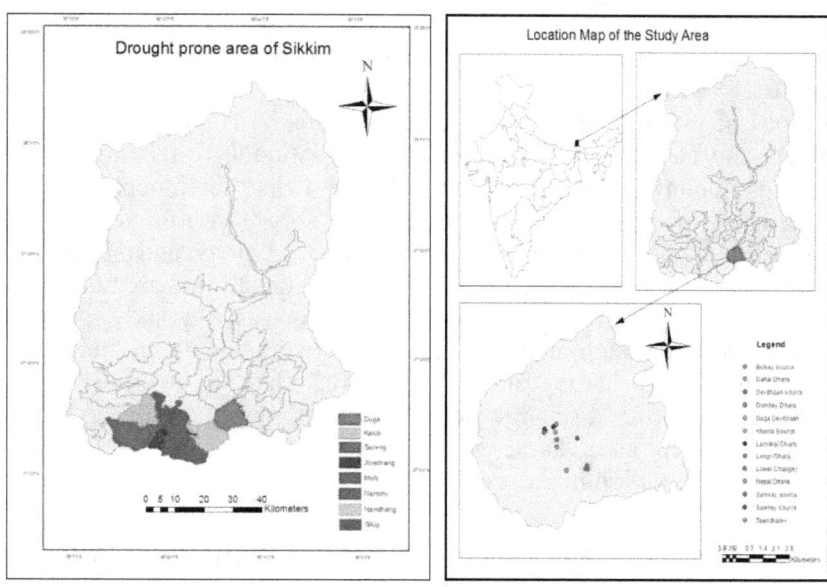

[Drought prone areas of Sikkim including Duga block (left), location map of study area with springs (right)].

Methodology

Water samples were collected from 13 spring sites across Central Pendam watershed in Duga block from March 2013 to March 2014. The discharge of the spring water is measured with the help of stop watch and jar (in L/Minute). Other parameters such as spring catchment area characteristics including geology, land use type, vegetation type, household dependency, land ownership and spring type were collected based on extensive field survey. The correlation between spring catchment area characteristics and spring discharge is being analyzed on EVIEWS software. The rainfall data of Duga is acquired from Automatic Weather Station (AWS) through ISRO. The graphical representation of rainfall and spring discharge is shown using

ORIGIN software. The co-ordinates of each spring are taken using GPS and showed their location in GIS platform.

Results and Discussion

Springs catchment area characteristics

The steep topography of Duga with and elevation ranges from 711 meters to 1830 meters suggests gravity springs are mostly available. Two types of gravity springs have been identified viz. Fracture (see plate 1.1) and Depression Spring which are continuously feeding by underlying unconfined aquifers. It is observed that catchment area characteristics of these springs varies considerably from one another with respect to elevation, land use, vegetation, geology and spring type etc. (see table 1.1 and 1.2). Most of the catchment areas are under multiple land use. The rainwater during monsoon season quickly runs off down slope through natural drainage networks, without much retention in the recharge zones. Therefore, there is a need to understand the spring discharge behavior as influenced by different recharge/catchment area characteristics to develop strategies for long term water conservation in the area.

Plate 1.1: A fractured lithology in the crest of Gadi (left), Outcrop of Gneiss in Devithaan source (right)

Table 1.1: Spring catchment area characteristics- elevation of springs, rock type and spring type

Sr. No.	Spring Name	Location	Elevation (in mts)	Rock type	Spring Type
1	Lamshal	Karmithang	1588.7	Gneiss	Fracture
2	Devithaan	Sajong	1453.8	Gneiss	Fracture
3	Dhalay	Bhurung	1447.7	Gneiss	Fracture
4	L. Changey	Deorali	806.5	Quartzite	Fracture
5	Bhulkey	Deorali	811	Quartzite	Fracture
6	Duga Devithaan	Duga	952	Quartzite	Depression
7	Teendharay	Bhurung	1128	Gneiss	Fracture
8	Khanal	Karmithang	1509.2	Schists	Fracture
9	Sawney	Karmithang	1389.6	Schists	Fracture
10	Nepal Dhara	Bhurung	1514	quartzite	Fracture
11	Dorkhey Dhara	Bhurung	1275	quartzite	Fracture
12	Samkey	Deorali	702.8	Schists	Fracture
13	Langri Dhara	Karmithang	1486	Quartzite, Schists	Fracture

Linkages between spring catchment area characteristics and spring discharge

It found that catchment area characteristics such as geology, spring type, vegetation, and land use type are the main controlling factor for recharge-discharge regime of springs. The degraded land with high biological interference and grazing lands has negative impacts on spring recharge discharge regime [2].

Table 1.2: Spring catchment area characteristics- household dependency of each springs, land ownership, land use in the catchment area and observed vegetation types

Sr. No.	Spring Name	Land use in Catchment	HHD*1	Vegetation in the spring catchment area (Botanical names)2
1	Lamshal	Agricultural field, thin vegetation cover.	27	Ficus Bengalensis, Musa Sapiendis, Arundinasia recemosa, Datura surveolens.
2	Devithaan	Dense vegetation, agricultural field.	70	Terminalia myriocarpa, Schima wallichii (M), Betula alnoides, Acer oblongum.
3	Dhalay	Dense vegetation, agricultural field.	25	Datura surveolens, Bombax ceiba, Acer oblongum, Albizzia procera, Spondias axillaris, Arundinasia recemosa.
4	L. Changey	Agricultural waste land and thin vegetation cover.	12	Bombax ceiba, Bauhinia purpurea, Grewia optiva, Ficus bengalensis.
5	Bhulkey	Agricultural field, wasteland and thin vegetation cover.	13	Albbiza procera, Ficus bengalensis, Gmelin arborea, Bombax ceiba,
6	Duga Devithaan	Dense vegetation, agricultural	12	Ficus bengalensis, Arundinasia racemosa, Bischofia javanice,

---

[1] *Household Dependent on natural springs.

[2] CRC World Dictionary of Medicinal and Poisonous plants: Common names, Eponyms, Synonyms and Etymology, published by CRC Press, May 2012. It is written by Umberto Quattrochhi.

		field.		Elaeocarpus Ganitrus Roxb, Schima wallichii (M), Terminalia myriocarpa.
7	Teendha ray	Agricultural field, thin vegetation cover.	120	Ficus Bengalensis, Thysanolaena maxima,
8	Khanal	Agricultural field, thin vegetation cover.	40	Ficus Bengalensis, Ficus, infectoria, Schima wallichii (M), Juglans regia, Arundinasia racemosa, Albizzia procera.
9	Sawney	Agricultural field, thin vegetation cover.	30	Ficus, infectoria, Terminalia myriocarpa, Brassiopsis hainl, Alnus nepalensis, Bombax ceiba.
10	Nepal Dhara	Dense vegetation, agricultural field.	30	Arundinasia racemosa, Datura surveolens, Arundinasia racemosa, Ficus rosenbergii, Brassiopsis hainl, Prunus cerasoides.
11	Dorkhey Dhara	Dense vegetation, agricultural field.	25	Erythrina stricta, Ficus Bengalensis, Ficus infectoria, Ficus bengalensis, Arundinasia racemosa, Schima wallichii (M),
12	Samkey	Agricultural field, wasteland and thin vegetation cover.	40	Ficus bengalensis, Albizzia procera, Ficus religiosa, Bombax ceiba, Arundinasia racemosa, Bauhinia purpurea.
13	Langri Dhara	Agricultural field, thin vegetation cover.	80	Arundinasia racemosa, Musa Sapiendis, Bauhinia purpurea, Datura surveolens, Brassiopsis hainl.

A positive correlation (r= 0.156966) has been found between geology of the catchment area and spring discharge (see table 1.3). This means geology is the main controlling factor for influencing amount and pattern of spring discharge. Likewise, the land use type also has a positive relationship with spring discharge (r= 0.171235), which means the changes in land use type by a unit results increases or decrease in spring discharge. It implies that spring catchment area under agricultural land and forest cover found to be conducive for spring recharge- discharge process than the area under wasteland and high biological interference.

Table 1.3: Correlation matrix of spring type, rock type and land use type with spring Discharge

Item	Spring Discharge	Spring Type	Rock Type	Land use Type
Spring Discharge	1			
Spring Type	-0.13678	1		
Rock Type	0.156966	0.030429	1	
Land use Type	0.171235	0.365148	-0.35	1

However, a negative correlation (r= -0.13678) has been found between spring discharge and spring type. The different vegetation types have different capacity to hold the water and also have varied evapotranspiration capacities. Negi et al., found that oak forest are conducive for spring recharge. The large variety of vegetation type in spring catchment area could not allow drawing relationship with spring discharge or recharge, which requires further study to see the level of impacts.

Rainfall and Spring Discharge Analysis

Rainfall trend of Duga

The local climatic condition and orographic features plays an important role in rainfall pattern as such Duga block lies in rain shadow zone of Darjeeling hills and receives relatively less rainfall than other parts of the state. The southwest monsoon, from the months of July to September, is responsible for 80% of the total annual rainfall in the state.

The rainfall trend of the last three years of the study area shows that rainfall starts increasing from June to August and diminishing trend starts from onset of September (see figure 3.14). The period from January to May is driest period. The highest mean rainfall has been recorded in August 2010 (1466±233) and the same month of 2011 (886±74). It is also shown that the amount of rainfall has been decreased from 2010 to 2013. High rainfall variability has seen in the area. An intense rainfall has been observed from the month of June to August, leaving other months with relatively less rainfall. This indicates the high surface run off and less water infiltration, which further indicates less water for recharging aquifers.

Linkages between rainfall and spring discharge

The spring discharge has increased drastically following the rainfall trend in the area. Springs like Devithaan source, Dhalay Dhara, Duga Devithaan source, Nepal Dhara, Lamshal Dhara and Dorkhey Dhara showed a high discharge exactly coinciding with high rainfall in month of August and drastic decrease in discharge as rainfall goes down. The mean rainfall of August 2013 was 400 mm and their discharge was 98, 27, 96, 188, 98 and 32 L/ Min respectively. In the following month (October), mean rainfall decreased to 26 mm and the spring discharge also decreased as Devithaan source with 13.8, Dhalay Dhara with 15, Duga Devithaan source with 15, Nepal Dhara with 13.5, Lamshal Dhara with 15 and Dorkhey Dhara with 27 L/Min.

Figure 1.1: Rainfall and spring discharge Figure 1.1.1 Rainfall trend of Duga from relationship

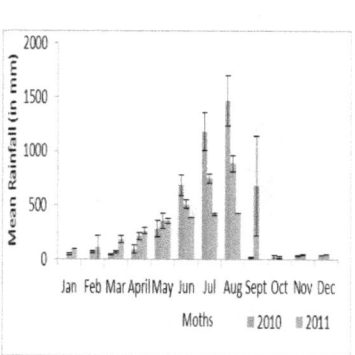
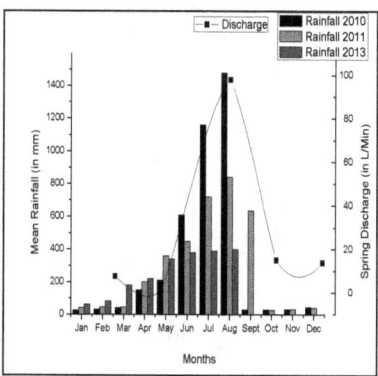

Figure 1.1.2: Lamshal Dhara Figure 1.1.3: Devithaan Source

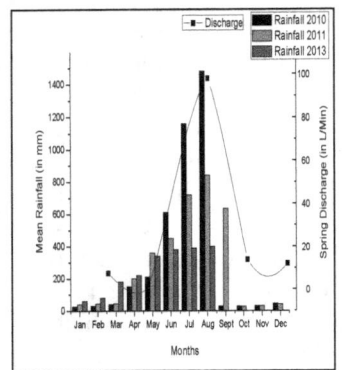 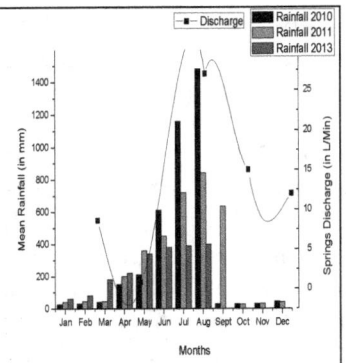

Figure 1.1.4: Dhalay Source Figure 1.1.5: Lower Changey

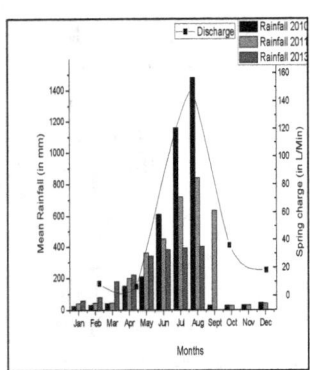 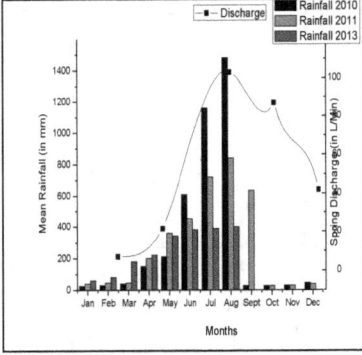

Figure 1.1.6: Bhulkey Source Figure 1.1.7: Duga Devithaan

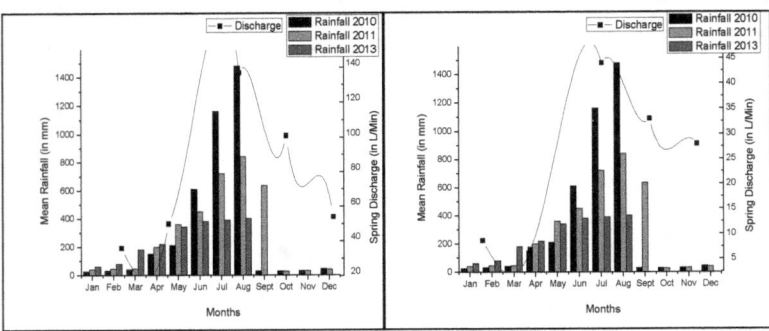

Figure 1.1.8: Teendharey source   Figure 1.1.9: Khanal Dhara

Figure 1.1.10: Sawney Source   Figure 1.1.11: Langri Dhara

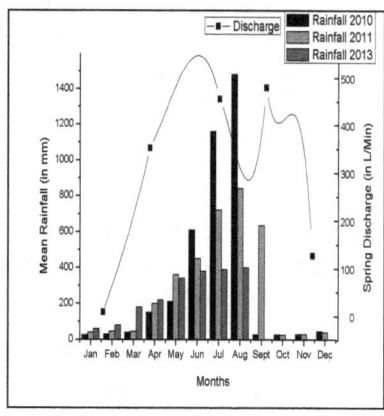 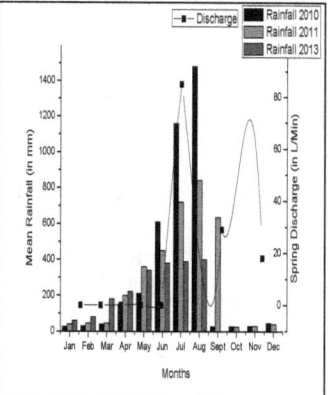

Figure 1.1.12: Samkey Source   Figure 1.1.13: Nepal Dhara Figure

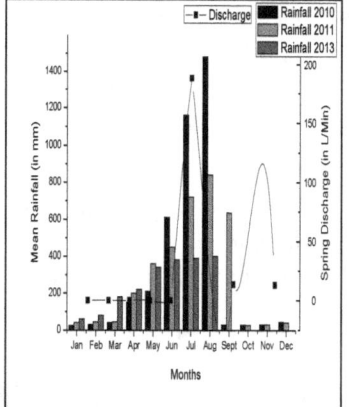 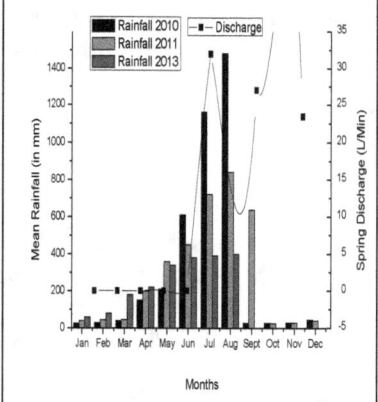

[Relationship between rainfall (in mm) and spring discharge (in L/Min)].

Other springs like Lower Changey source, Sawney source and Samkey had slow decrease of discharge in post monsoon period with 36, 33 and 29 L/Min. Some springs such as Teendharay source, Khanal Dhara and Bhulkey Source had good discharge rate in post monsoon period. In August (peak period), their discharge was 137, 340, 103 L/ Min respectively. It was decreased to 101, 163, 87 L/Min respectively in month of October. It is also observed that Langri Dhara is the only spring which had high discharge in post monsoon period. In peak month (August), the discharge was recorded to be 456 L/Min and in post monsoon period (October), the discharge was increased to 480L/Min.

The lowest discharge of the springs recorded in the month of March-May. The discharge of Lamshal Dhara, Devithaan source and Dhalay Dhara was recorded less than 1 L/Min during same month. Likewise, the highest discharge was recorded in the month of August. It is observed that high spring discharge coincides with peak rainfall period. Other important observation is the pace of increase in spring discharge following the rainfall pattern is slower than pace of decrease. In other words, in case of post monsoon period the discharge of spring decreased drastically except one spring (Langri Dhara).

However, it is observed that spring discharge did not increase immediately after onset of rainfall. This means, aquifers that are feeding natural springs needs considerable time for recharging it.

Plate 1.2: Spring discharge during peak rainfall period (left) and lean period (right), Khanal Dhara   Duga block

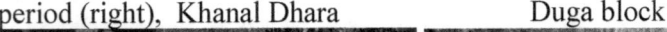

Findings and Discussion

The catchment area of springs found to be heterogeneous from one another. However, the catchment area characteristics are being found positively correlated with spring discharge pattern. This further implies that catchment area characteristics such as geology and type of land use are the controlling factor and has strong linkages with spring recharge and discharge regime. The catchment area with healthy vegetation cover and agricultural land are found to be conducive for good spring discharge than waste land and barren land with little vegetation. However, a negative relationship has been found between spring type and spring discharge. This may be due to occurrence of only one depression spring and dominant of fracture spring. The inclusion of more type of spring may give better results.

The rainfall trend and the discharge pattern of the springs show high interdependence. The most of springs have followed the rainfall trend there by indicating rainfall as the main source of water for recharging the aquifers underlying below. The analysis of last three years rainfall data shows decreasing trend of rainfall amount in the area.

This further indicates less amount of rainfall is able to percolate into the grounds and it may have probable impacts on discharge pattern. Over the last few years, the discharge from the spring as observed by the local community has shown a marked decline as well [6]. This decrease of spring discharge has resulted in an acute shortage of drinking water and a shift in land use pattern.

Conclusions

The Duga block with its steep and irregular topography presents variability in catchment area characteristics including geology, land use, vegetation, spring type and rock type. Interplay of all these factors affects the water yield and nature of both perenniality and seasonality of springs. The precipitation pattern is the main controlling factor which largely affects the rain fed springs. The impact of climate change leading to marked decline in amount and intense rainfall has exacerbated the condition. The occurrence of intense rainfall in short period of time indicates high run off and low percolation into the surface. This further means low chances for recharging the ground water. Analyzing the hydrogeological aspects of springs, paper suggests developing spring sanctuaries. It is an also suggested to strengthen the artificial measure based on rainwater harvesting to rejuvenate and augment the spring discharge of lean period. The rainwater trapping structures such as trenches, pit dams, walls will not only help to recharge the aquifers but also reduce mud flow and landslides.

References

[1] Sandeep Tambe, Ghanashyam Kharel, M. L. Arrawatia, Himanshu Kulkarni, Kaustubh Mahamuni and Anil K. Ganeriwala, Reviving dying springs: climate change adaptation experiments from the Sikkim Himalaya, International Mountain Society, Mountain Research and Development, 32(1):62-72. 2012.

[2] G.C.S. Negi and V. Joshi, Rainfall and Spring Discharge Patterns in two Small Drainage Catchments in the Western Himalayan Mountains, India, The Environmentalist, 24, 19-28.2004.

[3] Sri Subhra Suchi Sarkar, Md. Amjad Ali and Gargi Bhattacharya, Geology and Mineral Resources of Sikkim, General Geology, (Director General, GSI, 27 J. L. Nehru Rd. Kolkata -700016, 2012) 6-24.

[4] K Seetharam, Climate change scenario over Gangtok, Mausam 59 (3):361-366, 2008.

[5] G.C.S Negi and V. Joshi, Geohydrology of spring in mountain watershed: The need for problem solving research, current science, vol. 71 no 10, 25. 1996.

[6] Basanti Rai, Conservation and Management of Water Resources: A Case study of Duga, Sikkim Himalaya, V.P Sati (Ed.), Management of Natural Resources for Sustainable Management: Challenges and Opportunities, (New Delhi: Excel India Publisher, 2014) 101-108.

[7] Mirjam Macchi and the Team, Climate Change Impact and Vulnerability. InternationaCentre for Integrated Mountain Development GPO Box 3226, Kathmandu, Nepal, June 2010.

[8] Larry Mays, Ground and Surface Water Hydrology, (United States of America, Don Fowley, 2011).

[9] C.W Fetter, Applied Geohydrology, Fourth Edition, (New Jersey, Prentice Hall: Inc., 2001).

[10] Kirk Bryan, Classification of Springs, The journal of Geology, 522-561. 1919.

[11] G.C.S Negi and V. Joshi, Drinking Water Issues and Development of Spring Sanctuaries in a Mountain

Watershed in the Indian Himalaya, Mountain Research and Development, 2002.

[13] Quattrochhi, Umberto. CRC World Dictionary of Medicinal and Poisonous plants: Common names, Eponyms, Synonyms and Etymology. CRC Press, May 2012.

Chapter-II

Is Climate Risk Affecting Cropping Pattern of Nepal? A study of Hattibangai VDC of Rupandehi District

Dhanej Thapa*

Abstract

With growing consensus on climate change impacts and its negative implications to agriculture, farmers of developed nations are adopting different new changes in agriculture. However it is still area to explore whether farmers of least develop countries have changed agricultural practices considering climate change impact or not. Therefore, the main objective of this research was to analyze changing cropping practices introduced by the local farmers of Hattibangai Village Development Committee (VDC) of Rupandehi district, Nepal. A mixed method approach was used for the study. Logit model was used to identify the determinant of agricultural changes. The qualitative data was obtained by key informant interview, focus group discussion, semi-structured household interviews, historical timeline and observations. Our research findings suggest that farmers have perceived climate risk such as drought and erratic rainfall and increasing summer temperature. However, their changes in current agricultural practices are not influenced by climatic risk. Multiple drivers such as market services, land holding and extension services etc. are critical factors to change current agricultural practices. Research finding also suggest that current change in cropping system is not sufficient for adopting long term sustainable agriculture practices. Farmers must need authentic climate information and alertness to adapt local consequences of climate change.

Key words: Climate Change, Risk, Perceptions, Cropping Pattern, Rice-Wheat System

---

* South Asia Institute of Advance Studies (SIAS), Kathmandu, Nepal

Introduction

Climatic risk is in every sector but agriculture is most sensitive sector to climate change and variability (Aggarwal, 2008), as it can be affected by change in temperature, radiation, rainfall, soil moisture and carbon dioxide (CO_2) with complex relationships (Zhai and Zhuang, 2009). Different climate change impact and sensitivity analysis conducted in global and regional level have suggested decline in global food production (Rosenzweig and Parry, 1994; Grace et al., 2003; Parry et al., 2004). However, climate change impact in agriculture is not uniform to all regions (Warren, 2006). South Asian agriculture suffers more as three-fifth of the cropped area is rainfed; annual success of the monsoon determines well-being of millions of farmers (Kelkar and Bhadwal, 2008).

Nepal, amongst the South Asia, is highly vulnerable and is ranked as a fourth most climate vulnerable countries in the world (Maplecroft, 2010). Its fragile agro-ecology, flood prone Terai region, weak infrastructural status, and poor economic condition put country to vulnerable state (Ministry of Environment [MOE], 2010).Agriculture, which is largest contributor to Gross Domestic Product (GDP) of Nepal, is highly climate sensitive since only 40 percent of arable lands have year round irrigation facility (Karkee, 2008). Since rice-wheat rotation dominates the cropping system of Nepal; performance of rice-wheat crops determines the food security of Nepal. Rice-Wheat occupies more than 2.2 million hectare of land of Nepal (Ministry of Agriculture and Development [MOAD], 2012). It is the common cropping pattern of southern lowland region of Nepal. It is practiced in low land areas due to abundant fertile alluvial soils. However rice-wheat is also grown in lower altitude terraced hills and mountains, which provides substantial food to hill communities (Pandey et al., 2001; Pandey et al., 2009). In order to improve resilience on agricultural activities against ongoing and future climate change, we need to understand the impacts of climate on agriculture.

Climate change researches in Nepal are largely dominated by meteorological data analysis at national and sub-national levels (Shrestha et al., 1999; Practical Action, 2009; Department of Hydrology and Metrology [DHM], 2007). While understanding changes in agriculture practices and linkage with climatic stresses, farmer's perceptions are essential component.

Farmers are likely to perceive and monitor changes in climate systems to improve their farm management practices. They are particularly aware of local context and have good knowledge about the changes in climate and occurrence of climate related extreme events that need to be documented (Devkota et al., 2011). Linking scientific knowledge with farmer's perception can give insights which helps to measure the response of local people against climate change. Hence this research aims to understand how farmers of Terai region are cognized to climatic risk; and how they perceived such climatic stresses. The research also focused on the responses of local people against these stresses so as to adapt better cropping practices.

Methodology

Mixed method approach was taken for inquiry. As far as possible, my research questions quantified different changes in rice-wheat system such as different new cropping practices, production of different crops. Quantifying perceptions of people is not always possible. Qualitative approach gathers human experiences as a subjective experience, in different social context, and in historical timeline (Creswell, 2003). It is more about to uncover knowledge about how farmers think and feel about different climatic stresses and their adoption of new practices in local circumstances in which they find themselves.

The study site is Hattibangai village which is five kilometers northwest of Siddhartha municipality has been taken for detail study. It is well accessible by Lumbini highway that crosses through the middle of the village and all wards are also well connected with gravel roads. Tinau River, which is largest river of Rupandehi, passes through Hattibangai VDC. It almost touches more than four wards. Mixed caste group of Madhesi (Brahmin, Yadav, Kewat, Harijan, Kurmi, Hajjam) community is well dominant ethnic setting followed by Chaudhary and hill migrants (Bhramin, Chhetri and Magars). There are altogether 976 households among which only 28 hhs are headed by women. Ward no 4 is densely populated with more than 28 percent of total households. It comprises of religious diversity of Hindu, Muslim and Christian. Multi caste group of Madhesi community along with Chaudhary and hill migrants can be seen in this village consisting of multilingual, multiethnic and multi religious society.

However, there was overall dominance of Madhesi community in VDC. (Fig.1).

Figure 1: Map of Nepal and Rupandehi District

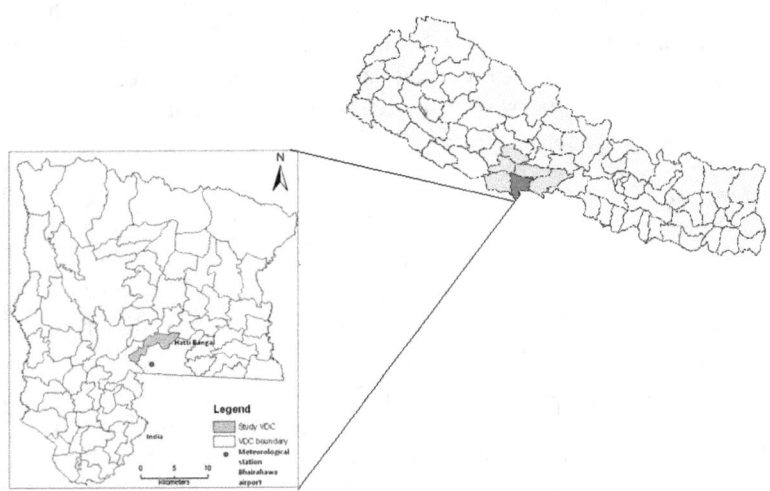

For the primary data collection, Hattibangai VDC was selected. There were altogether 976 households in the VDC. Simple random sampling was done with the assumption that all the households are more or less involved in agriculture or they were involved in past. Also possible adverse climate events are similar to every one of the VDC. I chose 97 hhs which is 10 % of total hhs for sample survey. As thumbs of rule, I assumed that 10 % will represent the overall households of that area. In some household surveys 5 to 10 % of total households were taken as a standard size of sample (e.g., Turner, 2003). The key informant interview was taken with district level agricultural agencies, experts and leaders of farmer networks. Key informant interview at district level helped to select research site of district. Informal interview with key informants was carried out to know about changing cropping pattern, water availability, extreme climatic events and uncertainties etc. This also helped to cross check of farmer's experiences regarding different changes in cropping system. Focus group discussion was conducted with farmers' group (banana growers, vegetable growers and rice-wheat growers) who had initiated new agricultural practices.

Each focus group session was started with a very general and open discussion, their past and current cropping practices and problems faced by the group or villagers. Historical Timeline was done to draw noticeable changes in agricultural practices, different disasters, climate extreme events, epidemic of insects/pest were collected from old farmers. This would help to know about introduction of new cropping practices and its linkage with theses extreme events. Many relevant information were being obtained from the direct observation and transect walk during field survey. It helped for qualitative assessment of existing situation of the village and gather wide range of other information about settlement patterns, village resources, land use systems, new cropping patterns, crop stands etc.

For the data analysis and interpretation, the data collected from the respondents using structured interview and literature was subjected to descriptive statistical analysis such as frequently counts, percentage and mean. Qualitative data was assigned certain weightage and then converted into quantitative data. The data collected was analyzed by mean derived from five-point Likert's type scale as the following: 5 = strongly agree, 4= agree, 3 = don't know, 2= disagree, 1 = strongly disagree. Responses were rated according to their perceptions and the cut-off mean score was determined by adding the ratings up 5 +4 + 3 + 2 + 1 = 15) and dividing the sum by 5 to give 3.0 as the cut-off mean score. For each statement, the total score was divided by the number of respondents, for instance a statement like summer has become hotter' have responses of strongly agree (f =16); agree (f = 42); don't know (f = 19); disagree (f = 20) and strongly disagree (f = 0). It will now be worked as 16 x 5=80, 42 x 4=168, 19 x 3 = 57, 20 x 2=40 and 0 x 1 = 0. Then the sum of total score (80 + 168 + 138 + 47+0) becomes 345. The sum was divided by the total f thus, 345 / 97=3.55. In this case, 3.55 are the mean score which is greater than the cut-off mean score of 3.00. The ranking was done according to the mean values. The farmers were given choices to rank their perception on different indicators of changing cropping pattern.

Logistic regression analysis was done to analyze the climatic factors and non-climatic factors to influence farmer's choice to switch new crops. Binomial Logit (Acquah andOnumah, 2011; Fosu-Mensah et al., 2012). In Nepalese context, Shrestha (2011) used this logistic model to analyze changing cropping pattern in Central Hills and Central Terai of Nepal.

For the detail procedure and result interpretation Saha (2011) was useful.

He discussed about applying logistic model to interpret examination result data Qualitative data obtained from different tools like focus group discussion, key informant interview, field observation and open ended questions asked to household were translated, edited and categorized to different themes of changing cropping pattern, factors responsible for new changes and linkage with climatic stresses. These data were compared and analyzed with quantitative data obtained from survey. Few skeptic views were also kept in boxes.

Results

Major Agricultural Changes

Over the past several years, a number of farm level changes took place. The survey results showed significant changes in agricultural management practices at farm level.

More than 73 % HHs reported that they grow cereals crops as a major crop. Similarly, more than 37 % of HHs were growing fruits crops. Livestock and vegetable growers were also comparatively higher. Around 24.7 % respondents produced vegetable crops, while 29.9 % HHs were growing livestock crops. Famers were very less involved in poultry and fisheries (Figure 2). Most of the HHs practicing cereals before 10 years ago were significantly decreased in current year. While proportions of HHs adopting vegetables were significantly increased in recent years as compared to last 10 years. Similarly proportions of HHs adopting fruits were increased. Though different types of crops were practiced by farmers, the rice-wheat system still dominated the cropping pattern of Hattibangai area. However use of chemical was increased by 16 % as compared to 10 years ago. The use of chemical pesticides was even more. Farmers were aware of the bio-pesticides, they never used them and but depended on chemical pesticides.

Figure 2: Proportion of HHs on Different Types of Agriculture Practices 10 Years Ago and at Present

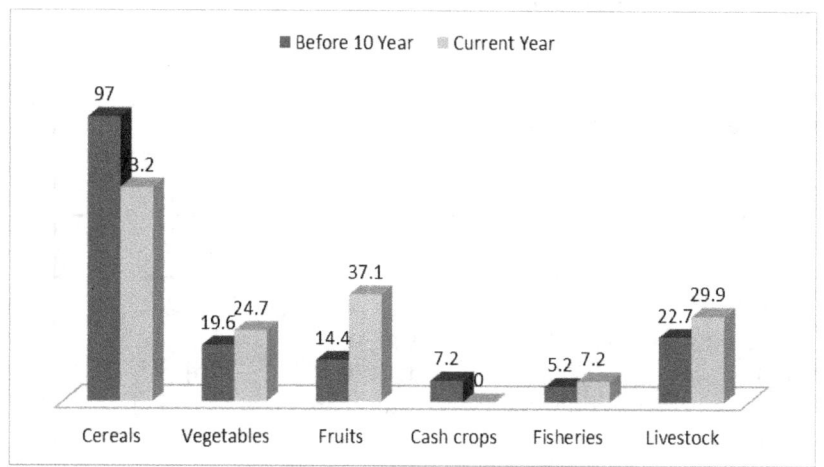

As Hattibangai village is a peri-urban area, it is gradually moving towards market agriculture. There was increasing trend of banana production, winter vegetable production, fruits crops, seed production of wheat crops and grain production of rice and wheat. Few traditionally growing crops such as gram, pigeon pea and others legume crops were being limited in lentil crops. However there was only 11 % increment in commercial growers. Subsistence farmers have slightly decreased (Fig. 2).

Figure Showing Status of Farmers

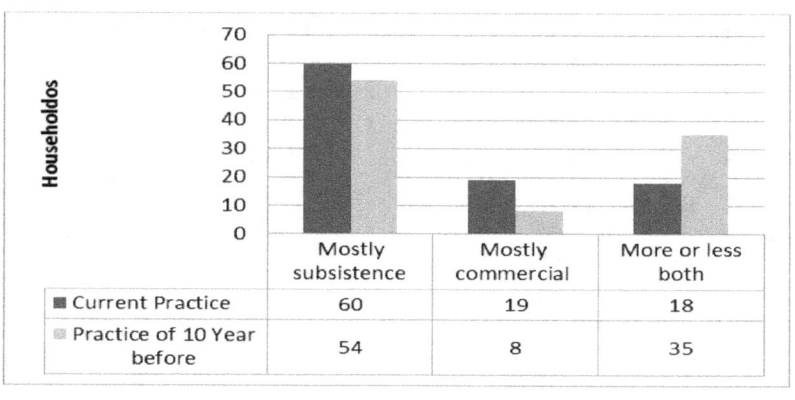

Source: Field Survey, 2013

Among rice-wheat growing farmers who didn't prefer to change different commodity, about 53.6 % of farmers have changed the varieties and use new pesticides in their farms.

Table 1: Status of Rice-Wheat crops and Change in the Varieties

Varieties of Rice-Wheat Crops			
10 years Ago		Current Year	
Rice	Wheat	Rice	Wheat
Sarju-49, S-52, Japani, Baburam, Sawa-Mansuli, Sabitrijanaki, Mansuli and Durga,	UP-62, UP-65, UP-92, Bhrikuti, Siddhartha RR-21, UP-262, NL-297, Sidhartha and Kundan	Gorakhnath, Radha-4, Jawahar, Hardinath, Loktantra, Barkhe-2	NL-297, UP 62, Bijay, Bhrikuti ,

Previously, farmers were cultivating rice-varieties like Sarju-49, Sabitrijanaki, Mansuli and Durga. Similarly, wheat varieties such as Bhrikuti, Siddartha, RR21, UP-262 and NL-297 were grown before a decade. In recent years, Sawa Mansuli, Gorkanath and Radha-4 varieties of Rice and Bijaya Brikuti variety of wheat were more popular and grown widely (Table 1). Similarly, rice-wheat farmers also changed previously practicing technologies and time of their cultural activity as compared to last 10 years. Wheat farmers felt that wheat growing season is being delayed. Around 91 % of farmers reported that they changed technology of preparing land. Similarly technological changes for harvesting were done by 70 % of farmers. While technological changes in pesticides and new agri-implements were done by 72 % and 66 % of respondents respectively. While analyzing the change of time of performing different cultural activity, 60 % of farmers changed time of land preparation.

Similarly 68 % of farmers changed harvesting time. While 69 % and 51 % of farmers have changed irrigation time and new varieties respectively (Table 2). Out of all eight agricultural practices mentioned, farmers continuing similar crops changed their crop management practices. However time related changes (changing time of agronomic management practices) were very less as compared to technological changes of crop management practices. Around 39 % of farmers have changed in sowing and transplanting technologies. More than 80 % of farmers were using Indian hybrid rice (Gorakhnath) and Nepali Radh-4 rice varieties.

Table 2: New changes in Agriculture Management Practices

Agriculture management practices Changes in		Percentage of HHs Changes
Land Preparations	Time	60
	Technology	91
New crops	Time	31
	Technology	54
Varieties	Time	70
	Technology	55
Sowing/transplanting	Time	39
	Technology	31
Use of pesticides	Time	51
	Technology	70
Irrigation	Time	69
	Technology	50
Harvesting	Time	68
	Technology	72
Post-harvest operations	Time	24
	Technology	51

New Practices: Changes in time of activity in cropping calendar and techniques use in performing different agronomic practices

Changing Dynamics of Agriculture of Gargatti Village

Farmers reported most noticeable changes within their farm during focus group discussion:

- Sowing of more than 2-3 varieties of each cereal crop by single farmers was common but now only one variety of rice or wheat was grown by most of the farmers.

- Use of single improved and high drought resistance varieties.

- Few large holders' farmers brought new machines from India and other small farmers taking spill over benefit from these machines.

- Use of short duration rice crops like hybrid Indian rice and Radha 4 rice. (Both giving higher yield and drought resistance).

- Vegetables and banana producing farmers were increasing. However, suffering with diseases and problem of insect pest infestations were increased.

Driver of Agricultural Change

It was noticed that none of the farmers cultivated cash crop. Framers reported that they used to grow sugarcane in large scale. But after political instability and continuous strike at sugar mill factory, farmers were compelled to leave out sugarcane farming. Famers remembered comparative benefit of sugarcane. Farmers of Maubari-6 said, "It used to give more profit and lesser burden to farmers. Once we transplant sugarcane, there is no necessary to replant for three years and also it needs very less intercultural operations". After the shutdown of sugar mill in Rupandehi, farmers have shifted to alternatives crops like banana, and many of them returned to rice-wheat system. It was found that all the farmers were growing mixed crops in their fields and no one had relied on single crops. Few selected smallholder and landless farmers were doing vegetable farming in active support of few NGOs. Similarly other households were also involved in vegetable farming as a kitchen garden.

Contribution of different NGOs and government program and VDC level program of vegetable seeds distribution has influenced the vegetable cultivation practices. Farmers were reluctant with previously growing rice-wheat crops for low income and increased risk of climate and market. Though different options like sugarcane cultivation was initiated by farmers. But it was left over after shutdown of sugarcane factory. With the initiation of few innovative farmers, they started new venture of commercial banana farming.

Usually the farmers used to seed wheat during final week of Mangsir. But now they shifted to the first week of Poush. Senior Scientist from National Wheat Research Program (NWRP), Mr. Nutan Raj Gautam told us that generally November 15 is used to be the appropriate time for wheat sowing, but now wheat sown 10 days later gives more yield.

In recent years, farmers started to use tractors for land preparation. After decline of bullocks, use of tractors became common among farmers. However, introduction of tractor is not new in Nepal; a large number of farmers were also using tractors previously. In addition, farmers were also using new machines like rotavetors for land preparation during winter season for wheat crops. This minimized the multiple tillage practices. Similarly, use of rotavetors solved the water stress problem for low soil moisture by multiple tillage practices. Larger holders' farmers introduced tractors and rotavators who could also earn money by leasing to fellow farmers. Most of the small-holder farmers used those machines for hour basis rent.

Market, especially agro-vet, food self-sufficiency situation, land holdings, climate awareness and GOs support were taken as dummy independent variables to influence farmers to switch new crops.

Table 3: Logistic Model: Different Non-Climatic Factors

Different Factors	B	S.E.	Wald	df	Sig.	Exp (B)
Landholding	1.312	.468	7.863	1	.005	3.714
Subsistence Farming	.414	.465	.790	1	.374	1.512
Climate Change awareness	-.081	.461	.031	1	.860	.922

Agro-vet	1.573	.729	4.657	1	.031	4.821
Contact with GOs	-1.160	.898	1.667	1	.197	.314

Field Survey, 2013

While analyzing five different non-climatic factors, contact with government organizations, climate awareness, subsistence farming were insignificant in explaining the influencing factors to switch new crops. In addition, small landholding farmers were 3 times more likely to switch new crops. Similarly, farmers consulting agro-vet were 4.8 times more likely to switch towards new crops (See Table 3).

Climate Risk and Linkage with Changing Cropping Practices

The results showed that an overwhelming majority of farmers perceived risk of climate to their existing cropping system.

Table 4: Perception of Farmers on Possible Change in Climate

Aspects of Climate change	HHs (%)	Negffects Hs) %)
Summer has become hotter	60	72
Winter has become colder	49	81
Winter has become hotter	41	42
Monsoon starts later	70	82
Monsoon rainfall difficult to predict	92	98
Overall monsoon rainfall period decreased	67	88
Wind damage to crop has increased	12	100
Drought has increased	50	68
Flood occurs more frequently	31	29
Hailstone has increased	11	20

In overall analysis, 60 % farmers reported that summer temperature has increased. Among of them, 72 % of farmers felt negative impact to their agriculture (Table 3). Rise of temperature during the summer can increase flow of heat wavers. This can negatively affect the grain formation of wheat seeds.

Even farmers have failed to analyze the chronological changes in temperature and precipitation of local areas. Farmers are confused within themselves and they are not able to map the exact change in climatic parameters. Some farmers experienced one kind of adversity of climate while other farmers felt different kinds of change in climatic parameters. About 68 % farmers experienced that monsoon starts earlier. Interestingly 70 % farmers mentioned that monsoon rainfall has delayed. More than 72 % famers believed negative impact on agriculture by delay rainfall. However 82 % farmers believed that negative impact due to delay rainfall. Overwhelmingly 92 % respondents told that it was difficulty in monsoon rainfall prediction and 98 % of farmers have felt negative impact on their agricultural decision making process. This ultimately affected their agriculture production. Talking about monsoons, 67 % farmers believed that overall monsoon rainfall was declined. Similarly 50 % percent farmers said that drought has increased and 68 % of farmers accepted negative impact on their agriculture. In case of floods, only 31 % farmers told that increase of rainfall. In the case of hailstone only 11 % farmers said that there was increment of hailstone occurrence. In case of wind damage to crop, only 12% famers told about damage by hailstone (Table 4).

Since climate perceptions were more complex and contested, it was difficult to draw conclusion about change in climatic parameters. So Famers' perception on climate change and overall ranking taken from weighted mean showed five major climate related changes perceived by farmers. Among the eleven different indicators of possible change in climate, only five of them were considered as important observation (See Annex II). Monsoon rainfall was difficult to predict, summer has become hotter, cooler winter and increasing winter temperature and drought were ranked from first to fifth.

In case of other climatic parameters, very few percentages of farmers perceived as a risk. Farmers reported flood, wind damage and hailstone as less important observations. However farmers reported some damage of hailstone and floods, which are discussed in later section.

While doing focus group discussion, farmers remembered different climate extreme events in different time periods. Farmers have also shared their memory and disorientation about climate extreme events and its negative effect to agriculture.

Farmers have experienced both drought and floods in different yearly intervals. Hailstone damage was also noticed by farmers during 1997. However its frequency of occurrence and damage was not noticed after that. While examining the trend of extreme events, we could observe that problems of flood were more till mid 90s whereas drought was more after mid 90s. Drought problem of 2007 was more severe and heavily damaged crops (Table 5).

Table 5: Historical Timeline of Climate Extreme Events

Year	Extreme Events
1981	Flood
1984	Floods
1989	Floods
1992	Drought
1995	Drought
1997	Hailstone
1998	Floods
2002	Hailstone damage (Insect pest infestation)
2007	2007 driest year
2008	drought
2011	drought

District stakeholder also emphasized that drought was increased in last 20 years, which adversely affected crop production. In recent years, especially three years ago, unpredictability of monsoon rainfall (and delay of rainfall) had largely affected agriculture leaving a large area of paddy cultivation fallow. District Agriculture Development Office (DADO) Officer of Rupandehi was puzzled with change in climate rainfall pattern.

Different people perceived climate related stresses very differently. Farmers linked their climate related learning with their local agricultural system. Rice growers were worried about uncertain monsoon rainfall. Delayed and uncertain monsoon left farmers in dilemma specially in raising the nursery bed. One of the farmers of Gargatti village of Rupandehi remembered:"It used to be delay in monsoon rainfall in the past years but this year it was early rain and we did not have rice seedlings for transplanting. Rainfall was continuous but we were unable to transplant rice".

However this is always not the case. In last few years, farmers have suffered with delay rainfall causing an over maturing problem of rice seedling prior transplantation. Chief of District Agriculture Development Office (DADO) added, "monsoon came early in last year and very less precipitation was seen in August and September, causing a drastic reduction in mid and late varieties like Sawa-Mansuli and Sunaulo Sugandha varieties of rice" Most of the farmers accepted the changes of climate in different manner. They have understood climate change phenomena according to their local farming system and their surroundings. While doing focused group discussion with farmers, they raised following climate issues and problems for their current agricultural practices (Table 6).

Table 6: Farmers General Perceptions on Climate and Weather

Most people said that rain this year started earlier.
In past year rain used to fall little bit later.
Overall duration of rain fall was short.
Everybody agreed that summer have become hotter and winter colder.
None of the farmers could tell us about the effect of temperature on crops.
Flood, hailstone and storm were not noticed from few years back.

Farmers opine that there used to be a regular pattern of monsoon in the past. Now without irrigation, they cannot plant their crops. Three years ago, a commercial banana farmer left his paddy field of five katthas fallow. He didn't care paddy rice. Irrigation from tube well was not sufficient. Famers who shifted to banana farming from rice-wheat remembered the damage of hailstone to entire crop. In the year of 1997, a banana farmer of Maubari area had grown banana in 6 bigha of land. Intense rainfall and hailstone damaged his entire banana crops. After that case, he and many other farmers have downsized their own cropping area. Now they have diversified there cropping areas with rice and wheat in some of the agricultural lands.

Risk and Uncertainty of Rainfall

While asking famers about their future risk perception, 49 % farmers said drought as very serious risk in future as well and 44 % percent farmers feel that somewhat serious. In case of flood, more than 38 % of farmers told that flood was very serious and 61 % of farmers said as somewhat serious (Table 7).

Table 7: Climate Fear/Suspect in the Future

Future Risks	Very Serious (%)	Somewhat Serious (%)	No Change (%)
Drought	49	44	7
Flood	38	61	1
Uncertainty of rainfall	22	77	1
Higher temperature in summer	27	72	2
Lower temperature in winter	17	83	0

Source: field survey 2013

In case of higher temperature in summer, 22 % of farmers said it is very serious and 77 % of farmers told that it is somewhat serious. Finally in case of low temperature in winter, 17 % of farmers reported that it will very serious while 83 % of farmers told that somewhat serious.

There was very negligible number of farmers saying no change for these five climatic risks for future.

Logistic regression model was used to identify influencing climatic factors that influence to switch to new crops. Late monsoon and hotter winter were insignificant to explain influencing climatic factors to switch crops. Farmers experiencing drought were 5.5 times more likely to switch new crops as compared to those who didn't experience drought as a problem. Similarly, farmers experiencing early winter more severe were 8 times more likely to switch new crops. Since the study was conducted in rain fed area, farmers significantly used tube wells for irrigation. Hot summer was significant but farmers were 0.144 times less likely to switch crops as compared to that respondent who didn't experience hot summer.

Table 8: Logistic Model: Different Climatic Factors

Climatic factors	B	S.E.	Wald	df	Sig.	Exp (B)
Drought	1.709	.563	9.225	1	.002	5.524
Monsoon Start Later	-.534	.585	.832	1	.362	.586
Summer Hotter	-1.941	.564	11.847	1	.001	.144
Post Winter Hotter	-.313	.777	.162	1	.687	.731
Winter More Severe	2.124	.810	6.878	1	.009	8.364

Source: Field Survey, 2013

Discussion

Market and Profit Factors

Though farmers of Terai are traditionally rice-wheat growers, farmers have either shifted to different agricultural practices or adopted new crop management practices. In overall, farmers are attracted towards vegetable production and kitchen gardening and fruits crops. Some of them are earning a bit from these enterprises. The annual report of district agriculture office showed that farmers of Rupandehi have gone through series of agricultural experiments in farm like, cash crops, vegetables, banana, fish and other new management practices (DADO, 2012). CCAFS sites in Rupandehi exhibit the highest levels of diversity in production, with over 50 % of surveyed households producing more than 8 different products (Kristjanson et al., 2011).

However, within the household, diversity of different products and crop variety was declining. Ojha et al. (2012) showed five major noticeable changes of rice-wheat system; technological changes in rice-wheat system, shift to short duration crops, new perennial crops replacing rice-wheat crops, new fish farm and agricultural land conversion to real state purpose. Farmers have experimented with and adopted alternative varieties of crops that are more resistant to risks or give better yields. Varieties of wheat like Bijay, Adhitya and Brikuti with such characteristics as early maturing, drought resistance, and tolerance to pests and diseases are popular among farmers of Rupandehi district (NWRP, 2011).

Farmers have adopted many improved varieties of rice and wheat crops of India as well. Some of them are released and registered varieties in Nepal, while some are not. Imported improved varieties of rice from India are Sarju-52, Sarju-49, Sawa-Mansuli and Gorakhnath Gold. Similarly fish farming, which gives a higher return in a shorter period than rice farming, has also been adopted by farmers as a response to the repeated problems of floods washing away the rice crops. As a result, farmers' income has increased due to fish farming but at the cost of a decreasing rice plantation area (Manandhar et al., 2010).

Market and profit factor played significant role in changing cropping practices. In similar research, Shrestha (2011) used this logistic model to analyze changing cropping pattern in Central Hills and Central Terai of Nepal. Due to expansion of urbanization, introduction of advanced technology in the agriculture systems and low returns in traditional farming systems, farmers of the Central Development Region of Nepal were compelled to change the traditional farming systems to modern systems. Famers consulting agro-vet get exposure on benefit from new crops as well as technical inputs for growing new crops. Farmers growing vegetable usually get technical information by agro-vet (e.g.Yadav Agrovet of Hattibangai).

Farmers were more attracted towards Indian varieties of crops. These were heavily subsidized from Indian government. Easy access of Terai farmers encouraged to adopt new Indian varieties. A related research of Tanzania shows that changes from cotton to rice and the increased use of manure as chemical fertilizer was due to change in factor prices, related to the removal of subsidies (ICRA,1990).

Market driven changes were also noticed in Hattibangai village. New changes from sugarcane to Banana were only possible after shutdown of Sugarmill. Farmers didn't get any market to supply their sugarcane. A research conducted by Connelly (1994) in Rusinga Island of Kenya showed that farmers abandoned many traditional intensive agriculture due to labor scarcity and the growing emphasis on the fishing industry. This study highlighted the importance of understanding not only the local ecology but also the broader political and economic environment in order to explain farmers' decisions and the process of agricultural change.

In our study as well, farmers are changing different cropping practices to cope with multiple stresses. However they have also equally emphasized market related opportunity. While categorizing their choices of cropping practices, comparatively smallholder farmers had done more number of changes in agricultural practices. Changing numerous practices helped them to gain higher economic return. Shifting from rice-wheat to sugarcane and then return to rice-wheat and finally to banana showed more number of changes.

Climate Risk and Agricultural Change

Manandhar et al. (2010) analyzed the climate data of 1977 to 2004 of Bhairahawa. The analysis of 30 years of temperature data showed slight increase in minimum temperatures while maximum temperatures remained the same. Few farmers' perceptions were matched with climate while others didn't. Around 42 % of respondent reported that intensity of rainfall was increasing. While precipitation analysis showed decline of rainfall during last 10 years. However in the precipitation of Butwal station, sharp increase in rate precipitation was observed (Annex III). Hence we can conclude that rainfall within district was also not evenly distributed. Rainfall data analysis of 30 year collected from the nearest meteorological station (Bhairahawa airport) highlighted the decreasing trend of precipitation in the area (Manandhar et al., 2010). This is linked with farmers' perceptions on increasing drought condition and increasing summer temperature.

Interestingly, drought was more emphasized by key informants and district stakeholders. Few leader farmers had emphasized the problem of drought. However our survey finding revealed drought as fifth important observation. This might be due to excess use of ground water for irrigation. Farmers were using their boring water for irrigation. Farmers in Hattibanagi area perceived decline of water table. Farmers reported that deep tube wells/ boring sets need to be further deepening for harvesting water. According to farmers' perceptions, water table declined from 180 feet to 280 ft. A research conducted by Dahal et al. (2012) suggested decline of water table in nearby areas. Even some of the Shallow Tube Wells (7.62 m) were dried during dry season (from April to June) in many cases in the vicinity of the Tinau River. However drying of Shallow Tube Wells (STW) was linked with excess riverbed extraction of Tinau River.

In same paper, it was clearly argued that decline of water table of deeper STW depths from 28.96 m to 36.58 were not affected by the extraction in the Tinau River. In case of Hattibangai and nearby VDCs, Bhairawa Lumbini Groundwater Project constructed numerous deep boring sets for irrigation purpose. Excess of ground water was harvested by deep boring sets. In case of declining precipitation, water table failed to recharge as per required. So we can conclude that decline of water table is more linked with decrease of precipitation.

Similar with our research finding, another research of Gauchan and Gumma (2009) showed that drought incidence has increased in Nepalese context. This study analyzed production and productivity by analyzing satellite images taken spatially and temporally on rice crops, drought years. This can be predicted that, with increasing climate change, such situation can be further devastating. Amgain et al. (2006) in their simulation study in Indian context indicated that increments in both maximum and minimum temperatures by 40 C decreases rice yield by 34 % and wheat yield by 4% as compared to base scenario with current weather data.

In case of Rupandehi, Manandhar et al. (2010) noticed possible climate adaptation options like new improved varieties, seasonal fluctuation and shift of more than month in cropping calendar of sowing and harvesting of rice and wheat crops. New varieties of rice crops and wheat crops can provide better yield in context of adverse climate context of very sparse rainfall.

In case of shift in cropping calendar, during normal rainfall, rice is grown from 1st week of June to 2nd week of October.

Similarly, wheat is grown from 3rd to 4th week of October to 2nd week of May. In case of late rainfall, rice is transplanted in 2nd week of August and harvested during 2nd to 3rd week of November. Wheat is sown in 1st to 2nd week of January and harvested during 2nd week of May. However, these practices adopted by farmers were short term strategic actions to cope with late rainfall. Permanent shift in cropping calendar was not observed. In our research, it was observed that farmers were adopting multiple new agricultural practices within rice-wheat cropping system. Some farmers switched to new crops when they found risk of drought and higher chances of crop failure.

Some farmers switched to new crops when they saw higher benefit in next crops. In addition some of the farmers shifted to new crops when they found climatic risk in pre-existing crops and saw benefit in new crops. In few cases, farmers' perception towards climate risk like drought encouraged them to search for alternative options such as ground water harvesting. Very few farmers shifted to new time of sowing rice-wheat crops or switched to new-crops after perceiving risk of climate.

Farmers have changed different new varieties to cope with different climatic stresses. Through survey finding and interaction with group of farmers, it was known that they have adopted new varieties to cope with drought problem and uncertainty of rainfall. However climate stress was not sole factor to change cropping practices. Farmers responded multiple stresses to adopt new cropping practices. Also multiple strategies were taken by farmers to adopt with climatic stresses. Same farmers were doing multiple activities for a single problem. So there was not clear linear relationship with climatic parameter and its changing new cropping practices.

So in overall, we can conclude smallholders' famers are more likely to switch new crops. Compared to the services provided by government, farmers were more influenced by market activities. Farmer's decisions were influenced mainly by agro-vet available in market. Above logistic model suggests that farmers who have experienced drought are more likely to switch crops. However their decisions are much more influenced by their landholding size and extension services provided by agro-vet.

Cropping System and Sustainability

The analysis of changing dynamics of agriculture system has identified issues in relation to the sustainability and effectiveness of such practices. Several fault lines are seen in changing cropping practices and its process. The intensive monocultures of wheat and paddy have displaced other crops like pulses, maize and mustard and other cash crops which were grown earlier. Though few farmers have shifted to new crops but most of the farmers are still doing rice-wheat crops. Currently farmers are more encouraged for mono-cropping of single varieties of rice and wheat.

It was noted that more than 80 % or rice field was dominated with Indian hybrid rice and Nepali drought tolerant Radha-4 varieties. Current agriculture is more climate sensitive as compared to previous farming system of diversified local crops and varieties.

Similarly, if the intensive cropping with harvesting ground water for irrigation continues then problem of water scarcity may arise in days to come. The case of Punjab is in front of us where the depth of water table ranged from 8.7 to 23.89 meters during pre-monsoon and from 9.95 to 22.41 meters during post monsoon. Declining water table was a major problem in Sangrur due to excessive use of water for paddy cultivation and poor recharge (Ojha et. al., 2012). Farmers of Rupandehi has also felt water table decline of their deep tube well and boring sets. An increment of 20-30 feet depth is necessary in current days to reach water table. Similarly, sharp decline in livestock production has also encouraged farmers to use more chemical fertilizers. Increasing trend of use of chemical fertilizers and less use of FYM could create serious soil problem in days to come. Farmers are already suffering with less water holding properties of soil. Continuous growing of banana with wheat in every three years could further degrade soil quality. A previously practiced legumes crops is completely abandoned by banana famers. Ecological sustainability could be a great issue in days to come. Excess use of chemical fertilizers, pesticides and mono-cropping of banana could create soil problem in banana farms. In terms of achieving higher economic return, farmers might suffer with negative consequences of mono-cropping. Farmers adopting mono-cropping and using excessive pesticides created wider health and environmental effects. Market driven changes are not always agriculture friendly.

A research conducted by Connelly (1994) in Rusinga Island of Kenya shows that farmers have abandoned many traditional intensive agricultural practices and shifted to fish farming which led to a chronic shortage of food on the island.

In overall, agricultural changes has several fault lines which must be seriously considered. Issues like mono-cropping, decline of legume crops and excessive use of ground water can have several negative implications. This needs in-depth analysis on the dynamics of changing cropping practices in the study area.

Conclusion

Firstly, my study shows that farmers of Hattibangai are changing cropping practices. However, their agriculture changes are their short-term strategic action. Farmers are more attracted towards few crops and varieties in terms of achieving higher economic benefit. Current shift in rice-wheat system to vegetables, fruits, new varieties of rice-wheat and adoption of new machines shows that agriculture practices are increasingly changed in this part of Nepal have some serious future challenges. Continuous harvest of ground water for irrigation, mono-cropping, and increasing use of chemical fertilizers and pesticides have shown some negative implications in current agricultural practices.

Secondly, farmers change cropping practices when they find risk in their current practices. Comparatively, more number of changes are done by food insufficient households. However their choices of new practices are shaped by different local institutions and market. Role of private agro-vets and support from government played significant role in changing cropping practices. Farmers learn and do experiment in their agriculture practices. They change their cropping practices after some shock/disorientation felt in their existing cropping practices. However multiple risks can influence cropping practices. In context of Hattibangai, farmers have experienced market related shock of sugar mill shutdown. They have also suffered with scarcity of popular wheat seeds and chemical fertilizers. They have experienced the disasters of climate extreme events and epidemics of insect pest infestation. So farmers are always in search of more secure and sustainable agriculture. Farmers speculate such risk and search for new interventions. They have perceived possible change in climate and taken it as a threat for their agricultural depended livelihood.

However their current changing cropping practices are less influenced by climatic risk perceived by farmers. Farmers' perception towards climate is not part of their systemic analysis of long-term changes in climate. Farmers are aware of noticeable variation in weather patterns. Basically their perceptions towards change in climate are induced with negative effects in their local agriculture such as epidemics of insect pest problem, farmers suffering in transplanting of rice and sowing of wheat seeds.

Farmers linked their problems with hot summer days, erratic nature of monsoon rainfall and drought. Besides autonomous induced perceptions, farmers do not have access to knowledge developed by climate scientist. Their climatic perceptions vary with each other and match with only some climate data. Additionally, their perceptions contradict with long term changes in climatic parameters like precipitation and temperature.

Finally I argue that though farmers are adopting different practices to adapt to current environmental change and other socio-economic drivers, this is not sufficient for adopting long term sustainable agriculture practices. Farmers need authentic climate information and alertness to adapt local consequences of climate change.There is no doubt that farmers are active agent of change; they speculate the changing circumstance and adopt new changes. However, their concerns are more on addressing short term changes in their agricultural field.

Reference

1. Acquah, H.D. and Onumah, E.E. (2011). Farmers perception and adaptation to climate change: a willingness to pay analysis. Journal of Sustainable Development in Africa, 13(5), 150-161.
2. Aggarwal, P.K. (2008). Global climate change and Indian agriculture: Impacts, adaptation and mitigation. Indian Journal of Agricultural Sciences, 78, 911-919.
3. DADO. (2012). Annual progress report, district agriculture development office. Rupandehi, Nepal.
4. Dahal K. R., Poudyal C.P., Adhikari, P., Sharma, S., and Ghimre, J. (2012). Effects of riverbed extraction on ground water resources in the vicinity of Tinau river, Rupandehi, Nepal Journal of Science and Technology, 13(2), 133-140
5. Department of Hydrology and Meteorology (DHM). (2007). Climate change scenarios for Nepal based on regional climate model RegCM3. Kathmandu, Nepal: DHM.
6. Devkota, R.P., Bajracharya, B., Maraseni, T.N., Cockfield, C., and Upadhyay, B. P. (2011). The perception of Nepal's Tharu community in regard to climate change and its impacts on their livelihoods. International Journal of Environmental Studies, 68(6), 937-946.
7. Fosu-Mensah, B.Y., Vlek, P.L.G., and MacCarthy, D.S. (2012). Farmers' perceptions and adaptations to climate change: A case study of Sekyedumase district in Ghana. Environment, Development and Sustainability, 14(4), 495-505.
8. Grace, P.R., Jain, M.C., Harrington, L., and Robertson, G.P. (2003). Long term sustainability of the tropical and subtropical Rice-Wheat System: An environmental perspective. Improving the productivity and sustainability of Rice-Wheat Systems: Issues and Impacts.ASA Special Publication 65, ASSA-CSSA-SSSA, USA.

9. Kelkar, U. and Bhadwal, S. (2008). South Asian Regional Study on Climate Change Impacts and Adaptation: Implications for Human Development. Human Development Report 2007/2008, UNDP.

10. Kristjanson, P., Garlick, C., Ochieng, S., Förch, W. and Thornton, P.K. (2011).Global summary of baseline household survey results. CGIAR Research Program on Climate Change, Agriculture and Food Security (CCAFS). Copenhagen, Denmark.

11. Kristjanson, P., Neufeldt, H., Gassner, A., Mango, J., Kyazze, F.B., Desta, S., Sayula, G., Thiede, B., Förch, W., Thornton, P.K. and Coe, R. (2012). Are food insecure smallholder households making changes in their farming practices? Evidence from East Africa. Food Security, 4(3), 381–397.

12. Manandhar, S., Vogt, D.S., Perret, S.R., and Kazama, F. (2010). Adapting cropping systems to climate change in Nepal: A cross-regional study of farmers' perception and practices. Regional Environmental Change, 11, 335-348.

13. Maplecroft. 2010.<http://maplecroft.com>Accessed on January 12, 2013.

14. Ministry of Agriculture and Cooperative (MOAC). (2010). Statistical information, a year book. Kathmandu, Nepal: MOAC.

15. Ministry of Agriculture and Development (MOAD). (2012). Statistical information on Nepalese agriculture, Kathmandu, Nepal: MOAD.

16. Ministry of Environment (MOE). (2010). National adaptation program of actions to climate change, Nepal. Kathmandu, Nepal: MOE.

17. Ministry of Finance (MOF). (2010). Economic survey- fiscal year 2008/09 Kathmandu, Nepal: MOF.

18. National Wheat Research Program (NWRP). (2010). Annual Progress Report, Bhairawa Rupandehi, Nepal: NWRP

19. NWRP. (2011). Annual Progress Report, National Wheat Research Program, Bhairawa, Rupandehi, Nepal.

20. Ojha, H., Rasheed, S.V., Sultana, P., Thapa, D., Dahal, K.R., Mittal, N., and Dhungana, H. (2012). Climate adaptive innovation: a study of agricultural adaptation and innovations in the Indo-Gangetic Plains. Kathmandu: Southasia Institute of Advanced Studies and CCAFS South Asia.

21. Palaniappam, S.P. and Shivaranam, K. (2006). Cropping system in Trophics: Principle and Management. Revised 2nd Edition, New Age International Publishers.

22. Pandey, P.R., Pandey, H.and Nakagawa, M. (2009). Assessment of rice and maize based cropping systems for rural livelihood improvement in Nepal. Journal of Agriculture and Environment, 10, 67-75.

23. Pandey, S.P., Pande, S., Johansen, C. and Virmani, S.M. (2001). Rice-wheat cropping systems of Nepal: Rice-Wheat Consortium Paper Series 12. New Delhi 110 012, India: Rice-Wheat Consortium for the Indo-Gangetic Plains; Patancheru 502 324, Andhra Pradesh, India: International Crops Research Institute for the Semi-Arid Tropics. pp.24.

24. Parry, M.L., Rosenzweig, C., Iglesias, A., Livermore, M. and Fischer, G. (2004). Effects of climate change on global food production under SRES emissions and socio-economic Scenarios. Journal of Global Environmental Change, 14,53–67

25. Practical Action. (2009). Temporal and spatial variability of climate change over Nepal. Practical Action, Kathmandu, Nepal.

26. Regmi, H.R. (2007). Effect of unusual weather on cereal crops production and household food security. The Journal of Agriculture and Environment, 8, 20-29.

27. Rosenzweig, C. and Parry, M. L. (1994). Potential impact of climate change on world food supply. Nature, 367,133-138.

28. Saha, G. (2011). Applying logistic model to examination results data. Journal of Reliability and Statistical Studies, 4,105-117

29. Shrestha, A.B., Wake, C.P., Mayewski, P.A. and Dibb, J.E. (1999). Maximum temperature trends in the Himalaya and its vicinity: An analysis based on temperature records from Nepal for the period 1971-94. Journal of Climate, 12, 2775-2787.

30. Shrestha, R. (2011). Factors affecting the cropping patterns in hills and plains of the central development region. Nepal Journal of Science and Technology, 10, 199-203

31. Timilsina, J. and Connor, D.J. (2001). Productivity and management of rice wheat cropping systems: Issues and challenges. Field Crops Research, 69, 93-132.

32. Tiwari, K.R., Ingrid, I., Sitaula, B.K. and Paudel, G.S. (2008).Analysis of the sustainability of upland farming systems in the Middle Mountains region of Nepal. International Journal of Agricultural Sustainability, 6 (4), 289-306

33. Warren, R. (2006). Understanding the regional impacts of climate change, Research Report Prepared for the Stern Review, Tyndall Centre Working Paper 90, Norwich, 2006

34. Zhai, F. and Zhuang, J. (2009). Agricultural impact of climate change: A general equilibrium analysis with special reference to Southeast Asia. ADBI Working Paper 131. Tokyo: Asian Development Bank Institute.

Annex I

Perception of Farmers on Possible Change in Climate (Likert Scale)

Indicators of climate change	Perception	Number of farmers	Weighted mean	Overall rank
Summer has become hotter	Strongly agree	16		
	Agree	42		
	Do not know	19	3.46	2
	Disagree	20		
	Strongly disagree	0		
Winter has become colder	Strongly agree	8		
	Agree	40		
	Do not know	9	3.16	3
	Disagree	40		
	Strongly disagree	0		
Winter has become hotter	Strongly agree	23		
	Agree	18	3.04	4
	Do not know	0		
	Disagree	52		
	Strongly disagree	4		
More intense rains during the monsoon	Strongly agree	4		
	Agree	14		
	Do not know	20	2.23	10
	Disagree	22		
	Strongly disagree	37		
Monsoon starts earlier	Strongly agree	3		
	Agree	18		
	Do not know	4	2.50	7
	Disagree	72		
	Strongly disagree	0		
Monsoon starts later	Strongly agree	11		
	Agree	38		
	Do not know	10	2.69	6
	Disagree	30		
	Strongly disagree	8		
Monsoon rainfall difficult to predict	Strongly agree	8		
	Agree	80		
	Do not know	7	3.96	1
	Disagree	2		

	Strongly disagree	0		
Drought has increased	Strongly agree	11		
	Agree	38		
	Do not know	5	3.02	5
	Disagree	28		
	Strongly disagree	15		
Wind damage to crop has increased	Strongly agree	5		
	Agree	7		
	Do not know	13	2.15	11
	Disagree	40		
	Strongly disagree	37		
Flood occurs more frequently	Strongly agree	8		
	Agree	22		
	Do not know	9	2.36	8
	Disagree	37		
	Strongly disagree	21		
Hailstone has increased	Strongly agree	5		
	Agree	6		
	Do not know	2	2.30	9
	Disagree	79		
	Strongly disagree	11		

Field Survey, 2013 Cut-off score = 3.0 (> 3.0 = important observation, < 3.0 = not important observation).

Annex II:

Average Annual Rainfall of Butwal Area (1998-2011)

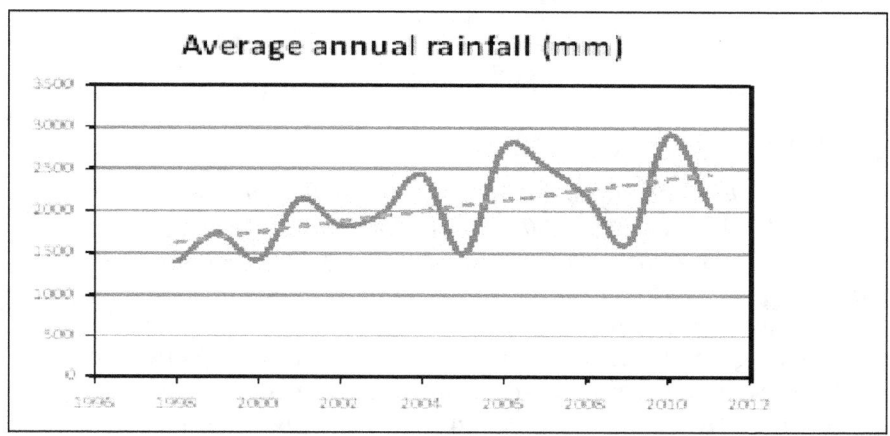

Source: (Dahal et al., 2012)

ANNEX III:

Monsoon Precipitation of Bhairahawa (1977-2007)

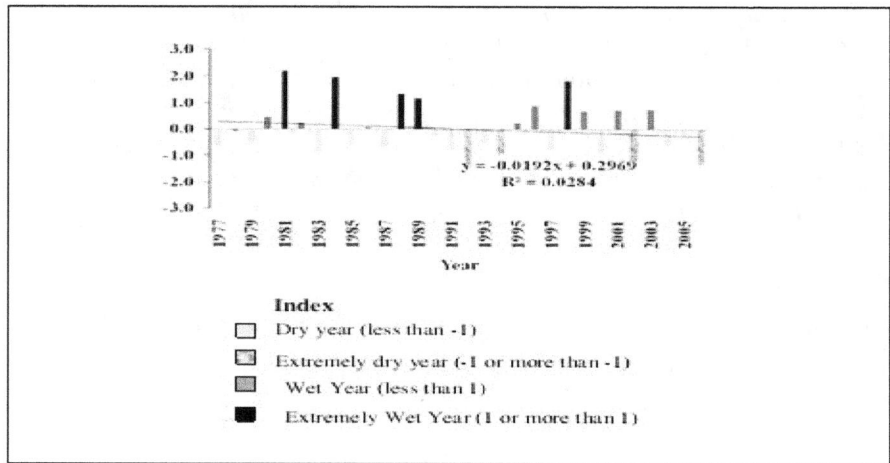

Source: (Manandhar et al. 2010)

Chapter-III

Eutrophication: A Major Issue- A Case Study of Rohtak District, Haryana

Gulab Singh*

Abstract

Today we face many problems like as air pollution, noise pollution, soil pollution and water pollution etc. Degradation of water quality, loss of biodiversity. This study base on water pollution. Water pollution affected our life in various ways. Eutrophication such as type of water pollution. Eutrophication is the natural process driving the ecological succession of fresh water, estuaries and marine ecosystem. This problem is worldwide problem and many researchers work on it. Some water species have been died by this problem. Here with the help of Remote Sensing and GIS techniques find out the problem in study area and give some suggestions to control it. For this purpose, used LISS IV and Cartoset imageries of different time series. Toposheets of study area also used in this paper. GPS and others technical instruments also used in this study. Main objective of the present study is to find out the problem of eutrophication in Rohtak district and mapping the affected area. In the study area the problem of eutrophication highly increased past fifteen years. Mostly water bodies of study area have been polluted by this problem. This study gives an idea to improve our environmental condition and also give some suggestions to control this problem in the study area as well as in world.

Keywords: Eutrophication, Pollution, Remote Sensing and GIS techniques, GPS and Imageries.

*Research Scholar, Department of Geography, M.D.U. Rohtak, Haryana

Introduction

Environmental pollution and other issues related to environment are on the hot seat of discussion these days. Presently, eutrophication of waters bodies is probably the most important environmental effect. The effects of nutrient enrichment thoroughly change equator ecosystems and occur virtually worldwide. The increase in human population, the use of fertilisers, increased intensity in agriculture, logging and increased atmospheric deposition is the main cause for this intensification.

Eutrophication is the natural ageing process of water bodies. This very slow process, which ultimately transforms aquatic environments into terrestrial habitats, begins with the addition of nutrients into the system. Nutrients enter aquatic environments as dissolved solutes and compounds to and inorganic responsible. Nutrients enter rivers and streams from both point and non point sources. Point sources are those from which nutrients are directly being released into the environment. A sewage discharge pipe draining into a river is an example of a point source of nutrients.

Two of the most important nutrients responsible for eutrophication are nitrogen and phosphorus. Phosphorus is commonly found in aquatic environments as phosphate. Human factors affecting the concentration of phosphorus in aquatic environments are wastewater and septic system effluent, detergents, fertilizer run-off, animal waste, development/paved surfaces, industrial discharge, phosphate mining, drinking water treatment, forest fires, and synthetic material. Harmful algal blooms are usually produced under eutrophic or hypereutrophic conditions. Cyanobacteria and dinoflagellates are examples of phytoplankton responsible for surface scum, oxygen depletion, and consequent fish kills.

Meaning of Eutrophication

Eutrophication is made by Greek word Eutrophia this mean healthy and it developed by German word Eutrophia (more precisely hypertrophication), is the ecosystem response to the addition of artificial or natural substances, such as nitrates and phosphates, through fertilizers or sewage, to an aquatic system.

Definitions of Eutrophication

The term 'eutrophic' means well-nourished; thus, 'eutrophication' refers to natural or artificial addition of nutrients in water bodies. When the effects are undesirable, eutrophication may be considered a form of pollution. It is a most popular issue in the world eutrophication is a very slow process which occurs in water bodies like ponds (Johars), lakes, rivers etc. it is harmful to environment and almost every animal. Water eutrophication is one of the most challenging environmental problems in the world. The investigation from the United Nation Environmental Protection (UNAP) indicates that about 30 per cent to 40 per cent of the water bodies and reservoirs have been affected more or less by water eutrophication all over the world.

Importance of the study

The study has devoted particular attention to the control of nutrients and phosphors uses. When we use bio fertilizers in the agriculture then we control the eutrophication problem. Eutrophication is a major issue in present time. Historically, the control of algal growth in reservoirs has received much attention, primarily because of problems relating to taste, odor, and filtration associated with certain algal types.

If we see all around us, we find that much natural and cultural pollution like air pollution, traffic pollution and water pollution etc. water pollution is the main purpose of this study we discuss about a small area of Rohtak district (Haryana, India). We find many water ponds in this area but most of water ponds are it full of eutrophication pollution because the farmer uses more and more fertilizers in agriculture fertilizers cause of nutrients and phosphorus. Nutrients and phosphorus cause of algae and algae cause of eutrophication. This study provides us an idea to improve our environment condition which provides scientific data for planning and regulatory agencies to address environmental problems in this area.

Present study aims to provide the correct and real time information about the increase in eutrophication process in the Lakhan Majra block in Rohtak district. Remote sensing has strong tools for water and eutrophication studies and others studies.

There are sources from which one can do the water and eutrophication studies, one is aerial photographs and another is satellite imagery.

Water and eutrophication studies depends on technological and scientific discipline for sensing, modeling, representing, visualizing, monitoring, processing, and communicating geo-information in support of water management. The main focus of the study is to represent the present status and scope of mapping, planning and management of the selected block area with the help of available satellite data.

Study Area

Lakhan Majra is a small village and block in Rohtak distrct which situated in northern part of Rohtak district at Highway No. 71. Lakhan Majra block is spread between 28°55'50" N to 29°05'50"N latitude and 76°23'0" E to 76°35'10" E longitude in the National Capital Region (NCR) of Haryana (Fig. 5.1). The block has 13 villages and the total population in 2011 was 67562 and total area is 143.082 km².

Location Map of Study Area

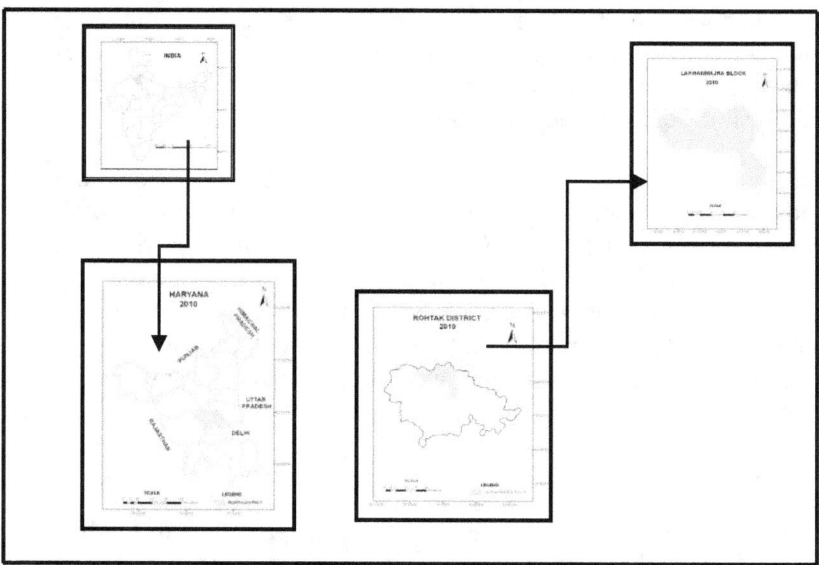

Fig. 5.1

The block is a part of Indo-Genetic alluvial plain ranging from Pleistocene to recent age. The geological structure of the block consists of alluvium (Recent), loam (Bhangar and Nadrak) and coarse loam (Daher and Chaeknote). The sediments comprise of clay, sand and kankar mixed in different proportions. No exposure of hard rocks forming the basement are seen in the area which one as deep as three hundred meters. The average elevation of the block is about 225 meters above mean sea level. Many canals and Rajbahas are passing through the block which irrigate the agricultural fields as well as used for drinking purposes. Most part of the study area is covered by sand. Soil formation of study area is very fertile.

The climate of Lakhan Majra block is sub-tropical, semi-arid, continental and monsoon type. Thus, it has hot summers, cool winters and small rainy season. The winter season starts towards the latter half of November and extends till about the middle of March followed by summer, which continues till about the end of June when maximum temperature reaches up to 45° C. Dust cyclones are common during summer months. After hot summer season, South-West monsoon arrives. The monsoon remains active between July to September. The post monsoon months are October and November constitute a transitional period from monsoon to winter season. The climate is ideal for agricultural development which is the base for all activities in the block. Limited rainy season, good and healthy climate is also suitable for industrial development also.

Annual rainfall is about 58 centimeters. Rainy season starts from July and ends in mid of September. About 80 per cent of the total rainfall is received during this period. Some amount of rainfall is received from western disturbances during winter season. Land use pattern is heavily inclined towards agriculture. Some part of the study area is also covered under natural vegetation. Due to continuous seepage from water channels, water lodging and salinity problem is increasing day by day.

Aim and Objectives

The main aim of the study is to identify the eutrophication in Lakhan Majra Block with the help of Geo-Informatics tools and monitoring the impact on animals and environment. The major objectives are below:

- To map out the spatial problem of water bodies (Johars) in study area.

- To identify the problem of Eutrophication in water bodies.

Methodology

Data source and methodology is a central part of any research work which gives us help in scientific description and explanation of reality. The present study is based on secondary data sources and uses GIS and Remote Sensing techniques to reach to conclusion. The present study focuses on the increasing problem of eutrophication in water bodies (Johars) of Lakhan Majra block of Rohtak district. For this purpose, LISS- IV (2002) and LISS-IV (2010) satellite data Survey of India (SOI) Topo-sheets of the same area has been used. Toposheets used in this study have been Geo-coded by converting them into Polyconic (Everest 1965, India/Nepal) projection with the help of ERDAS image 9.0. Using of supervised classification method identified the problem. Finally the maps are generated in Arc GIS 9.3, and interpretation and analysis have been made (Fig. 7.2). Given flow chart (Fig. 7.1) show using methodology:

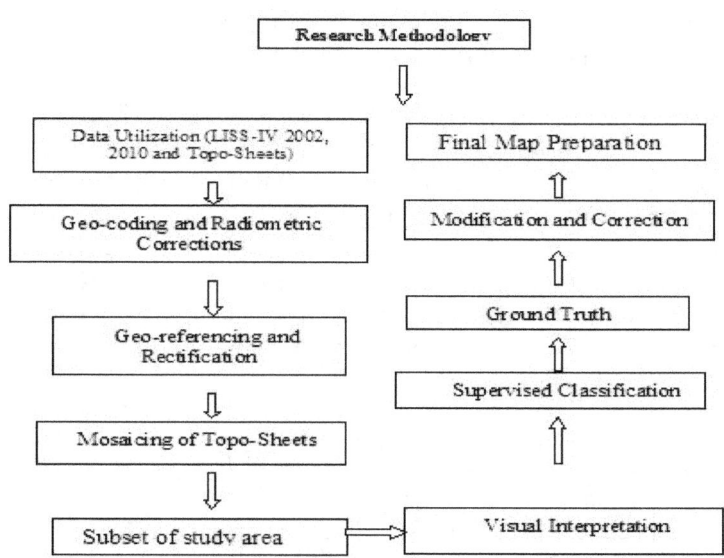

Fig. 7.1 Flow Chart Showing the General Methodology

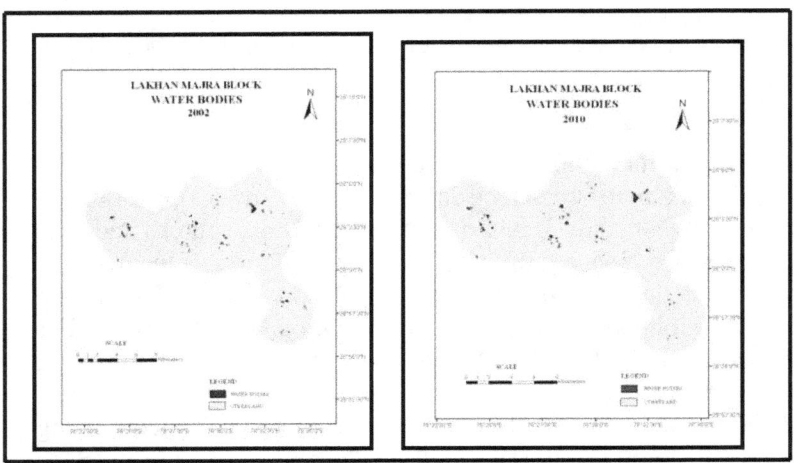

Fig. 7.2

Results and Discussion

Aerial Extent of Eutrophication in water bodies in Lakhan Majra block in 2002. There are 13 villages in Lakhan Majra block. All villages have more than one pond.

The ponds play a very important role in the rural economy. These are mainly being used for drinking animals as well as other domestic purposes. Out of 143.082 km² area in the block, 2.083 km² areas come under water bodies However, the problem of Eutrophication in Lakhan Majra Block is occurring in last few years. Level of eutrophication has been analyzed by Supervised classification technique in Lakhan Majra block. Out of total area under water bodies are 2.083 km² and 0.252 km² has been affected by Eutrophication (Table 8.1 and Fig. 8.1).

Table 8.1:- Area under water bodies in km² (2002)

Serial No.	Total Area	Water Bodies	Eutrophication
1	143.082	2.083	0.252

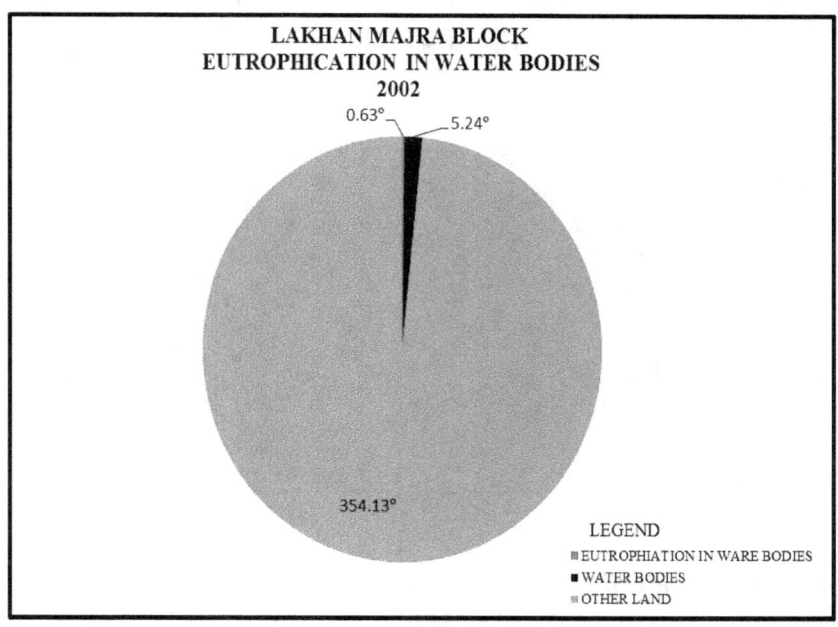

Fig. 8.1

Aerial Extent of Eutrophication in water bodies in Lakhan Majra Block in 2010. The present study aim to identify the eutrophication in water bodies in Lakhan Majra block. Level of eutrophication has been analyzed by supervised classification technique in Lakhan Majra block. Out of total area under water bodies are 1.868 km² and 0.734 km² has been affected by Eutrophication. (Fig. 8.2 and Table 8.2).

Table 8.2:- Area under water bodies in km² (2010)

Serial No.	Total Area	Water Bodies	Eutrophication
1	143.082	1.868	0.734

Fig. 8.2 Showing Eutrophication in water Bodies-2010

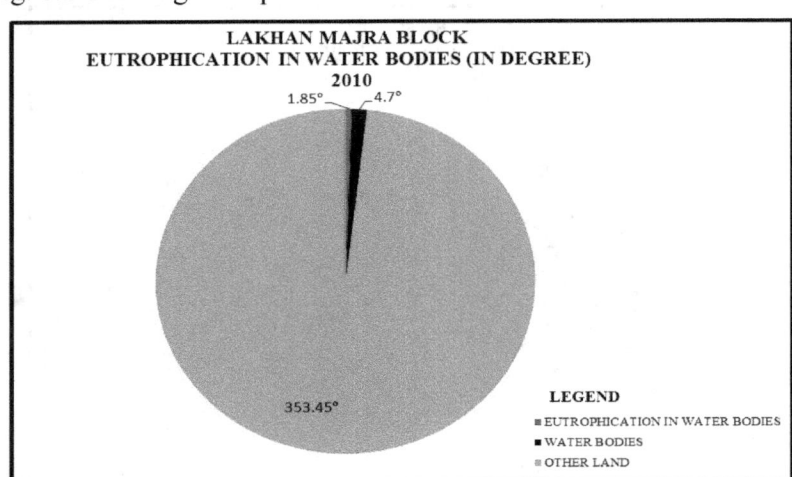

Status of Eutrophication in water bodies (2002 – 2010)

Eutrophication of waters bodies is probably the most important environmental effect human civilization facing today. The effects of nutrient enrichment of water body ecosystems are occurring virtually worldwide. Nutrients move across the land-water at such a high rates that water bodies have become the most fertilized ecosystems on the earth. The increase in human population, the use of fertilizers for agricultural purposes, increased intensity in agriculture, logging and increased atmospheric deposition is the main cause for this intensification.

The aim of present study is to see the impact of Eutrophication process on water bodies of Lakhan Majra block. There are 13 villages in Lakhan Majra block. The supervised classification algorithm has been applied on LISS IV image to find out the extent of Eutrophication during 2002 and 2010 (Fig. 8.3). The study area is facing twin problems related to water bodies. On the one hand, the water bodies (Johars) are shrinking due to pressure of population on land resources, at the other hand the problem of Eutrophication. In existing water bodies is alarmingly increasing very fast. The data in Table 8.3 reveals that area under water bodies has decreased to 2.083

km² in 2002 to 1.868 km² in 2010. At the same time the Eutrophication has increased. The Eutrophication process in the water bodies has increased from 0.252 km² in 2002 to 0.734 km² in 2010.

After calculation we find that in the Lakhan Majra block many ponds are full of Eutrophication. The area under water bodies has decreased from 2.083 km² in 2002 to 1.868 km² in 2010. At the same time the Eutrophication in water bodies has increased from 0.252 km² in 2002 to 0.734 km² in 2010.

Table 8.3:- Area under water bodies and Eutrophication in km² (2002 - 2010)

Year	Water bodies	Eutrophication
2002	2.083	0.252
2010	1.868	0.734

Fig. 8.3 Showing Eutrophication in Water Bodies from 2002 -2010

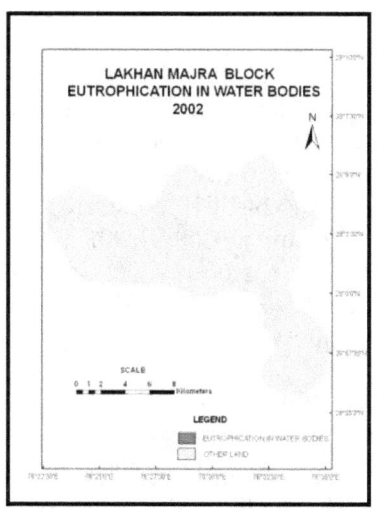
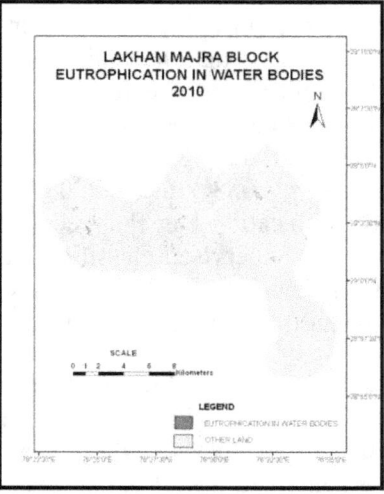

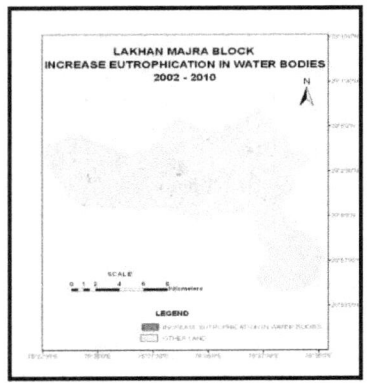

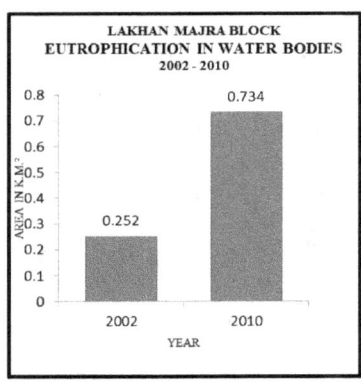

Conclusion and Suggestions

Conclusion

The population of Lakhan Majra block is continuously increased; it results in the increasing in agricultural techniques and uses of fertilisers. It directly as well as indirectly affected the water bodies in Lakhan Majra block. Due to increasing uses of fertilisers in agriculture, the eutrophication area in water bodies is increased very fast. It is observed that the rapid uses of insecticides and fertilisers in agriculture, the area of eutrophication has increased 0.252 km^2 to 0.734 km^2 during this period. It shows that area of water bodies has been decreased during this period. The area of water bodies has changed from 2.083 km^2 in 2002 to 1.868 km^2 in 2010. The area under eutrophication has changed from 0.252 km^2 in 2002 to 0.734 km^2 in 2010. Supervised classification technique has been successful to study the changes in eutrophication area and water bodies. This technique has help to identified eutrophication in water bodies.

Remote Sensing Satellite, with repetitive and synoptic viewing capabilities together with GIS is an important tool to map assesses and monitors the changes in eutrophication as well as water bodies. A database generated from Remote Sensing imageries in Erdas software and thematic maps prepared using Arc GIS which could be helpful for sustainable planning.

Suggestions

To manage the problem of eutrophication in water bodies in Lakhan Majra block, it is suggested that the use of Remote Sensing and GIS in combination with geospatial data is of vital importance. Therefore, there is need for the use of eutrophication and water bodies information database that can be generated using Remote Sensing an GIS techniques. Programme on Eutrophication is massaged and manipulated into regionally relevant criteria. Indeed, by introducing the concept of impairment of human water uses and public perceptions, there would appear to be a danger that eutrophication assessment and control could drift completely from its scientific and technical roots. This can be successfully when both government and local people participate at a great level. The government, private and local agencies should be involved in to controlling water related problem.

References

1. Biddanda, B., M. Ogdahl and J. Cotner (2001) "Dominance of bacterial metabolism in oligotrophic relative to eutrophic waters. Limnology and Oceanography" 46,730-739.
2. Biggs, B.J.F. (2000) "Eutrophication of streams and rivers: dissolved nutrient-chlorophyll relationships for benthic algae". Journal of the North American Benthological Society. Page 19, 17-31.
3. Burkholder, J.M., Tomasko, D.A. and et al (August 2007) "Seagrasses and Eutrophication"
4. Carr, G. M., A. Morin, and P. A. Chambers (2005) "Bacteria and algae in stream periphyton along a nutrient gradient". Freshwater Biology 50, 1337-1350.
5. Khan, F. A. and Ansari, A. A. (2005) "Eutrophication: An ecological vision. The Botanical Review". 71,449-482.
6. Roll, S. K., S. Diehl and S. D. Cooper (2005) "Effects of grazer immigration and nutrient enrichment on an open algae-grazer system". Oikos 108,386-400.
7. http://en.wikipedia.org/wiki/Eutrophication
8. http://toxics.usgs.gov/definitions/eutrophication.html
9. http://www.wri.org/project/eutrophication/about
10. http://www.enotes.com/science/q-and-a/what-eutrophication-288561
11. http://en.wikipedia.org/wiki/Rohtak_district
12. http://cgwb.gov.in/District_Profile/Haryana/Rohtak.pdf
13. http://www.mcrohtak.gov.in/history.htm
14. http://www.globalcoral.org/Eutrophication%20and%20Water%20 quality.html
15. http://zju.edu.cn/jzus; www.springerlink.com
16. http://www.lenntech.com/eutrophication-water-bodies/introduction.htm
17. http://www.lenntech.com/eutrophication-water-bodies/eutrophication-sources.htm
18. http://www.answers.com/topic/alga
19. http://new.coolclassroom.org/files/adventures/1/Eutrophication_Teacher.pdf
20. http://rainforestdeforestationeutrophication.blogspot.in/2011/05/introduction-to-eutrophication.html

Chapter-IV

Migration in House Dust Mites: A Review

Kiran Lata Damle*

Abstract

Throughout the animal kingdom collective migration occurs in a wide range including insects during foraging, fish, birds, and other vertebrates. Animals migrate during their nomadic phase, shelter, overcrowd during swarming occur. But how individual move in groups. The mechanism underlying collective migration is poorly studied. Here a study on mite migration movements from one area to a new area was triggered. Migration of house dust mites fluctuate with the human occupation fluctuation with temperature and relative humidity which is the most favorable locations for mites which change constantly and repeatedly. Mites migrated from a starting area to the second area in Diamond form of equal length between two branches. Here both the local air dryness and the distant water source were necessary to trigger the collective migration. Males and nymphs migration was higher than the larvae and females. By following simple rules the migrating individuals can start a coordinated migration that induces a positive feedback loop. It was also observed that mites lay an attractive trail which reinforced by the followers and the consistency of the collective choice is higher as the number of migrants increase. We observed that dust mites migration are similar for sub-social or eu-social species as a collective phenomenon and may lead to similarities in their pattern of migration.

Keywords: feedback loops, fluctuation, migration, relative humidity, temperature.

---

* *Associate Professor, Dept. of Zoology. Govt. Digvijay College, Rajnandgaon, (C.G.). India*

Introduction

Mites are of micro to macro group of living organisms having cosmopolitan distribution and are having free to parasitic mode of life. Mites are among the oldest of all terrestrial animals with fossils known from the early Devonian, nearly 400 million years ago (Norton et al., 1988). They found in everywhere and eat flakes of skin in addition to other things. Although tiny themselves, mites belongs to the largest, the Arthropods. Within the arthropods, mites are the most diverse representative of an ancient lineage (Walters & Proctor, 1999). Mites belong to the order acarina of subclass acari and class Arachnida. The scientific study of mites is called acarology. Most of the Dust mites are the most infamous members of the family Pyroglyphidae. Mites are ubiquitous and have plasticity of habitats, and because of their microscopic size go largely invisible. Many of the mites live freely in the soil or water (fresh & marine), but there are also a large number of species that live as parasites on plants, animals (invertebrate & vertebrate), some are predator while still others found beneficial symbionts (Halliday, et al., 2000). Insects may also have parasitic mites. About 48,200 species of mites have been described. A large number of mites are found in the dust of homes, offices, hospitals and other human and animal environment. They live in our rugs, furniture, mattresses, bedding, and other areas that accumulate organic detritus and maintain a high level of humidity and feed on the 350-400 grams of skin shed by person, mice, cats, and dogs and mould annually (Nayer, et al. 1974). Kern (1921) discovered Dermatophagoides pteronyssinus in house dust as allergen in U.S.A.

Migration in House Dust Mites

Throughout the animal kingdom collective migration occurs in a wide range including social insects such as ants during foraging (Holldobler & Wilson 1990), fish (Sumpter 2009), birds (Bajec & Heppner 2009), and other vertebrates (Couzin & Krauze 2003). Animals migrate during their nomadic phase (Gotwald 1995), in search of a new suitable shelter (Mallon et al. 2001), when their dwelling place become overcrowd (Seeley & Buhrman 1999; Visscher & Camazine 1999) and during swarming; (Seeley & Visscher 2004) occur.

How Individuals Moves in Groups?

The movement of individuals in the group move as an integrated social unit (Dyer 2000). It is sometimes thought that collective migration is organized by a sophisticated system of communication among individuals belonging to highly organized societies such as ants and termites (Holldobler & Wilson 1990). Although previous studies have shown that collective migration actually does not necessarily follow on a complex organization (Deneubourg & Goss 1989; Bonabeau, et al. 1997) and can simply be achieved through amplification processes that result from simple interactions between individuals (Camazine, et al. 2001; Jeanson, et al. 2004). Migrating individuals can start a coordinated migration by following simple rules that induce positive feedback loops.

Mechanism of Migration

House dust mites (Dermatophagoides pteronyssinus) are widespread in the furniture and mattresses of homes (Trouessart 1897) that causes allergic symptoms (Colloff 2009). Dust mite migrates as a collective phenomenon which is similar for sub social or eusocial species and may lead to similarities in their patterns of migration (Buhl, et al. 2006; Costa 2006) regardless of their degree of social organization. A social spider Anelosimus eximius that produces silk threads that is followed by nest mates during displacement (Furey 1998) is an example of an amplification process leading to coordinated migration. This silk-laying behaviour leads to the formation of silk 'highways' that ensure group cohesion as well as collective decision-making processes during swarming (Lubin & Robinson 1982; Avile & Tufino 1998; Mailleux, et al. 2008). This mites feed on human skin scale and is found in the locations where this scale collects, such as in bedding, carpets and padded furniture (Murray, et al. 1985).

Factors affecting Migration

The dust mite population size is mainly influenced by the physical factors of temperature and humidity, which are known to affect both reproduction and development rates (Arlian 1992; Crowther, et al. 2001). In mattresses, humidity and temperature show large daily variations related to human occupation (Arlian 1992). Consequently, the most favourable locations for mites constantly shift.

The mites move away from dry conditions up a humidity gradient (Crowther, et al. 2000, 2001). There is evidence for the migration of mites between microhabitats within the home (Mollet & Robinson 1995) but nothing is known about migrating dust mite populations that have been poorly studied, although migration must be a crucial phase for the survival of dust mites (Glass, et al. 1998).

Discussion

Dust mite migration is a crucial phase for their survival. The determinant factors of the migratory behavior of dust mites were identified which are humidity gradient, developmental stage and sex. Also the local dryness strongly influences migration dynamics. This might be attributed to differences in the individual response thresholds to environmental conditions. However the hygrometric conditions may not matter, nymphs and males were more inclined to migrate than to stay in the initial arena, these were always more numerous. On the other hand, females and larvae had a lower tendency to migrate. These differences between the proportion of migrating males and females were not linked to their respective walking speeds that are similar. Arlian, et al. (1998) showed that females are more resilient at a low relative humidity than males and are therefore more likely to survive a reduced relative humidity. This could be because of their bigger body size and hence their lower surface or volume ratio that makes them less vulnerable to dehydration than males. The larvae walked slowly but the length of the experience was long enough for them to reach the arrival arena.

Therefore, their low walking speed did not explain their low migration rate. Individual variability in the tendency to migrate can be explained by qualitative and quantitative variations in individual responsiveness (Beshers & Fewell 2001). Responsiveness of an individual is regulated by internal factors such as genetic predisposition, physiology, developmental stage, sex and age (Robinson 1992; Page, et al. 1997). The responsiveness of an individual can also depend on several external factors, such as the relative humidity and light intensity in the laboratory. Anne-Catherine Mailleuxet, et al. (2010) identified three factors that modulated individual responsiveness in house dust mites: an environmental factor (relative humidity), and two internal factors (sex and developmental stage).

Dust mites possess a spectrum of migration and invasion mechanisms including both individual and collective strategies. As mites move, it is likely that they passively lay chemicals on the substrate that then guide the followers (as observed on spiders by Jeanson & Deneubourg 2006 a, b). The two main species of dust mites, D. pteronyssinus and Dermatophagoides farinae, are highly aggregative and this behaviour might significantly reduce individual water loss (Glass, et al. 1998). The collective migration offers them the possibility of forming aggregates to protect them from dehydration (Wharton, et al. 1979). In general, forming such aggregates has many advantages for both the individual and the group because it provides easier access to food and mates as well as protection against predators (Wertheim 2005). It also presents disadvantages since forming aggregates means sharing food, mates and living space, and can result in inter-individual conflicts (Wertheim, et al. 2004; Prokopy & Roitberg 2005). Acari present the basic features required for the emergence of coherent migration and collective decision making, such as mutual nonspecific attraction, spatial proximity and spatiotemporal overlap of generations. Despite these prerequisites, in Acari there is little evidence of social behaviours apart from aggregative behaviours and they are mainly found in spider mites building silk nests (Kotaro & Saito 2004).

Conclusion

The collective migration is organized by a sophisticated system of communication. The hypothesis was that the interplay between the distribution of individual responsiveness in the group and the environmental conditions determines the proportion of mites that migrate and lay a trail leading to an amplification process. Therefore, individual and collective migration modes might represent temporary states that can interchange depending on this interplay. The four stages: female, males, larvae and nymphs might have had a different responsiveness to the presence of the other mites, Mite migration is commonly understood as the solitary movement of individuals, triggered by and directed towards environmental gradients. Therefore, their low walking speed did not explain their low migration rate. Is this stage more sedentary? Are they influenced by the presence of females? These questions maybe the matter of new quiriocity.

References

1. R. A. Norton, Phylogenetic perspectives on genetic systems and reproductive modes of mites, New York: Chapman and Hall (1988), 8-99
2. R. B. Halliday, B. M. Oconnor, and A.S. Baker, Global diversity of mites. In Peter H. Raven & Tania Williams. Nature and human society: the quest for a sustainable world (2000).
3. E. Nayer, M. Lal and A. Dasgupta, The prevalence of mite Dermatophagoides pteronyssinus and its association with house dust Allergy. Indian J. Med. Res. 6, (1974), 11-14.
4. Kern. Dust sensitization in bronchial asthma. K. Clin.N.America. 5 (1921), 751-758.
5. B. Holldobler & E. O. Wilson, The Ants. Springer- Verlag, Berlin. Jeanson, R. & Deneubourg, J. L. 2006a: Discrete dragline attachment induces aggregation in spider lings of a solitary species. Anim. Behav. 67, (1990) 531—537.
6. D. J. T. Sumpter, Group behaviour: leadership by those in need. Curr. Biol. 19, (2009) 325—327.
7. L. Bajec & F. H. Heppner, Organized flight in birds. Anim. Behav 78, (2009). 777—789.
8. D. Couzin, & J. Krauze, Self-organization and collective behaviour in vertebrates. Adv. Study Behav 32, (2003). 1—75.
9. W. H. Gotwald, Army Ants: The Biology of Social Predation. Comstock Pub. Associates, Ithaca, NY. (1995)
10. E. B. Mallon, S. C. Pratt, & N. R. Franks, Individual and collective decision-making during nest site selection by the ant Leptothorax albipennis. Behav. Ecol. Sociobiol 50, (2001). 352—359.
11. T. D. Seeley & S. C. Buhrman, Group decision making in swarms of honey bees. Behav. Ecol. Sociobiol. 45, (1999) 19—31.

12. P. K. Visscher & S. Camazine, The mystery of swarming honeybees: from individual behaviors to collective decisions. In: Information Processing in Social Insects (C. Detrain, J. L. Deneubourg, & J. M. Pasteels). Brikhau¨ ser, Basel, (1999) pp. 355—378.

13. T. D. Seeley & P. K. Visscher, Quorum sensing during nest-site selection by honeybee swarms. Behav. Ecol. Sociobiol. 56, (2004) 594—601.

14. F. C. Dyer, Group movement and individual cognition: lessons from social insects. In: On the Move: How and Why Animals Travel in Groups (Boinski, S. & Garber, P. A., eds). Univ. of Chicago Press, Chicago, (2000) pp. 127—164.

15. J. L. Deneubourg & S. Goss, Collective patterns and decision-making. Ethol. Ecol. Evol. 1, (1989) 295—311.

16. E. Bonabeau, G. Theraulaz, J. L. Deneubourg, S. Aron, & S. Camazine, Self-organization in social insects. Trends Ecol. Evol. 12, (1997) 188—193.

17. S. Camazine, J. L. Deneubourg, N. R. Franks, J. Sneyd, G. Theraulaz, & E. Bonabeau, Self-Organization in Biological Systems. Princeton Univ. Press, Princeton, NJ. (2001)

18. R. Jeanson, J. L. Deneubourg, A. Grimal, & G. Theraulaz, Modulation of individual behavior and collective decision-making during aggregation site selection by the ant Messor barbarus. Behav. Ecol. Sociobiol. 55, (2004) 388—394.

19. M. J. Colloff, Dust Mites. CSIRO Publishing, Springer, Dordrecht, the Netherlands (2009).

20. J. Buhl, D. J. T. Sumpter, D. Couzin, J. J. Hale, E. Despland, E. R. Miller, & S. J. Simpson, From disorder to order in marching locusts. Science 312, (2006) 1402—1406.

21. J. T. Costa, The other Insect Societies. Harvard Univ. Press, Cambridge, MA (2006).

22. R. E. Furey, Two cooperatively social populations of the theridiid spider Anelosimus studiosus in a temperate region. Anim. Behav. 55, (1998) 727—735.

23. Y. Lubin & M. H. Robinson, Dispersal by swarming in a social spider. Science 216, (1982) 319—321.

24. L. Aviles & P. Tufino, Colony size and individual fitness in the social spider Anelosimus eximius. Am. Nat. 152, (1998) 403—418.
25. C. Mailleux, R. Furey, F. Saffre, B. Krafft, & J. L. Deneubourg, How non-nestmates affect the cohesion of swarming groups in social spiders. Insect. Soc. 55, (2008) 355—359.
26. D. Crowther, T. Oreszczyn, S. Pretlove, I. Ridley, J. A. Horwood, P. Cox & B. Leung, Controlling house dust mites through ventilation: the development of a model of mite response in varying hygrothermal conditions. Proceedings of Biocontaminants. International Society of the Built Environment, Dijon, France (2001).
27. B. Murray, M. B. Ferguson, & B. J. Morrisson, Sensitization to house dust mites in different climatic areas. J. Allergy Clin. Immunol. 76, (1985) 108—112.
28. L. Arlian, Water balance and humidity requirements of house dust mites. Exp. Appl. Acarol. 16, (1992) 15—35.
29. D.Crowther, J. A. Horwood, N. Baker, D. Thomson, S. Pretlove, I. Ridley & T. Oreszczyn, House dust mites and the built environment: a literature review; Hydrothermal Model for Predicting House-Dust Mite Response to Environmental Conditions in Dwellings. Report for the EPSRC Project: T (2000). pp.34.
30. D. Crowther, T. Oreszczyn, S. Pretlove, I. Ridley, J. A. Horwood, J. A. Cox & B. Leung, Controlling house dust mites through ventilation: the development of a model of mite response in varying hygrothermal conditions. Proceedings of Bio contaminants. International Society of the Built Environment, Dijon, France. (2001)
31. J. A. Mollet, & W. Robinson, Use of marked mites to study the dispersal of the American house dust mites (Dermatophagoides farinae) In: Mites, Astham and Domestic Design II (Tovey, E., Fifoot, A. & Sieber, L., eds). Univ. of Sydney, Sydney, (1995) pp. 19—21.
32. D. Morgan, Trail pheromones of ants. Physiol. Entomol. 34, (1995, 2008) 1—17.

33. E. V. Glass, J. A. Yoder & G. R. Needham, Clustering reduces water loss by adult American house dust mites Dermatophagoides farinae (Acari: Pyroglyphidae). Exp. Appl. Acarol. 22, (1998) 31—37.

34. L. Arlian, J. S. Neal & S. W. Bacon, Survival, fecundity and development of Dermatophagoides farina (Acari: Pyroglyphidae) at fluctuating relative humidity. J. Med. Entomol. 35, (1998) 962—966.

35. S. N. Beshers & J. H. Fewell, Models of division of labor in social insects. Annu. Rev. Entomol. 46, (2001) 413—440.

36. G. E. Robinson, Regulation of division of labour in insect societies. Annu. Rev. Entomol. 37, (1992) 637—665.

37. R. E. Page, J. Erber & M. K. Fondrk, The effect of genotype on response thresholds to sucrose and foraging behaviour of honeybees (Apis mellifera L.). J. Comp. Physiol. A 182, (1997) 489—500.

38. Anne-Catherine Mailleux, Aina Astudillo Fernandez, Gilles S.Martin, Claire Detrain & Jean-Louis Deneubourg J. Schneider doi: 10.1111/j. (2010)(1439-0310.

39. R. Jeanson & J. L. Deneubourg, Discrete dragline attachment induces aggregation in spider lings of a solitary species. Anim. Behav. 67, (2006a) 531—537.

40. R. Jeanson & J. L. Deneubourg, Path selection in cockroaches. J. Exp. Biol. 209, (2006b) 768—4775.

41. G. W. Wharton, K. M. Duke & H. M. Epstein, Water and the physiology of house dust mites. Recent Advances in Acarology, vol. 1 (Rodrigues, J. G., ed.). Academic Press, London, (1979) pp. 325—335.

42. B. Wertheim, Evolutionary ecology of communication signals that induce aggregative behaviour. Oikos 109, (2005) 117—124.

43. E. Ranta, H. Rita & H. Lindstrom, Competition vs. cooperation: success of individuals foraging alone and in groups. Am. Nat. (1993) 142, 42.

44. B. Wertheim, E.-J. A. Van Baalen, M. Dicke & L.Vet, Pheromone-mediated aggregation in non social arthropods: an evolutionary ecological perspective. Annu. Rev. Entomol. 50, (2004) 321—346.
45. J. Prokopy & B. Roitberg, Joining and avoidance behavior in non social insects. Annu. Rev. Entomol. 46, (2005) 631—665.
46. M. Kotaro & Y. Saito, Nest size variation reflecting anti-predator strategies in social spider mites of Stigmaeopsis (Acari: Tetranychidae). Behav. Ecol. Sociobiol. 51, (2004) 201—206.

Chapter-V

Environmental Problems Due to Land Use Changes in the Coastal Areas of Bangladesh: A Review

Md. A Mannan* Bidita Beg**

Abstract

The present paper describes the causes of major changes in land use pattern and aggravation of environmental parameters in the coastal zone of Bangladesh; obviously considered as a man-made disaster. The paper shows that landuse in the coastal areas are gradually changing i.e. diverse, competitive and alarming. Lands are using there in different purposes viz. agriculture, shrimp farming, salt production, forestry, ship-breaking yards, ports, industry, settlements, wetlands etc. The study also reveals that about 1950, land are mainly used for paddy cultivation but human interference to natural drainage system and climate change are responsible for water and soil pollution in the area which reduced productivity decades to decades. Finally, the paper highlights the suggestive measures to address the problems in land management.

Key Words: erosion, land use change, man-made disaster, water logging, ecosystem

*Lecturer; Geography and Environment & Political Science; Govt Syed Hatem Ali College, Barisal; Bangladesh

Introduction

Land use refers to the uses of land serves in different purposes viz. wildlife habitat, forest agriculture, settlement etc. It plays a vital role for many planning and management activities concerned with the surface of the earth. The coastal area of Bangladesh covers nineteen coastal districts, continental shelf and the Exclusive Economic Zone (EEZ) of the Bay of Bengal. Natural disasters have direct and indirect impacts on land resources and its various uses. The trend of land uses in coastal areas of Bangladesh is remarkable over the last half century. In these areas the major land uses comprise agriculture, shrimp farming, forestry, urban development and other settlement needs. There is demand for expansion of all current land use, while the need for new exploitation is also emerging with a huge number of populations. Moreover, land is being degraded and lost due to the effects of increased salinity intrusion, inundation of low-lying marshy land, floods and land erosion by the unplanned and haphazard land use of people. However, much remains to be done in implementing the recently adopted Coastal Zone Policy (2005) and the establishment of Integrated Coastal Zone Management (ICZM) - coordination, demarcation of land zoning, mangrove forestation through community participation, better preparedness against disaster and the introduction of modern land management systems.

Study Area

The coastal zone of Bangladesh selected as a study area in this research. The coastal areas cover the nineteen districts in the south and south-east parts of Bangladesh. It occupies 32 percent of the total area and 28 percent of the population of Bangladesh (Islam, 2004[1]). It covers an area from the shore of 37 to 195 k.m., whereas the exposed coast is limited to a distance of 37 to 57 k.m. (Islam et al., 2006[2]). The coastal belt of Bangladesh is divided into three distinct regions, i.e. the western, central and eastern regions. The western and central zones are very flat and low. The land here is criss-crossed by numerous rivers and channels with a large number of islands. The western zone of Satkhira, Khulna, Bagerhat, Perojpur is home to the famous mangrove forest, the Sundarbans. A submarine canyon, Swatch of No Ground runs NE-SW up to about 24 k.m. south of the western coast of the country. The central region of Barguna, Patuakhali, Bhola, Barisal, Lakshmipur, Noakhali, Feni is geomorphologically most active land formation process making a new shape of land features. These areas are facing a number of natural disasters i.e. cyclones, salinity intrusion, tidal surges, floods almost every year.

Moreover, the population is increasing at alarming rate in the coastal areas in Bangladesh. Agricultural labourers, small farmers, fisher folk and the urban poor make up 71 percent of the 6.85 million households (Ahmad, 2004[3]). Among them about 54% of the people of coastal areas are functionally landless and more than 30% are absolutely landless. Among the landholders, 80% are small farmers, 18% are medium farmers and only 2% are large farmers (PDO-ICZMP, 2004[4]). These have decisive impacts on major economic and livelihood activities, on land use and subsequently on the quality of land.

Map-1: The coastal zone of Bangladesh

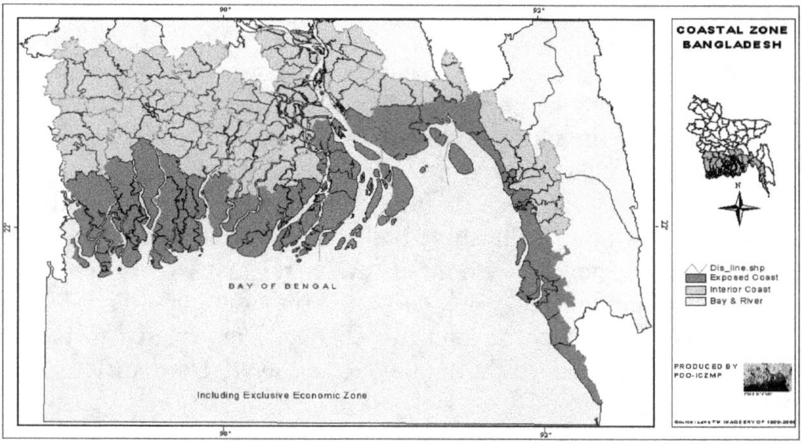

Source: Islam, 2006.

Objectives of the Study

It is well established that the process of land use change leads to the alteration of existing environmental conditions of any area.

The research is fully devoted to visualize the dynamics of land use change of coastal zone of Bangladesh and its consequential impacts on its land use and land evaluation and other environmental areas.

The specific objectives of the study are:

- to identify the existing land use pattern of the selected area;

- to explore the prime causes of land use change and its effects on the environment of the study area; and

- to give some suggestions based on the study findings.

Materials and Methods

The methods used for this research are a combination of physical and human parameters. Relevant data for detecting land use changes of the study area were collected directly from the field and also using a questionnaire which contained structured and open – ended questions. The sample size of the questionnaire was 120. The methodology adopted for the present study also makes extensive use of secondary material to build up and support the objectives of the study. Through reviewing available literature, a broad outline of different causal issues of land use changes and its consequential impacts on the environment have been gained. To fulfill the objectives of the study an attempt has been made to illustrate the current land use pattern and trends of land use change of the area. Cadastral maps of different periods and satellite images were used to bring out the trends of urbanization and the pattern of land use change. Data related to the previous land use of the study area were gathered from different secondary sources.

Results and Discussions

Major Land Uses in Coastal Zone

Land use in Bangladesh is generally determined by physiography, climate and land levels (Brammer, 2002[5]). However, lands in coastal areas in Bangladesh is used for agriculture, shrimp cultivation and fish farming, forestry, salt production, ship-breaking yards, ports, industries, human settlements and wetlands (Figure 2). As a result, land use in the coastal areas is diverse, competitive and often conflicting (Alam et al., 2002; Islam, 2006 [6]).

Agriculture

Like other parts of Bangladesh, coastal livelihoods are largely depended on agricultural crops, mainly rice i.e. agriculture predominates. The net cultivable land of areas in Bangladesh is 1.95 million hectares. However, it becomes limited at rainy season cropping because of highly soil salinity is in the dry season. Medium-high land dominates the coastal area, followed by highland, medium-low land and lowland. At present, coastal regions contribute approximately 16 percent of the total rice production of the country.

Fisheries

One of the main economic activities in the coastal area is aquaculture (Islam, 2003 [7]. In 2012 and 2013, the fisheries sub sector contributed 6.18 percent of the GDP of Bangladesh. A vast network of river systems, beels (natural depressions), boars (dead river sections), flood lands and ponds, low-lying marshy lands provide opportunities for both capture and culture fisheries. The main land uses in fisheries are pond aquaculture and shrimp cultivation. However, the significance of shrimp farming has grown rapidly over the last 30 years. Shrimp cultivation areas have expanded from 51,812 hectares in 1983 to 137 996 hectares in 1994 and 218 649 hectares in 2004 (DoF., 2005 [8].

Forestry

About 50 percent (7 869 000 hectares) forests of Bangladesh are in the coastal areas and it comprise both natural forests, including the Sunderbans, and planted forest. The natural forest area includes mangrove forest, mixed evergreen and deciduous forest and mixed thickets and forest in Teknaf, Ramu, Cox's Bazar, Ukhiya and Fatikchhari thanas of Cox's Bazar and Chittagong districts.

Map-2: Indicative coastal land zones of Bangladesh

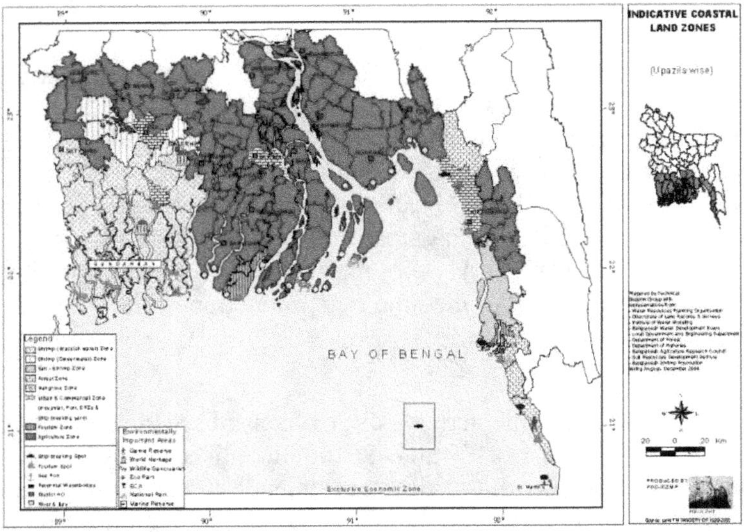

Source: Islam, 2006.

Salt production

In 1960, the Bangladesh Small and Cottage Industries Corporation started to produce salt on 2,742 hectares in Chittagong and Cox's Bazar districts in southeast of Bangladesh, where salt production continues to be concentrated. Since then, land use under salt production has been gradually increasing to meet the ever-growing demand. There are 41,000 listed salt producers. In 2003/2004, 0.9 million tonnes of salt were produced from 24,900 hectares land.

Other Land Uses

The Barisal, Chittagong and Khulna Metropolitan cities, 74 municipalities and other urban areas are located along the coastal areas of Bangladesh. As a result, a large area of the coastal zone in Bangladesh is using for urbanization. The coastal area of Bangladesh is covered with natural sceneries. Many tourist attractive spots are located in the coastal zone. Cox's Bazar is the only well-developed beach town and is the most visited, as it has both natural and cultural diversity. Kuakata beach, St. Martin's Island and the Chakaria Sundarbans is other important tourist destinations in this area.

The coastal zone possesses several ecosystems that have important conservation value. The world's largest uninterrupted stretch of mangrove ecosystem, the Sundarbans, is a World Heritage Site. However, coral ecosystems are found around St. Martin's Island.

Changes in Land Uses - Causes and Impacts

Land use in coastal Bangladesh was predominantly for paddy cultivation, especially low-yielding locally adapted varieties. In very limited areas of the south-western parts of Bangladesh, traditional shrimp culture was practiced. However, salt intrusion and tidal surges damage the crop almost every year. Crop failure due to saltwater intrusion or monsoon flooding has been reported in most areas once every three years (Nishat, 1988 [9].

Due to the green revolution in the 1960 the land of Bangladesh starts using for more intensive rice cultivation. The government recognized the need for protection of the coastal areas and construction of embankments was took place in the coastal areas of the country. The Coastal Embankment Project (CEP) was taken up, with assistance from the World Bank, in 1967. The embankments included regulators and other structures to control water intake and drainage of the emboldened area. The primary purpose was to increase agricultural production. During the first phase, 92 polders were constructed with 4022 k.m. of embankments and 780 drainage sluices. It became immediately apparent that emboldening increased the scale of production: The yields in certain places increased by 200 to 300 percent (Nishat, 1988[9]). The dominant land use, during the period, was still paddy cultivation, primarily of traditional local varieties, but modern paddy varieties and technological packages were also introduced. Other land uses and land cover remained the same, i.e. salt production, mangrove forest and traditional shrimp farming.

In the 1970 and 1980, the government continued large-scale polderization of coastal areas of Bangladesh. Polders became part of the natural coastal setting. A total of 123 coastal polders were constructed in this hydro-dynamically active delta. It was soon realized that internal water management had to be established within these polders in order to enhance further agricultural production. Changes in land use occurred due to intensification of paddy cultivation with attempted expansion of modern varieties and conversion of agricultural land to non-agricultural use.

During this time, coastal forestation was started with the objective of protecting the coast from cyclones and foreshore erosion, areas for industrial belts also started to expand.

Moreover, the study shows that in order to boost rice production in this area the World Bank and others helped with large-scale polderization in 1960–1980. As a result, artificial embankment hampered the drainage system and the whole low-lying marshy land became water logging which increasing the salinity intrusion within the next decade. Moreover, a historical tradition of shrimp farming, polders provided an opportunity for intensive shrimp farming. As a result, crop land and mangroves forest areas were gradually transferred to shrimp farming which created a social conflict in the locality.

Figure-3: Coastal polders set-up in Bangladesh

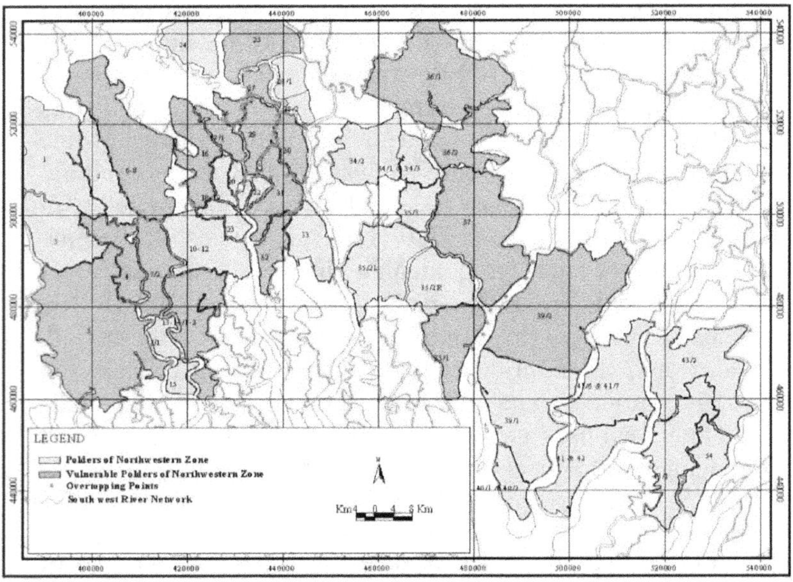

Source: Islam, 2006.

Population Pressure

Bangladesh has a population of 150 million living on a land area of 1, 47, 570 sq. km with an annual growth rate of 1.48 percent. In the coastal zone alone, the population is expected to increase from 36.8 million in 2001 to 43.9 million to 60.8 million in 2015. With the increasing population, land is being converted from productive purposes, such as crop cultivation, to other uses. Bangladesh is losing good quality agricultural land by approximately 80 000 hectares annually to urbanization, building of new infrastructure and implementation of other development projects (World Bank, 2005 [10]).

Degradation of Land

Land is being continuously degraded and lost owing to erosion, salinity, inundation and other anomalies. Moreover, at least 86,000 hectares of land were lost to river/estuarine erosion from 1973 to 2000 (MES, 2001[11]) although this was somewhat compensated for by land formed through accretion. Seventy percent of the land of Barisal and Khulna divisions are affected by different degrees of salinity, which reduces agricultural productivity. Fifty percent of coastal lands are subjected to inundation of varying degrees and frequency that limits their effective use. This situation is expected to worsen due to climate changes due to global warming.

Emergence of Commercial Shrimp Farming

Increased demand and the high price for shrimp at the international markets have led to increase commercial shrimp farming in the coastal areas in Bangladesh. The south-western parts of Bangladesh had a history of traditional shrimp farming, but polders provided a further opportunity to intensify this activity. The polders of the south-western coast of the country are experienced severe internal drainage congestion and heavy external siltation. Areas became unsuitable not only for agriculture, but in extreme cases, even for human habitation. It was termed as a "man-made disaster" (Rahman, 1995 [12]) resulting in increased poverty and out migration from the area. At the same time, polders provided new opportunities for expanded shrimp farming using the control structures of the embankments. Subsequently, the land devoted to shrimp farming expanded and encroached on agriculture and forest lands.

Many coastal polders, constructed to protect agricultural land from saltwater inundation, were turned into large shrimp farms. Saltwater was allowed into the polders in order to raise shrimps cultivation. Driven by commercial interests, land used for agriculture and mangroves was converted, often forcibly, to shrimp farming (Haque, 2004 [13]). This resulted in wide-scale land-use conflicts (Karim and Stellwagen [14], 1998; Deb, 1998 [15]), environmental pollution (Islam, 2003) and social unrest situations in these areas (Firoze, 2003 [16]).

Several studies reported a reduction in land for cattle grazing (Maniruzzaman, 1998 [17]), the death of trees and other vegetation, increased salinity of soil and water, and a reduction of the drinking water supply. Firoze (2003) and Majid and Gupta (1997) reported the social and environmental impacts of industrial shrimp culture. As agricultural lands were converted into shrimp farms, sharecroppers and landless wage labourers lost their livelihoods. They began movements to resist the introduction of shrimp cultivation into their areas. This often is resulted in violence. During the last two decades, more than 150 people have been killed and thousands injured in shrimp cultivation-related violence (Firoze, 2003 [16]).

Brackish water shrimp cultivation on an industrial scale has introduced large-scale environmental degradation (Islam, 2003 [7]). Shrimp polders retain saline water for months and the salinity seeps into adjacent paddy farms and salinizes the soil. The loss of mangrove areas to aquaculture is a common feature with Chakoria Sundarbans being the classic example. Between 1967 and 1988, Chakoria Sundarbans mangrove areas were reduced from 7,500 to only 973 hectares.

The coastal area along the Meghna Estuary is morphologically one of the most dynamic areas in the world (MES, 2001 [11]). Land erosion and accretion are common natural phenomena in the coastal zone. To find out the land erosion and accretion rates in the Meghna Estuary several LANDSAT satellite images were taken during the period 1973 to 2000 (MES, 2001 [11]) and analyzed. Land erosion and accretion of inter-tidal areas, i.e. mudflats, is not included in this analysis. The study shows an overall land gain for the Meghna Estuary system of about 50 800 hectares (Table 2). The average annual gain for the entire study period was 1 880 hectares/year.

Table-1: Erosion and Accretion Rate in the Meghna Estuary, 1973–2000

Periods	Erosion and accretion in ha and ha/yr					
	1973–1979	1979–1984	1984–1990	1990–1996	1996–2000	1973–2000
Accretion	50 175	45 550	33 505	56 520	23 850	137 168
Erosion	32 873	31 112	42 410	29 182	32 260	86 366
Net change	17 302	14 438	-8 905	27 338	-8 410	50 802
Annual rate of accretion	8 363	9 110	5 584	9 420	5 963	5 080
Annual rate of erosion	5 479	6 222	7 068	4 864	8 065	3 199
Annual rate of net change	2 884	2 888	-1 484	4 556	-2 103	1 882

Source: Meghna Estuary Study (MES), 2001.

Because of continual shifting of the coastline and erosion, shifting people are common in the community fabric of coastal Bangladesh. Hundreds of thousands People have been shifted to 14 times in a year.

Suggestive Measures

In consideration the problems, causes and prospects of the present study the following initiatives may reduce the hazardous situation and can play an effective role for ensuring a sustainable environment in the coastal areas in Bangladesh:

- to ensure immediate establishment of the ICZM coordinating arrangement, as approved under the Coastal Zone Policy 2005,
- to coordinate and harmonize different agencies active in the coastal zone,
- to demarcate of land zoning, as approved under the Land Use Policy, 2001 and enforcing laws to prevent encroachment,
- to prevent the deforestation at the coastal green belt by involving coastal communities in its maintenance,

- to establishment of Tsunami preparedness measures (including community-based awareness and preparedness) in the most vulnerable area where at least 4.7 million people remain at risk,
- to protect land reclamation through construction of cross dams,
- to take initiatives for studying the impact of land use change and review regularly for the socio-economic and environmental change detection,
- to ensure a continuous monitoring system to understand the Land use changes and identify the areas under Land use change,
- to ensure establishment of set-back distances along the coastline,
- to prevent and discourage human settlement in highly erosion-prone areas,
- to establish a network of expert groups on coastal and land-use planning and management,
- to arrange technical support for countries in the region to establish a modern GIS-based land record system and
- to set up a Commission for studying on "planning and practices of land zoning in the coastal Bangladesh" and land zoning should be identified as an important instrument for sustainable land management for decades, its implementation still remains a concern.

Conclusion

In recent years, coastal planning and land-use management have received serious attention by the Government of Bangladesh. Adoption of the Land Use Policy (2001), Coastal Zone Policy (2005), Tsunami Vulnerability Map (2005) and Coastal Development Strategy (2006) are some of the milestone achievements. However, implementation of policy and strategy directives remains a key issue otherwise it would be a man-made disaster in the coastal zone of Bangladesh in near future.

References

1. Islam, M R (Ed.) 2004. Where land meets the sea: a profile of the coastal zone of Banglades, The University Press Limited, Dhaka, p 317.
2. Islam, M.R. Ahmad, M. Huq, H. & M.S. Osman, 2006. "State of the coast 2006", Program Development Office for Integrated Coastal Zone Management Plan Project, Water Resources Planning Organization, Dhaka.
3. Ahmad, M., 2004. "Living in the coast: people and livelihood", Program Development Office for Integrated Coastal Zone Management Plan Project, Water Resources Planning Organization, Dhaka, March 2004.
4. PDO-ICZMP, 2004. "Areas with special status in the coastal zone", PDO-ICZMP project, Dhaka.
5. Brammer, H., 2002. Land use and land use planning in Bangladesh, The University Press Limited, Dhaka.
6. Alam, S.M.N. Demaine, H. & M.J. Phillips, 2002. "Land use diversity in south western coastal areas of Bangladesh", The Land, 6.3: 173–184.
7. Islam, M.R. & R. Koudstaal, 2003. "Coastal zone management: an analysis of different policy documents", Working paper 09, Program Development Office for ICZM, January 2003, p 52.
8. DoF., 2005. "Fishery statistical yearbook of Bangladesh 2003–2004", Fisheries Resources Survey System, Department of Fisheries, Dhaka.
9. Nishat, A., 1988. "Review of present activities and state of art of the coastal areas of Bangladesh", Coastal area resource development and management Part II, Coastal Area Resource Development and Management Association (CARDMA), Dhaka, pp 23–35.
10. World Bank, 2005. "Revitalizing the agricultural technology system in Bangladesh", Bangladesh Development Series - Paper No.7, Dhaka, World Bank, p 156.

11. Meghna Estuary Study (MES), 2001. "Hydro-morphological dynamics of the Meghna Estuary", Meghna Estuary Study (MES) Project, Bangladesh Water Development Board, Dhaka.
12. Rahman, A. 1995. "Beel Dakatia: environmental consequences of a development disaster", The University Press Limited, Dhaka.
13. Haque, A.K.E., 2004. "Sanitary and phyto-sanitary barriers to trade and its impact on the environment: the case of shrimp farming in Bangladesh", IUCN Bangladesh Country Office, Dhaka, p 63.
14. Karim, M. & J. Stellwagen, 1998. "Shrimp aquaculture", Fourth Fisheries Project, Department of Fisheries: Final report, Dhaka, Volume 6, p 101.
15. Deb, A.K., 1998. "Fake blue revolution: environmental and socio-economic impacts of shrimp culture in the coastal areas of Bangladesh", Ocean & Coastal Management, pp 63–88.
16. Firoze, A., 2003. "The southwest coastal region: problems and potentials", The Daily Star, Dhaka, XIV, Issue 215.
17. Maniruzzaman, M., 1998. "Intrusion of commercial shrimp farming in three rice-growing villages of southern Bangladesh: its effects on poverty, environment and selected aspects of culture", an unpublished Ph.D. thesis, University of the Philippines, Quezon City, Philippines.

Chapter-VI

Solar Energy Policies and Rural Electrification in India

Meenal Jain, Meenakshi Mital and Matt Syal*

Abstract

Today, India can well be identified as an energy guzzler. In an effort to meet the demands of a developing nation, the Indian energy sector has witnessed a rapid growth. But continuation of the use of fossil fuels is set to face multiple challenges: depletion of fossil fuel reserves, global warming and other environmental concerns. Renewable energy is the solution to the growing energy challenges as they are abundant, inexhaustible and environmentally friendly. Accelerating the use of renewable energy, particularly solar energy is also indispensable if India is to meet its commitments to reduce its carbon intensity. Given the vast potential of solar energy in India, all it needs is comprehensive policies. Government has taken a number of steps towards improving the adoption of solar energy at a large scale in the country and making the stakeholders aware of its benefits. Many programs and policies have been initiated at both the National and State levesl, but the use and production of solar energy in the country is still limited. On studying one of the major initiatives of National government, the "Remote Rural Village Electrification" in Chattisgarh as a case, it was found that there was a gap between the policies and the actual scenario. The awareness level among the beneficiaries was found to be very low. Thus, there is an urgent need to generate awareness among the stakeholders regarding the government initiatives, so that solar energy is widely accepted and used.

Keywords – Awareness, Government Policies, Solar Energy.

* Research Scholar and Professors, Department of Resource Management and Design Application, Lady Irwin College, University of Delhi

Introduction

Energy is inevitable for human life and a secure and accessible supply of energy is crucial for the sustainability of modern societies (Asif & Muneer, 2007). Energy has been recognized as one of the most pertinent contributors for economic growth and human development universally. There is a strong two-way relationship between economic development and energy consumption. On one hand, growth of an economy hinges on the availability of cost-effective and environmentally benign energy sources, and on the other hand, the level of economic development relies on the energy demand (India Energy Portal, n.d.). Today, India can well be identified as an energy guzzler. The demand for power is growing exponentially and the scope of growth of this sector is immense. In an effort to meet the demands of a developing nation, the Indian energy sector has witnessed a rapid growth (Ministry of New and Renewable Energy [MNRE], 2011a).

India is heavily dependent on fossil fuels for most of its demand. It is evident by the fact that coal accounts for almost 55% of the country's total energy supplies and about 75% of the coal in the country is consumed in the power sector. Coal is followed by crude oil and natural gas in terms of usage in the power sector (India Energy Portal, n.d.). Continuation of the use of fossil fuels is set to face multiple challenges: depletion of fossil fuel reserves, global warming and other environmental concerns, geopolitical and military conflicts and of late, continued and significant fuel price rise. Renewable energy is the solution to the growing energy challenges as they are abundant, inexhaustible and environmentally friendly (Asif & Muneer, 2006).

Accelerating the use of renewable energy is also indispensable if India is to meet its commitments to reduce its carbon intensity. The power sector contributes nearly half of the country's carbon emissions. On average, every 1GW of additional renewable energy capacity reduces CO_2 emissions by 3.3 million tons a year. Investing in renewable energy would enable India to develop globally competitive industries and technologies that can provide new opportunities for growth and leadership (Sargsyan, Bhatia, Banerjee, Raghunathan & Soni, 2010). As per Ministry of New and Renewable Energy, India is the 4th largest country with regard to installed power generation capacity in the field of renewable energy.

Wind, Hydro, Biomass and Solar are main renewable energy sources in India. The country has an estimated renewable energy potential of around 85,000 MW from commercially exploitable sources (MNRE, 2011b). Currently, India has an installed base of over 27,000 MW of renewable energy, which is around 17% of India's total power generation capacity (Abdullah, 2011).

If we try to look at all the renewable energy sources, it is seen that India is among top 5 destinations worldwide for solar energy development as per Ernst & Young's renewable energy attractiveness index (MNRE, 2011c). Because of its location between the Tropic of Cancer and the Equator, India has an average annual temperature that ranges from 25°C – 27.5 °C. This means that India has huge solar potential (Meisen, 2006). Most parts of India have 300 - 330 sunny days in a year, which is equivalent to over 5000 trillion kWh per year - more than India's total energy consumption per year. India is expected to have installed solar energy capacity of 20,000 MW by 2022 (MNRE, 2011d). Thus, if we look at the renewable energy potential, solar energy provides great opportunity to be tapped by India to have a sustainable energy scenario. Hence, it is important to understand the initiatives taken by the Indian government to promote renewable sources of energy, with specific reference to solar energy.

Significance

Review of literature has shown that there are many programs and policies which have been initiated by the Indian government, both at the National and the State level for promoting renewable energy, but the use and production of renewable energy in the country is still limited. It is important to understand the programs, policies and incentives started by the government in detail. Further, there is need to understand the awareness and satisfaction level of the end users or the beneficiaries of these renewable (solar) energy projects. The study also envisages to understand the impediments in implementing these initiatives from the perspective of the government and generate a framework for better acceptance and implementation of such programs and policies. Literature review showed that even though information on the policies, programs and incentives is available, the stakeholders' perspective is not yet studied. The present paper focuses on the impediments associated with solar energy policies from the stakeholders' perspective.

Methodology

The study was conducted in the state of Chattisgarh in India which is situated in Central India. Urban Chhattisgarh is one of the few states of India where the power sector is effectively developed. The Chhattisgarh State Electricity Board (CSEB) is in a strong position to meet the electricity requirement of the new state and is in good financial health. Talking about the rural areas of the state, deciduous forests of the Eastern Highlands Forests cover roughly 44% of the state and this is the reason these areas have not yet received grid connected power. Thus, Non conventional energy sources have been accorded very high priority. To cater to this issue, a special agency called CREDA (Chhattisgarh Renewable Energy Development Agency) has been set up, and over 1200 villages in dense forests are being electrified using off-grid energy. CREDA is the nodal agency of Ministry of New and Renewable Energy. This organization comes under the State Government but eventually implements the policies brought out by the Central Government (MNRE).

Four villages namely Kobahara, Rawan, Mahoda and Latadadar were selected which were electrified by solar energy under the Remote Village Electrification Programme. From each village, eight households were selected and one respondent from each household was interviewed based on their willingness to take part in the study. The respondents included both men and women. Also, government officials in CREDA were interviewed to take their perspective on the catalysts and barriers associated with solar energy policies in the state.

Government Programmes and Policies

Government of India has come out with a number of policies and programs for the promotion of renewable energy, and specifically solar energy, in India. The National Solar Mission is a major initiative of the Government of India and State Governments to promote ecologically sustainable growth while addressing India's energy security challenge. It will also constitute a major contribution by India to the global effort to meet the challenges of climate change. Solar is currently high on absolute costs compared to other sources of power such as coal. The Mission recognizes that there are a number of off-grid solar applications particularly for meeting rural energy needs, which are already cost-effective and provides for their rapid expansion.

It also states that off-grid decentralized and low-temperature applications will be advantageous from a rural electrification perspective and meeting other energy needs for power and heating and cooling in both rural and urban areas.

On March 3, 2001, the Prime Minister of India convened a meeting of all the Chief Ministers of states to build a national consensus, where rural electrification got the top-most priority. Important resolutions included in the consensus were (a) electrification of all villages and households is to be undertaken; rural electrification is to be treated as a basic minimum service, (b) rural electrification is to be completed by 2007, and electrification of all households by 2012 (Buragohain, 2012).

Taking the said missions forward, the National Action Plan on Climate Change was launched in 2008 which had eight missions under it, dealing with various issues. Under the National Solar Mission, one of the programmes for off-grid power solution is the Remote Village Electrification Programme, brought out by MNRE. This Ministry is implementing this programme for providing financial support for electrification of those remote unelectrified census villages and unelectrified hamlets of electrified census villages where grid-extension is either not feasible or not cost effective. Such villages are provided basic facilities for electricity through various renewable energy sources, particularly solar. The beneficiaries of this scheme are the village households which get solar power for their basic requirements of lighting. In addition, street lighting systems with 11 W CFL is also considered under the project.

The Ministry provides a subsidy of upto 90% of the costs of the Renewable electricity generation systems (including the cost of Annual Maintenance Contract (AMC), if any, for 5 years). The balance cost of projects can be financed through contribution from respective State Government/CSR funds/entrepreneurs investment/ loan/beneficiaries contribution or other sources other than Government of India fund. However, it will be necessary that at least half of the balance cost is met from State Government's funding (MNRE, 2011a). About 1,400 solar-powered villages in Chattisgarh, that are not connected to the national grid because they are in a remote area, have been enjoying the benefits of electrification under this Remote Village Electrification Programme.

Impediments in Solar Energy Policies

It was seen that most of the beneficiaries were farmers and belonged to low socio-economic status. The electricity being supplied through solar power was basically used for lighting in the households. Under the projects, basic lighting facilities with two light points (around 9 W each) and one socket (around 40 W) for operating electronic gadgets for each of the willing households in the village may be provided (flexibility of points may be allowed within total 58 W). Thus every household will be eligible for a maximum of 58 Watt unless the house owner himself wants less. The technology for such projects is simple and the source of power abundant, making it the obvious choice for electrification in rural areas. It was reported that the installation costs were borne by the government, both Central and State and the beneficiaries had to pay some monthly amount per CFL that they use. However, it was seen that there was a variation in the amount of money being charged from the villagers per CFL per month. Under the project, the households were eligible to get electricity for six hours a day. However it was reported that the electricity was available only for three to four hours a day.

Most of the respondents said that one of the major barriers in the current solar electricity they were getting was that it was not available during night when they needed it the most. Some reported that most of the important events like weddings etc. happen at night but electricity is not available at that time.

The villagers also reported that the electricity available to each household should be increased, i.e., they wanted to run more appliances like water pumps, fans, refrigerators and TV, than just a single light bulb. Also, most of the respondents said that they wanted light for the entire night for their kids to study. Thus, in the short time that the electricity was supplied, the families would start using a lot of appliances like lights, fans, TV etc. and thus, due to overloading, the plant would trip, leading to another problem of discontinuous supply of electricity. It was heartening to know that during the four hours schedule of electricity supply, it is effectively there for only half an hour to one hour. During data collection, the researcher also witnessed that the light kept going on and off.

It was found that although training programmes on use and maintenance of solar power plants are regularly organized by CREDA, the end-users were most negligent and thus, lacked awareness. CREDA was involved in training and capacity building of the local people for laying and maintaining the solar power plants. Every village had a plant operator who belonged to that village and was trained by CREDA. However, it was observed that most of the beneficiaries were not aware of solar energy. Although some of them knew that the electricity was coming from the power plant which was there in the village, few knew that the source was solar energy. Many of the respondents were not even aware of the power plant in their village. It was surprising to see that even the plant operator's wife was neither aware of the power plant, nor its source.The maintenance and upkeep of solar power plants were not up to the mark since the beneficiaries are the most negligent. Thus, major problems were there like thefts of PV panels, overloading and so on.

It was seen that cost is the biggest impediment in implementing solar energy policies. Since government is trying to increase capacity of solar power plants in each village, huge investment is required by the government. It was also found that the Nodal agency of each state has to fight with the Central and State governments for finances. Another barrier that was reported by CREDA officials was limited manpower available in the organization. This resulted in many problems associated with training of the local people, maintenance of the power plants and so on.

Thus, all the above came out as the main impediments in solar energy policies' and their implementation which need to be worked upon.

Conclusion

Continuation of the use of fossil fuels is set to face multiple challenges: depletion of fossil fuel reserves, global warming and other environmental concerns, geopolitical and military conflicts and of late, continued and significant fuel price rise. Renewable energy is the solution to the growing energy challenges as they are abundant, inexhaustible and environmentally friendly. Thus, government being the main regulatory body in the country, it has an important role to play in promoting renewable energy in the country. National Solar Mission was taken as the main policy initiative by the Government, under which attempt was made to understand the impediments associated with the Remote Village Electrification Programme in Chattisgarh.

After conducting the research, many major impediments came out both from the implementers' and the users' perspective such as lack of awareness, high costs involved, discontinuous supply of electricity, less capacity and so on. It is suggested that solar power projects be developed taking care of the local needs of the people. The local people ought to be involved at every stage to have a clear understanding of their requirements so that the project can be made to suit their needs.

Another benefit that it would incur is that when people are involved in something, they feel connected to it and thus, problems like overloading can be taken care of. In addition, when the problem of overloading is taken care of, the problem of erratic electricity supply would also be solved. Another major area of concern is monitoring of these solar power plants. Proper monitoring teams need to be made to overcome the problems of thefts etc. Also, the capacity of the solar power plants need to be increased so that more appliances could be run and problem of overloading could be taken care of. Another area that needs attention is the amount of time the electricity is supplied for. It is suggested that the electricity be supplied for at least twelve hours a day and especially during nights.

Awareness is a major area that requires immediate attention. Training programs needs to be developed in local languages, spreading education on the benefits of solar energy and proper use and maintenance of the plants being installed in the village. Local people can be trained to keep a track of the plants. Another important issue is the involvement of women. Women are the main end users of electricity in the households as they spend most of their time indoors and do most of the household chores. Empowering them would result into empowerment of the entire society. Thus, specialized training programmes need to be created for women and delivered from time to time. All these measures would help take this movement of solar energy to great heights.

References

1. Abdullah F (2011) India's Renewable Future: Challenges and Prospects.http://www.renewableenergyworld.com / rea/news/article/2011/02/indias-renewable-future-challenges-and-prospects. Accessed 22 May 2013.

2. M Asif, & T Muneer (2007) Energy supply, its demand and security issues for developed and emerging economies. Renewable and Sustainable Energy Reviews, 11(7):1388-1413

3. India Energy Portal (n.d.) Indian Energy Sector: An overview. http://www.indiaenergyportal.org/overview_detail.php. Accessed 2 February 2014.

4. India Energy Portal (n.d.) Overview of Indian Energy sector. http:// www.indiaenergyportal.org/overview.php. Accessed 2 February 2014.

5. International Energy Consulting Corporation (2011) India Energy Handbook. http://www.psimedia.info/handbook/India_Energy_Handbook.pdf. Accessed 22 January 2014.

6. Meisen P (2006) Overview of Renewable Energy Potential of India. http://www.geni.org/globalenergy/library/energytrends/currentusage/renewable/Renewable-Energy-Potential-for-India.pdf. Accessed 5 December 2013.

7. Ministry of New and Renewable Energy (2011a) Jawaharlal Nehru Solar Mission. http://www.mnre.gov.in/annualreport/2010_11_English/Chapter%206/chapter%206.htm. Accessed 5 December 2013.

8. Ministry of New and Renewable Energy (2011b) Power from Renewables: Grid Interactive and off grid Renewable Power. http://www.mnre.gov.in/annualreport/2010_11_English/Chapter%205/chapter%205.htm. Accessed 9 November 2013.

9. Ministry of New and Renewable Energy (2011c) Renewable Energy at a glance. http://www.mnre.gov.in/akshayurja/akshayurja-december-2011/52.pdf. Accessed 9 November 2013.

10. Ministry of New and Renewable Energy (2011d) Strategic plan for New and Renewable Energy sector for the period 2011-17. http://www.mnre.gov.in/policy/strategic-plan-mnre-2011-17.pdf. Accessed 16 October 2013.

11. Sargsyan G, Bhatia M, Banerjee, S G, Raghunathan K., & Soni R (2010) Unleashing the Potential of Renewable energy in India. http://siteresources.worldbank.org/EXTENERGY2/Resources/Unleashing_potential_of_renewables_in_India.pdf. Accessed 16 October 2013.

Chapter-VII

Adjusting Livelihood and Environment: Traditional Dairy Farming Practice of the Nepali Community in Lower Dibang Valley, Arunachal Pradesh

Puspa Komor & Jayasree Borah*

Abstract

The Eastern Himalayan foothill region of Lower Dibang Valley in Arunachal Pradesh is dotted with dairy farming units of the Nepali community, locally known as Khutti. Though the dairy units are located in Lower Dibang Valley, the dairy farmer's household is located in Sadiya, sub-division of the Tinsukia district of Assam. The economy of these dairy farming units mainly depends on their own unique traditional structure of cost and production, price and profitability, milk and milk products, networking and market. This dairy practice relies heavily on the traditional knowledge base of the Nepali Community. It has its own ecological, economic, geographical and social ramifications. Owing to frequent changing of the channels by the tributaries of the Brahmaputra River, floods, diminishing grazing lands and fodder availability coupled with other anthropogenic factors in the upper reaches of the Brahmaputra Valley, this community have shifted their dairy units to the Dibang Valley. This has augmented to a wide variation and complicated pattern of livelihood in terms of its spatial arrangement and temporal adjustment with the environment. The study is exploratory in nature. Both qualitative and quantitative methods are employed with appropriate PRA exercises. The findings of the study will help to identify gaps and set priorities for livelihoods improvement of the Nepali dairy farming community through the traditional knowledge and evaluate the impacts on the rural livelihood.

Keywords: Dairy farming, Khutti, Livelihood, Lower Dibang Valley, Traditional knowledge

---

*Research Scholar & Professor, Department of Geography, Cotton College, India

Introduction

The far east of India usually referred as the 'north east India' forms a heterogeneous ensemble of ethnicity, culture and linguistic groups. One such ethno-linguistic group is that of the Nepali community. With their own mother tongue i.e. Nepali, also known as Gurkhali, Khas Kura or Parbatiya, this community have a unique characteristic of being very a highly mobile community. There earliest migration to northeast India dates back to 730-750 AD [(1)] but the most significant migration took place after the Treaty of Sagauli (signed after the Anglo-Gurkha war, 1816-1817). The British started to recruit the Gurkha in the British army as the 'Gurkha battalion' (now Assam Rifles) and the presence of the Nepali community was started to be felt in the soils of Assam (now North-east India). The first Anglo-Burmese war in 1826 which led to the Treaty of Yandaboo incorporated Assam as a protectorate of the British government. Assam transformed into a land of opportunities with unlimited income and investment chances, converting Assam into a prime destination for people from outside and groups such as the Marwaris, Biharis and Nepalis found their way into the region [(2)]. The Nepali dairy farmers are the later group of migrants who began to migrate in the last part of the nineteenth century. They followed the 'beaten paths' laid down by the Gurkha soldiers recruited by the British to defend the Eastern frontier. This migration has continued in the post colonial period, with most migrants finding an easy source of survival in the business of dairy farming, as addition or alternative to other work [(3)].

To keep up with their traditional occupational practice, the Nepali settlers required wide extensive grazing lands. The virgin rolling alluvium tract of the upper Brahmaputra basin with abundant water availability attracted the early settlers as it would provide ample scope of fodder for their cattle. Thus, the Sadiya region became a suitable destination for the Nepali dairy farming community. With the changing demography of the Sadiya sub-division, the fodder availability started to shrink and the Nepalis dairyman started to move their herd further uphill. In no time at all, today, most of the cowsheds, locally known as 'Khutti' are located in the Lower Dibang Valley in Arunachal Pradesh. With their home in Sadiya, Assam and herds in lower Dibang Valley, Arunachal Pradesh their community surprisingly puts forward a very interesting semi pastoral sort of phenomena, adding substantially to the economy of the Nepali dairy farming community. In this factum, having established the conceptual and empirical background of the study, the present research paper attempts to study the nature and the dynamics of the functioning of Khuttis. It also tries to identify the gaps of this traditional livelihood. Further, it prudently explores the socio-economic condition of the Nepali dairy farming community in order to evaluate the resultant impact on the rural livelihood in the study area.

Study Area

The study area includes the Lower Dibang Valley district (27° 0′ 08″ to 28° 0′ 35″ N & 94° 0′ 06″ to 95° 0′ 24″ E) of Arunachal Pradesh and the Sadiya sub-division (27°20′ - 28°0′ N and 95°15′ and 96°0′ E) of the district of Tinsukia in Assam. The Lower Dibang Valley is a comparatively newly carved state. It was born on 16th Dec'2001. The river Dibang, one of the tributary of the mighty Brahmaputra flows through the district and hence, it is named so. The district is bordered by Upper & East Siang on West, Anjaw & Lohit on the East & Dibang Valley to the North. Sadiya, on the other hand is the confluence point of the three rivers, namely, Dibang, Dihing and Lohit which forms the mighty Brahmaputra. It is bordered by Lower Dibang Valley to the north; to its northeast lie the district of Lohit, Dhemaji to the west and to the south lies the Brahmaputra (Fig. 1) .

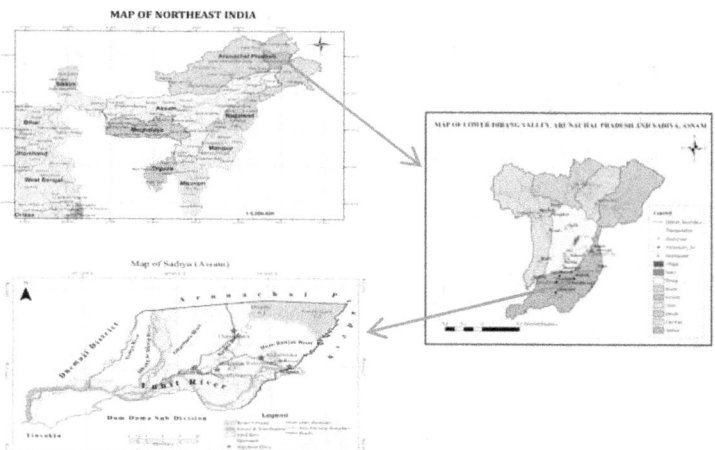

Figure 1. Locational Map of the Northeast India, Lower Dibang Valley and the Sadiya sub-division, Assam

Methodology

The field study was conducted during the period of 2009-11 at different phases in Lower Dibang Valley district of Arunachal Pradesh and the Sadiya sub-division of the district of Tinsukia, Assam. A total of 90 khuttis were surveyed, spreading over the 3 circles of the Lower Dibang Valley. The household of these khutti owners are located in 6 different villages in Sadiya. The study is exploratory by nature. Both qualitative and quantitative methods have been employed. For the qualitative study, PRA exercises, direct observation, interview with the key informant and group discussion with the dairy farm owners were conducted for assessing seasonality and understanding the role and nature of the functioning of the dairy farms. While for the quantitative methods, data were collected with the help of structured survey schedule. To assess the altitudinal variation, longitudinal and latitudinal position of the dairy farms Geographical Positioning System (GPS) has been used. Topographic maps and Satellite Imageries have been used in order to study the spatio-temporal aspects of the study area.

Socio-cultural Aspect of Dairying

It is a marked tendency of every cultural linguistic group to retain their tradition and occupation and maintain that traditional identity which has been passed on through generations. The Nepalese are no exception to this phenomenon. The Nepali community has been traditionally engaged in cattle rearing, sedentary agriculture and dairy farming. Livelihood simply connotes a means of securing the necessities of life and dairying as a source of livelihood to the Nepali community has been embedded in their culture and has become a way of life. The Nepali community has been broadly divided into two distinct racial groups. They are the Caucasoid and the Mongoloid. The Caucasoid speaks the Indo Aryan Nepali language (Bahun, Chetri, Newar and others) and whereas the mongoloids speak the 'Tibeto – Nepalese'. Of the 'Tibeto- Nepalese' a section (Tamang, Sherpas, Yotmus and others) follows Buddhism and the others (Rai, Limbu, Gurung, Magar and others) follow animists' faith. As a result, there exists no caste hierarchy in the latter. The social structure is egalitarian in nature unlike to that of the Indo-Aryan Nepali language speaking community [(3), (4)].

Dairying for the Nepali community is not only a source of economy but also at the same time is more of a cultural symbol and ethos. Ownership of a herd still symbolizes social acceptance and prestige and religious considerations cannot be ignored. Livestock are considered pious are an integral part of most of the ceremonies performed by the community. Marriages 'Biye' to the Cremation Ceremony 'Sarad' or Naming of child 'Naran', livestock are presented to the priest for the well being of the family or the concerned person. Further, the urine 'Gayunt' of a young calf is considered to be a purifying agent and is consumed after the cremation ceremony.

Irrespective of their languages and religious practices, the Nepali community in the study area has been traditionally engaged in cattle rearing, sedentary agriculture and dairy farming. The sampled dairy farm units in the Lower Dibang Valley are either Cow Khuttis or Buffalo Khuttis. But some of the dairy units have both cow and buffalo in the same dairy unit. Of the sampled Dairy Units, most of the Farm Type belonged to cow and buffalo rearing (44%) while only 16% of the dairy units rear buffaloes.

It has been witnessed that the maximum number of farms are of medium size (57%) of which 24% are found in Dambuk circle, 30% belongs to the small farm size and 13% accounts for the big size farms (Table 1).

Table 1: Distribution of Dairy Units according to Farm Type and Farm Size

Farm Type (FT)	No. of Farms	Percentage (%)
Farm type- Cow (FT-Co)	36	40
Farm Type- Buffalo (FT-Bu)	14	16
Farm Type- Cow & Buffalo (FT-CoBu)	40	44
Farm Size (FS)	No of Farms	Percentage (%)
Farm size- Big (FS-B) >200	12	13
Farm size- Medium (FS-M) 80- 200	51	57
Farm size- Small (FS-S) < 80	27	30

The dairy owners belonged to 6 different villages in Sadiya, viz., Ambhikapur, Chunpura, Ghurmura, Chapakhowa, Chunpura and Shantipur. These dairy units are spread over three circles of the Lower Dibang Valley, the other three circles Kronli, Hunli and Desali falls within the rugged topography of the Eastern Himalayas. The slopes are steep and terrain rugged. Owing to such conditions the dairy farm owners have settled for the foothill region of Lower Dibang Valley covering the circles of Roing, Dambuk and Koronu.

Sample Variable	Variables	Frequency	Percentage (%)
Age	Young (Below 30)	19	21
	Middle (31-50)	55	61
	Old (Above 50)	16	18
Education	Literates	78	87
	Illiterates	12	13
Occupation	Dairy farming	22	24
	Dairy farming & Agriculture	52	58
	Dairy farming & others	16	18
Owner's Caste	Bahun	23	26
	Chetri	29	32
	Newar	11	12
	Tamang	9	10
	Rai	10	11
	Gurung	8	9
Land	Landless	-	-
	Marginal (0.1- 2.5 acres)	31	34
	Small (2.51- 5 acres)	48	54
	Large (> 5 acres)	11	12
Source of Fund	Bank loan	0	0
	Own Source	79	88
	Money lender	21	12

Source: Fieldwork

Land is one of the most important assets in every village. Though the main source of livelihood for the Nepali dairy farming community is dairy farming, they depend on agriculture in the lean period. Moreover, the whole family is not involved with dairy farming. It is mostly the male folks in the family and a lady for the household chores moves to the dairy farms unit. The left out members back at the villages are engaged in agricultural activities.

Middle aged and more experienced member of the family generally takes over the dairy unit. 61% of the khutti owners belong to the middle aged group. But after 60 years the elderly member retires for spiritual pursuits and let the young members to take over. A significant 21% accounted for young dairy farm owners. The majority of the Khutti households own medium scale farms. 24% of the dairy farm owners rely solely on dairying for their livelihood. While 58% of the khutti owners are also depended on agricultural practices and the remaining 18% of them either have a temporary service holder back at home or is an ex-army man. Thus, we can see that the dairy farmers have not abandoned agriculture. Not of the dairy farm owners are landless. 54% are small scale land holders, 12% of them are large scale land holders. The dairy farmers generally practice rice cultivation. Dairy farming supports them only in the peak period of lactation and draught trade but in the dry period it is agriculture that they depend upon. The entire household surveyed grows rice. Production of rice is basically for there own consumption but people with large agricultural fields also sell it the in the nearby town. Apart from rice cultivation the Nepali dairy farming families are also engaged in fishery cultivation, ginger cultivation, sugarcane cultivation, pulses and other different crops.

Thus, we see that they practice agricultural activities and do have an ample amount of landholdings to support their families. The socio-personal profile (Table 3) also shows that 32% of the total dairy farm units belonged to the Chetri caste. Bahun comprised of 26%, Newar (12%), Rai (11%), Tamang (10%) and Gurung (9%). The study revealed that religious assimilation has developed a new type of faith. The household belonging to the Rai and Magar caste follow Hinduism but have not totally abandoned their animistic faith altogether. 87% of the Khutti owners are literate. But some of them does have formal education but can read and write. They are well versed and are well read in religious text and scriptures. For the establishment of the Khutti, 88% of the owners had invested the initial amount from their own source and the rest have arranged it either from the money lender or from the village head.

Table 2. Distribution of Dairy Unit in the Different Circles in percentage (%)

Circles	FS-B	FS-M	FS-S
Dambuk	7	24	12
Roing	4	18	13
Koronu	2	16	4
Kronli	-	-	-
Hunli	-	-	-
Desali	-	-	-

Nature and Functioning of the Dairy Economy

Economics of dairying is an applied field of economic science (5). Livestock keeping continues to be an integral part in most farming system thereby generating income and contributing to an improved livelihood in many farming household (6).

Open pastures are common phenomenon in Lower Dibang Valley but one still finds troughs in the yards for feeding the newborn. For the cow sheds the dairy farmers prefers an uphill location but as for the buffalo shed they prefer the downhill region. This is basically because of the buffaloes, as part of their typical animal behaviour requires wetlands for their survival. The prominent landscape elements that characterize the Khuttis in ad ditions to the cows and buffaloes themselves are the small huts of the dairy farmer, the cowshed adjacent to the hut and a small kitchen garden to supply them with the daily vegetables.

The Khuttis are located in the far off places where the influence of the settlement is very less, where there is an abundant supply of fodder for the livestock. Most of these Khuttis are located in the river islands of the River Dibang, locally known as 'Chouri'. None of the dairy units is connected to the nearest town by any roadways. They are connected by some beaten pathways, which the dairy farmers

'Guwalas' built by clearing the forest. Waterways are widely used by them for transporting their goods and products. The main objective of Khutti economy is to generate cash and kind i.e., milk, money and manure. But the economy of the Nepali guwalas is not entirely dependent on the economic factor only. A lot of social and cultural aspect of the community is interwoven intrinsically within the purview of the economy. The profitability or the justification of carrying on this traditional method of dairying can be assessed by comparing the total expected cost of each type of cattle against the total expected benefits of the same. Thus, an attempt has been made to determine if it is a sound investment by linking the functioning of dairy farm units to assess the Cost and Returns of Cows and Buffalo Farms in the Study Area to livelihood economy.

Income Pattern of the Dairy Units

Khuttis be it cow, buffalo or both dot the landscape of Lower Dibang Valley. But the production and income differ from each other. But this form of economy is seasonal. This is mainly because the cattle, be it, the cow or the buffalo gives milk only in the lactation period. The lactation period for the cows in this region is near about 170-180 days and for the buffaloes it is around 180-190 days of the year. The main objective of the Khutti economy is to raise cattle to produce milk. The milk is used in the original form or turned into butter, cream and clarified butter (ghee). The milk produced in the Khuttis is generally sold in the collection area at a particular time of the day. If they happen to be late the entire milk is wasted. The milkman who comes to collect the milk and its products are generally employed by the local trader for a monthly salary of Rs 1000. The trader buys the raw milk from these dairy farmers. The cow's milk fetches Rs 10 for the dairy owner and Rs 15 for buffalo milk per litre.

The production of milk depends upon the number of milk able cows and buffaloes. The khuttis have more female buffalo than the male once. Every buffalo khutti have a head buffalo for every herd. A bell is hung around the neck of the head buffalo so that the herder is aware of the herd's whereabouts. The other buffaloes simply follow the head buffalo wherever it goes.

Table 4 provides a detailed account of the income generated from milk from both cows and buffaloes. The income generated from cow milk is lower than that of the buffalo. This is because of the low fat content in the cow milk. Milk is not the only source of income from the Khuttis. Apart from the milk and milk products, the Nepali dairy farmers also supply draught animals for plough in the field and for pulling the cart. They also sell the draught animals to the local traders; these traders inturn sell the cattle to the middleman who supplies the cattle to the various slaughterhouses in the different districts (Nagaon, Morigaon etc) of Assam. The dairy farm owners earn a good sum of money by selling the cattle to the traders (Table 5). From table 5, we can clearly see that the income generated from selling the buffaloes for draught purpose is much higher to that of the cows. The present rate of a buffalo is Rs 10000 whereas a cow is sold off at Rs 3500.

Table 4. Income from milk

Livestock	Total number of cattle	Milching Livestock	Milk produced/ day	Income from milk /day (@Rs 10/litre)	Income from milk /day(@ Rs 15/litre)
Cow	9220	6449	9673.5	96735	-
Buffalo	2397	1927	3854	-	57810

Table 5. Income from selling of draught animals

Livestock	Total number of cattle	Male Cattle	To be sold for draught purpose	Income (@ Rs 3500/cow	Income (@ Rs 10,000/buffalo
Cow	9220	1908	1267	4434500	-
Buffalo	2397	470	365	-	3650000

Cost and Returns of rearing dairy cows and buffaloes in Lower Dibang Valley

The cost items includes the feed cost, labour cost, housing cost, veterinary cost and the tax that the dairy farmers have to pay to the land owner. Khutti economy does not mean that the farmers have to keep only the milch cows or the calf and the heifer but also the dry, old and sick cows. For estimating the cost of rearing cattle the feed cost forms the most integral part but in the study area there is no such cost for the feed. The cattle graze in the open fields and the green grass is plentiful in nature. Saw dust is brought to the Khuttis from their respective villages. The whole economy is run down by the family members and hence there is no extra expenditure for labour too. The only expenditure is the veterinary cost (be it modern or traditional), housing cost, and the tax on the cows and buffaloes. The veterinary cost is around Rs 2 for both the cow and buffalo. The housing cost remains the same.

The tax on a cow is Rs 30/year and Rs 45/year on a buffalo. It is noted that the average daily cost of rearing per dairy cow and buffalo is Rs 6.08 and Rs 9.12 respectively in the study area.

The return from dairy cow and buffalo was calculated on the basis of the return from milk yield and return from selling the animal for draught purpose. Hence, these items were used in computing the gross return from the dairy cows. Table 6 and Table 7 provides the detailed account of the returns from a cow and a buffalo in the study area. The return from selling the calves is based on the local market value set by the traders every year. Based on the present market rate i.e. Rs 3500 (cow) and Rs 10,000 (buffalo), the return/day/animal was calculated. After deducting the gross cost from the total returns we get the net return from the dairy farms. From table 6 & 7, we can deduce that the net return from the cow farms and the buffalo farms is Rs 18.92 and Rs 48.27 respectively and the cost benefit ratio is 1:3.1 and 1: 5.3 respectively.

Table 6. Cost and Returns of rearing a cow/ day in the study area

Items	Cost (in Rs)
Feed Cost	
Green grass	-
Saw dust	-
Labour Cost	2
Housing Cost	2
Veterinary cost	2
Tax	.08
Total	6.08

Returns from rearing cow/day

Return items	Unit	Quantity	Price in Rupees	Total
Milk	Litres	1.5	10	15
Draft animal		1	3500/year	10
Total				25

Gross Cost: 6.08
Net return: 18.92
Cost Benefit Ratio: 1:3.1

Table 7. Cost and Returns of rearing a buffalo/ day in the study area

Items	Cost (in Rs)
Feed Cost	
Green grass	-
Saw dust	-
Labour Cost	5
Housing Cost	2
Veterinary cost	2
Tax	.12
Total	9.12

Returns from rearing cow/day				
Return items	Unit	Quality	Price in Rupees	Total
Milk	Litres	2	15	30
Draught animal		1	10000/year	27.39
Total				57.39

Gross Cost: 9.12
Net return: 48.27
Cost Benefit Ratio: 1:5.3

Forward Linkages

The procured milk and its produce are then sold by the local trader to the local sweet shops and restaurants, which make milk cakes and other confectionaries. But the major portion of the milk is transported from this upper bank of the Brahmaputra to the lower bank.

The traders in 'Dholla', the commercial milk town in the district of Tinsukia, receive the milk. And from here the milk is sold in the restaurants in Tinsukia. The milk is also stored here as there is a cold storage facility. The milk here is then churned and transformed to curd and cream and is made ready for the local markets of Upper Assam districts of Tinsukia and Dibrugarh. The milk from khutti's also finds its way to the army camps in Dinjan Army Camp and also to the sweetshops in Bokakhat (a small town in Central Assam), which is famous for the sweet delicacy 'Peda'. So we see that these products are not necessarily made in the Khutti.

When the whole region is under the influence of the monsoons, the whole area downhill is flooded and the small pathways of the khutti dwellers are submerged underneath the floodwater. The Khuttis are cut off from civilization and the fodder availability too decreases leading to the decrease of per day production of milk. The milk then generally finds its way to their own household or to the households of friends and relatives.

Overall Management of the Diary Fram Units

The overall management scenario of the dairy farm units in the Lower Dibang Valley is very traditional. Modern methods of dairying are unknown in this part of the world. Traditionality plays a pivotal role in defining the nature, functioning and overall management of the dairy units. Table 8 provides an insight to the management practice of these traditional dairy farmers. As for the housing system, only 2% of the total dairy farm owners have tin shed and the rest 98% used straw shed to provide shelter for their cattle. 51% of them have a closed pattern of housing and 44% keep their cattle in a semi-closed housing pattern. But the buffalo on the other hand prefers to stay under the open sky. Stall-feeding is generally for the young ones, who cannot go out in the pastures. 51% advocated for grazing the cattle in open pastures. For feeding the young ones, 100% of the dairy farmers advocated for the sucking system. The Khutti owners till date have followed the age-old tradition of this form of economy. No technological developments have been adopted as yet and as for the breeding system, no cows were inseminated artificially as 100% were natural. It has been observed that 100% of the farmers in the Khuttis milked their cows manually and by using traditional methods and the milk is not stored at all.

Milking is generally hygienic (91%) and the farmers regularly use sanitizers (100%) such as the Phenyl, Potash and bleaching powder to clean their sheds. The cleaning is done with the help of buckets (100%). The dairy farmers get adequate supply of water and its main source is from the nearby river (79%). As for the manure, it is disposed in the open (78%). 88% of the respondents treat their livestock by a locally trained person. By veterinary surgeon they are generally unavailable in time of need but does consult them when and where possible.

Table 8. Overall Management System of the Khuttis

Information			Frequency	Percentage
	Type of Shed	Tin Shed	2	2
		Straw Shed	88	98
	Pattern of Housing	Open	4	5
		Closed	46	51
		Semi Closed	40	44
Feeding System	Type of Feeding system	Stall	12	13
		Stall + Grazing	32	36
		Grazing	46	51
	Types of Calf Feeding	Sucking	90	100
		Bottling	-	-
Breeding System	Breeding Methods	Artificial	-	-
		Natural	90	100
Overall Management System	Milking	Hygienically	82	91
		Un hygienically	8	9
	Milking System	Manual	90	100
		Mechanical	-	-
	Water Source	River	71	79
		Tube well	4	4
		Pond	7	8
		Spring	8	9
	Water Supply	Adequate	90	100
		Inadequate	-	-
	Cleaning done by	Bucket	90	100
		Pipe	-	-
	Cleaning	Regularly	90	100
		Irregularly	-	-
	Dairy equipment	Traditional	90	100
		Modern	-	-
		Semi Modern	-	-
		Storage of Milk		
		Freezing	-	-
		Not Stored	90	100

Isolation of Sick Cattle	Kept isolated	81	90
	Not Kept isolated	9	10
Disposal of manure	Out in the open	70	78
	Dug pits to dispose	17	19
	Used as fuel	3	3
Sanitizer Used	Phenyl	82	91
	Potash	2	2
	Phenyl + Potash	0	0
	Bleaching Powder	6	7
Treatment by	Veterinary surgeon	11	12
	Locally trained person	*79*	*88*

Communities's Perception on the Impact of Dairy Farming on Livelihood

The Khutti economy has so long been the basic source of livelihood of the Nepali dairy farming community. It has been an integral part of their culture and the people have embedded themselves in this economy. But the question is will it continue to be so in the future? The community expressed concerns over the depleting fodder availability, the rising population and the sudden floods occurring in both the Dibang and the Brahmaputra valley.

The erratic nature of floods has posed a threat not only to the khutti owners but also to the livestock. The younger generation is not much into this form of livelihood. They prefer to move out of the area and leave behind this traditional form of livelihood. They see no future in it. The cultural ethos and social safety of this livelihood is questioned by the youths. Owing to a number of reasons such as increasing workloads, erratic weather conditions, unpredictable income pattern, loss of livestock to floods and disease, lack of roadways and proper linkages to the collection centre etc have resulted to the decline of popularity of this form of livelihood among the youths.

The people of this community are not that educated and though economically sound the standard of living is low. The younger members of the family showed their eagerness towards education but the girls gave preference to marriage rather than education. They are good agriculturist and the production too is good but the agricultural products were basically for self consumption. From the above discussion, it may be concluded that they still practice the age old methods of dairy farming and the present management system of these small dairy farmers is also traditional. As for the economy the dairy farmers seemed satisfied with their traditional profession as the returns are good and has kept their family floating in times of economically dry days.

Conclusion

For the success of these dairy farms in this region the government should take up steps by providing financial assistance so that these farmers can rake in full benefits. Moreover, these farms should be registered and their products should get the appropriate fixed price recommended by the government from time to time. The price of the milk should be fixed at a reasonable level and the milk and draught animal marketing system should be improved by the intervention by the government. Short term training on dairy farming should be imparted in this region and a scheme of short term institutional loan should be implemented. And finally, veterinary care and services should strengthen. Moreover, lack of a dairy policy of the state is yet another lacuna for the development of these dairy farm owners. Therefore, appropriate policy measures should be adopted by the Arunachal Pradesh government for the upliftment of these dairy farm

owners. With the economic returns from this Khutti economy being so high this practice is to stay in the near future. But its sustainability in the long run can be questioned. If proper attention and necessary steps are taken from the government this traditional system of livelihood can certainly be established and maintained and can continue to be the major source of livelihood for the Nepali dairy farming community as it has always been.

References

[1] K.L Baruah, Nepali Migration to Northeast India (Guwahati, Assam), 1966.

[2] A. Dasgupta, Othering of the not-so- other: A study of the Nepalis in Assam. In A.C.Sinha and T.B. Subba (Eds) The Nepalis in Northeast India: a community in search of Indian Identity (New Delhi, Indus), 2003.

[3] L. Nath, 'Migration, insecurity and identity: The Nepali dairyman in India's Northeast', Asian Ethnicity, 2006, 7 (2), 129- 148.

[4] D. B. Bista, People of Nepal (Kathmandu, Ratna Pustak Bhandar), 1980.

[5] A. J. E Boer, Socioeconomic aspects of Dairying in Developing countries. In the symposium: Dairying in Developing Countries, 1981.

[6] F. Bashmann, Livelihood and Livestocks. Lessons from Swiss livestock and dairy development programmes in India and Tanzania. IC, 2004, Series, No. 4, 40pp.

Chapter-VIII

Plant Diversity of Mangroves in Estuarine Ecosystem of Uttrakannda District with Special Reference to Kali River

Puttaraju, K. & S. P. Bhanusri*

Abstract

India has 67,429 wetlands covering an area of 4.1 million hectare. Mangroves are salt tolerant forest ecosystem of tropical and subtropical intertidal regions near river mouths with high productivity. Karwar is a coastal district of Karnataka state situated in the Western Ghats of Sahyadry, Western coast of India. River Kali or Karihole is a major river of the northern Karnataka at lat.14 48'N and Long.74 07'E. Documentation, conservation and management of estuarine ecosystem have become an international priority because of its ecological, economical and social significance. Total 163 species of plants belonging to 101 genera and 40 families have been recorded of the 15 species of eumangroves reported from Karnataka, as many as 13 species were found growing here. Mangrove genera have been recorded from different biotopes of this Kali estuarine environment. The survey was carried out for a period of two year from November 2008 to October 2010. Monthly census of flora was done in order to know their seasonal flowering and fruiting occurrence. Mangrove ecosystem supports high secondary productivity to improve the fertility of the region. Mangrove forest and estuaries are the breeding and nursery ground for a number of marine organisms including the commercially important shrimp, crab and fish species. Decomposition of the litter contributes to the production of Dissolved Organic Matter (DOM), the recycling of nutrients both in the mangroves and in adjacent habitats and ultimately supports fishery resources. Hence loss of mangroves not only affects society indirectly, there are also direct economic repercussions through loss to the entire fishing industry.

Key words: Anthropogenic, Coastal, Endangered, Sustainable Development

*Kaiga Generating Station, Kaiga, Uttara Kannada, Karnataka, School of natural sciences Bangalore University

Introduction

India is blessed with enormous water resources in the form of numerous rivers, streams, wetlands, lakes etc. By virtue of its geographical position and varied terrain and climatic zones, it supports a rich diversity of inland and coastal wetlands. India has 67,429 wetlands covering an area of 4.1 million hectare. Mangroves are salt tolerant forest ecosystem of tropical and subtropical intertidal regions near river mouths with high productivity. Coastal Karnataka is the central part of the Malabar Coast which extends to Dakshina Kannada, Udupi and Uttarakannada. Mangrove formation is a tropical phenomenon mostly confined to tropical coastal areas, sometimes extending to subtropics. Van Rheede in the year 1943 reported for the first time about the mangrove plants in the Malabar Coast.

The total coastal line in Karnataka is approximately 320 km which presents varied geomorphologic features in the form of long beaches, some time intercepted by rocks forming attractive beaches. Sometimes coastal land is dissected by the rivers joining sea with the formation of shallow lagoons or estuaries. We can also see the elevated sandy ridges which are called sand dunes with a height of about 8-10m. Sharavathi, Aghanashini, Gangavali and Kali are the major rivers of Uttarakannada districts joining the sea. Karwar is a coastal district of Karnataka state situated in the Western ghats of Sahyadry, Western coast of India. River Kali or Karihole is a major river of the northern Karnataka at lat.14 48'N and Long.74 07'E. Documentation, conservation and management of estuarine ecosystem has become an international priority because of its ecological, economical and social significance. Kali estuary extending from Kodibag (S) and Devbag (N) at the river mouth up to Kunnipet Kaiga township (S) and Kardra (N), stretching to a distance of about 35kms. Another small river called Mavinahalla also joins this estuary, converting it into an estuarine complex. So far, 163 species of plants belonging to 101 genera and 40 families have been recorded (table 1) of the 15 species of eumangroves reported from Karnataka, as many as 13 species were found growing here. Mangrove genera have been recorded from different biotopes of this Kali estuarine environment. This includes the major mangrove genera such as Avicennia (3 species), Bruguiera (2species), Rhizophora (2 species), Sonneratia (2 species) and one species each of Aegiceras, Excoecaria, Lumnitzera and Kandelia. Among these Sonneratia alba, Rhizophora apiculata and Avicennia officeinalis are the most dominant species. All details of plants found in Beaches and Mangroves of Karwar- Kaiga are provided in Table 1. Estuarine environment provides a functional role of those different benthic faunal components as a part of their bioturbatory activities and as an integral component of litter decomposition vis–a vis biogeochemical cycles in this estuarine ecosystem functioning. Maximum biogenic alteration of the sediments by virtue of burrowing, feeding, defecation, tube like shelter building etc leading to modification of physical, chemical , biological properties of sediments, have been made by Brachyuran crabs, followed by polychaetes, molluscs, brachiopods and cnidaria. However, the functional role of different micro arthropods in the decomposition of mangrove plants litter have been found to be maximum than other macrobenthic faunal components. Besides, survival strategies based on different behavioural manifestation of all such benthic fauna have been found to import profound effects on sediment-water-faunal-floral linkages and helped maintaining the ecological health of estuarine ecosystem.

This estuarine complex formed by rivers Kali and Mavinahalla (Uttarakannada District of Karnataka) along the West Coast, supports mangrove vegetation along its shores and mud flats. Floristic studies have revealed that the isolated and remnant patches of mangrove forest of this area are rich in species diversity of both eumangrove and mangrove associate plants.

Climate

The climate in the coastal region is characterized by high humidity nearly all the year round. The summer from March to May, the monsoon season from June to September, the post –monsoon season from October to November and low temperature season from December to February. The average rainfall in Karwar is 3,680mm. Majority of the mangrove forest of Karnataka have declined due to anthropogenic pressures in the recent years. During the last 25 years some reduction in Mangrove cover of Karnataka has been due to human interference and development activities. Some of the major problems face by the shore front areas of Karnataka coast are related to coastal erosion, siltation, pollution, destruction of mangrove swamps, salt marshes, sea level rise, landslides and slope failure, pressure of population, industrialization, road transport etc.

The earlier studies do not give the estimation about the number of plant species and area covered. So objective of present paper is to study plant diversity of mangroves along coast of Karwar district for conservation of estuarine ecosystem and mangroves for sustainable development. Different estuaries of Karwar were visited frequently for study. Plants were identified with the help of standard literature and floras. The studies reveal that Karwar district shows biodiversity of Mangroves with 163 species of plants belonging to 101 genera, and 40 families have been recorded. Sonneratia, Avicinnea are the more common genus. Granatum species has been categorized as least concerned in the IUCN red list the conversation notes on it emphasis on its declining population all over the country due to severe habitat loss. More efforts should be made by the government, concerned authorities, policy makers etc to conserve estuarine ecosystem and biodiversity of mangroves by different methods such as education and awareness programmes to local people about ecological values of mangroves for sustainable development.

Material and Methods

The survey was carried out for a period of two year from November 2008 to October 2010. Monthly census of flora was done in order to know their seasonal flowering and fruiting occurrence. The population of flora was estimated from 6.00 am to 8.00 am by direct counting method. Documentation/Checklist was done by using boat, Raft for the island on the either side of the Kali river and rest of the area by road, around 9 small island were visited during the period and flora were recorded within a transect of 20m in various sites.

Study Area

Kali River (figure1) originates at Diggi, near Ambikanagar in Joida taluk. It flows in south - western direction and receive many halla or hole on its journey before it discharges in to Arabian see at Karwar in Uttarakannada district. Most of the area are Evergreen to Semi-Evergreen forest are confined to the western part of the basin. Many of the hills are covered with heavy forests while ravines and valleys produce luxuriant trees known for their great height and size. Areca nut, also called betel nut is a widely used article of consumption and is grown in valleys.

The study area encompasses extending from left bank of the river Kunnipet Kaiga township (S) and right bank of the river Kardra(N), stretching to a distance of about 35kms Kodibag(S) and at the river mouth up to Devbag(N). following are the villages/places where checklist done, Kunnipet, Mallapur, irpage, Bolve, Kerwadi, Katar, Kadiye, Devalmakki, Bargal, Wylwada, Kharge and Kharge jug, Halga jug, Siddar, Umli jug, Kinner, Shirvad, Makheri, Kadwad, Sunkeri, Nandangadda, Kodibag, Nadibag all are on the left bank of the river and on the right side of the river is Kadra, Satar sare, Bore, Gotegali, Wayl balni, Sakal balni, Byre, Hapkarni, Hoti, Shingudda, Ambrayi, Barge, Ulga, Katne, Bhouvri, Madewada, Halga, Pile wada, Basung, Agali, Halge jug, Gopshitta, Bolshitta, Hankon, Amle, Hotegali, Asnoti, Kolge, Dhol, Sadashivgad, Devbag.

Habitat and Productivity

The coastal areas with diversified habitats within a radius of 5 km are characterized by estuarine systems, mangroves, rocky, sandy, tidal flats and coral reef patches. The occurrence of such different habitats within narrow region probably brings about higher degree of interactions among the different habitats and supports high species diversity. Mangrove ecosystem supports high secondary productivity to improve the fertility of the region.

Mangrove forest and estuaries are the breeding and nursery ground for a number of marine organisms including the commercially important shrimp, crab and fish species. Decomposition of the litter contributes to the production of Dissolved Organic Matter (DOM), the recycling of nutrients both in the mangroves and in adjacent habitats and ultimately supports fishery resources. Hence loss of mangroves not only affects society indirectly, there are also direct economic repercussions through loss to the entire fishing industry.

In many coastal areas, mangroves are substitute for fodder. Thus mangroves reduce pressure on scarce pastureland. Till recently mangroves were the main source of tannin for the leather industry and are still exploited in many areas in India for this purpose. Mangrove wood has a high caloric value and burns very well. This character has become a curse; in many areas both rural and urban communities are heavily dependent on mangrove wood for fuel. Honey collection from mangrove area is exclusively practiced in Bengal and Orissa. The finest honey is collected from mangroves which fetches a good price.

Pioneering investigation are now showing the mangrove and their associated fauna can be source of valuable products like black tea, mosquito ides, Gallo tannins, microbial fertilizers, antiviral drugs, anti tumor drugs and UV-screening compounds (Ravi & Kathiressan, 1999: Premanthan et al, 1992).

Family	Genus	Species
Rhizophoraceae	Rhizophora	R.apiculata
		R.mucronata
	Bruguiera	B.gymnorrhiza
		B.cylindrica
	Kandelia	K.candel
Avicenniaceae	Avicennia	A.officinalis
		A.alba
		A.marina
Sonneratiaceae	Sonneratia	S.caseolaris
		S.alba
Combretaceae	Lumnitzera	L.racemosa
Euphorbiaceae	Excoecaria	E.agallocha
Myrsinaceae	Aegiceras	A.corniculatum
Acanthaceae	Acanthus	A.ilicifolius
Pteridaceae	Acrostichum	A.aureum
Fabaceae	Caesalpinea	C.crista
		C.bonduc
	Dalbergia	D.spinosa
	Derris	D.trifoliata
		D.scandens
	Acanthospermum	Acanthospermum hispidum L.
		Achryanthes corymbosa L.
		Achyranthes aspera
		Acrocephalus indicus
		Aerva lanata
		Aeschynomeme indica
		Ageratum conyzoides

		Alternanthera sessilis
		Alysicarpus vanginalis
		Amaranthus spinosus
		Ammannia baccifera
		Anacardium occidenatale
		Bacopa monnieri
		Blumea lacera
		Blumea oxyodonta
		Blumea virens
		Boerhavia diffusa
		Borassus flabellifer
		Borreria articularis
		Borreria pusilla
		Brachiaria ramose
		Bulbostylis barbata
		Calophyllum inophyllum
		Calotropis gigantean
		Canavalia rosea
		Cardiospermum helicacabum
		Cassia tora
		Cassytha filiformis
		Casuarina equisetifolia
		Cerbera odollam Gaertner
		Ceriops decandra
		Chromolaena

		odorata
		Cleome viscose
		Cocos nucifera
		Coldenia Procumbens
		Corchoorus aestuans
		Crotolaria nana
		Crotolaria retusa
		Crotolaria striata
		Crotolaria verrucosa
		Croton bonplandianus
		Cyanotis cristata
		Cynodon dactylon
		Cynosurus aegyptius
		Cyperus arenarius
		Cyperus compressus
		Cyperus malaccensis
		Cyperus rotundus
		Cyperus stoloniferus
		Dactyloctenium aegyptium
		Datura metel
		Dentella repens
		Derris scandens
		Desmodium triflorum
		Digitaria bicornis
		Digitaria longiflora
		Echinochloa frumentacea
		Eclipta alba
		Emilia sonchifolia

		Epaltes divaricata
		Eragrostis riparia
		Eragrostis tenella
		Eragrostis tremula
		Eragrostis unioloides
		Erythrina veriegata
		Euphorbia articulate
		Euphorbia hitra
		Evolvulus alsinoides
		Fimbristylis argentea
		Fimbristylis cymosa
		Fimbristylis ferruginea
		Fimbristylis polytrichoides
		Geissapis cristata
		Glinus oppositifolius
		Grangea maderaspatana
		Hedyotis corymbosa
		Hedyotis herbacea
		Hedysarum bupleurifolium
		Heliotropium indicum
		Hybanthus suffruticosus
		Hydrophylax maritima
		Hygrophila auriculata
		Hyptis suaveolens

		Ipomoea maxima
		Ipomoea pes caprae
		Ischaemum aristatum
		Ischaemum indicum
		Ischaemum semisagitatum
		Justicia prostate
		Justicia simplex
		Launaea sarmentosa
		Leea indica
		Lindernia atipoda
		Lindernia ciliata
		Lindernia crustacea
		Ludwigia hyssopifolia
		Mariscus pedunculatus
		Mariscus squarrous
		Merremia tridentate
		Murdannia nudiflora
		Ocimum tenuiflorum
		Opuntia dillenii
		Pandanus tectorius
		Panicum repens
		Paspalum vaginatum
		Perotis indica
		Phyla nodiflora
		Phyllanthus amarus Schummann

		Physalis minima
		Polycarpaea corymbosa
		Poreteresia corymosa
		Portulaca oleracea
		Premna latifolia
		Pycreus polystachyos
		Rungia pectinate
		Salvadora persica
		Sarcostemma acidum
		Scaevola plumieri
		Scaevola taccada
		Scoparia dulcis
		Seasamum orientale
		Sesuvium portulacastrum
		Sida acuta
		Sida cordata
		Solanum nigrum
		Solanum surattense
		Spermacoe pusilla wallich
		Sphaeranthus indicus
		Spinifex littoreus
		Sporobolus virginicus
		Stachytarpheta jamaicensis
		Tephrosia hamil tonii
		Thespesia populnea
		Tridax procumbens

		Triumfetta rhomboidea
		Urginea indica
		Vernonia cinera
		Vitex trifolia
		Waltheria indica
		Wedelia biflora
		Ziziphus mauritiana
		Zornia gibbosa spanoghe
		Zoysia materlla

Conclusion

It is believed that if the mangrove communities along the banks of estuaries and coastlines were disturbed or destroyed, there would be no habitat or food to support the organisms in the areas. Further more, the loss of these mangrove-related ecosystems would disturb natural ecological systems over a considerable area and result in large-scale economic loss and socio-cultural change in coastal communities (S.Aksornkoe 1991, IUCN). There is a belief that the increasing floods in Bangladesh are due to the loss of mangroves in the past few decades and there is not much disagreement regarding this view in the scientific community. More efforts should be made by the government , concerned authorities , policy makers etc to conserve estuarine ecosystem and biodiversity of mangroves by different methods such as education and awareness programmes to local people about ecological values of mangroves for sustainable development.

References:

1. Naskar, KR and Mandal,R.1999,ecology and biodiversity of Indian Mangroves, vol.1 & 2.Daya publishing New Delhi

2. Rao, TA and Suresh, PV.2001.Coastaql Ecosystem of the Karnataka state, India.1.Mangroves. Karnataka association for the advancement of sciences, Bangalore.

3. Selvam V.et al., 2006. Toolkit for Establishing Coastal Bioshield, MS Swaminathan Research Foundation, Chennai.

4. Costanza R., Kemp; W.M. and Boynton W.R. (1993). Predictability, scale, and biodiversity in Coastal and Estuarine Ecosystems-Implications for management.Ambio 22 88-96

5. Ducrotoy J.P and Elliott M (2006). Recent Developments in esturine ecology and management. Marine Pollution Bulletin 53 1-4

6. Frenchy J. (2006) Tidal marsh sedimentation and resilience to environmental change: Exploratory modeling of tidal, sea-level and sediment supply forcing in predominantly allochthonous system, Marine Geology 235 119-136.

7. Shankar D. (2010) Nature of freshwater influx in Indian estuaries. Presentation at the Symposium on the Indian Estuaries, 76th Annual Meeting of the Indian Acdemy of Sciences, Bangalore.

8. Shetye S.R., Dileep Kumar M. and Shankar D.(Eds.)(2007) The Mandovi and Zuari Esturies. Bangalore: Lotus Printers, 145 p.

9. Venkataraman K.and Wafar M.V.M (2005) Coastal and biodiversity of India.Indian Journal of Marine sciences. 34: 57 - 75

Chapter-IX

Conservation Value of Ruralscape in South - East Rajasthan

Rakesh Vyas*

Abstract

The paper deals with the concept of conservation value and try to present it in a fresh light in context of ruralscape in south-east Rajasthan. It was found that the ruralscape invariably comprises of three or four interdependent ecosystems and it's their interplay which enhances the conservation value of the whole as well as of its each entity. The issue is discussed in line with the accepted criterions to ascertain the conservation value of an ecosystem. The shortcomings of the present policy or the lack of it is discussed, and the importance of local culture and religious beliefs in conservation has been presented. This paper is the result of years of field study of the birds and ecology of the study area and presents it in a fresh perspective.

Key Words – Conservation value, Ruralscape, Endemic, Endangered, Bio-indicators

* Environmentalist, Hadoti Naturalists Society, Kota NGO Washleigh – Manor, Rustam Bagh, Bangalore, India

Introduction

The present day scientific studies are being aimed at looking in to the conservation value of Landscapes, Seascapes and many other conglomerates of ecosystems. In a ruralscape, we find an interplay of different ecosystems - natural, man made and man altered. There is a concerted effort by the scientists all over the world to utilize birds as the bio-indicators of the health of the ecosystem or a habitat and establish the conservation value of even a degraded habitat. Kati and Sekercioglu (2006 [8]) tried to construct a model of monitoring the populations of certain indicator bird species to cost effectively and efficiently judge the state and quality of the habitat of entire land bird community, thereby integrating the knowledge of community structure in to conservation decision making. Peh et al (2006 [7]) in their study quantified the conservation value of three degraded habitats for forest bird species.

The efforts are also being made to understand and increase the awareness of avian ecological functions and services. Birds are one of the most diverse groups of ecosystem service providers, whose ecological functions range from creating soil to shaping primate behavior. Given the ongoing declines in avian functional groups, there is a pressing need to compare avian ecological functions to those of other taxa, to understand how these functions translate to ecosystem services and to estimate the ecological implications of bird declines (Sekercioglu, 2006 [3]).

If we look in to the global land use, it is dominated by agricultural systems and the proportion of global land area covered by cropland is expected to further grow, as the demand for food for growing human population will necessitate conversion of forestland, grassland and even wetland in to cropland. Although the habitat loss is the major cause of the loss of species throughout the world but some agro-ecosystems ca harbour a substantial portion of the biodiversity of the original land cover (Vandermeer & Perfecto, 1997 [5]). In the Indian context, a village landscape comprising of cropland, scrubland, wetland and human habitation can act as a buffer and complement the protected areas in conservation of endemic, vulnerable or endangered species. Such efforts have yielded encouraging results in Australia for conservation of native animals (Claridge et al, 2003 [1]).

In the recent times, a concept of 'high conservation value forest' is being propagated and followed in a number of countries. For this purpose, the Forest Stewardship Council criterions are followed and any forested area fulfilling one or more criterion is considered of 'high conservation value'. The whole thing has been designed to protect areas of value to endemic and endangered species, areas providing basic ecological services and is of economical, ecological, cultural and religious significance to local communities. The high conservation value area need not be a large one, but just a part of the habitat, in this case, the forest habitat that fulfils the criterions. The same principles may be effectively applied to a ruralscape and shall be discussed ahead.

A typical ruralscape in south-east Rajasthan will invariably have human habitation, wetland, cropland and grassland (more aptly scrubland). In addition, there may be a grove of trees surrounding a temple and protected by religious sentiments. Together these ecosystems support a bird community comprising of forest dwelling birds, wetland birds, and scrub and grassland birds utilizing one or more than one habitat. Traditionally it would be thought that a ruralscape is a disturbed area in need of restoration to its pristine state to protect its avian diversity. The present state of affairs in India would not allow such drastic measures of protection and alienation of human interests. Therefore with a pragmatic view, I decided to look in to the years of data from the study areas and found that the ruralscape offers great opportunity of survival to a diverse group of endemic and endangered bird species, thereby enhancing the conservation value of the ruralscape.

Study Area

The Kota division in south-east Rajasthan is situated on Hadoti plateau and has Aravali mountain range in its west, Malwa plateau on its east, Chhappan plateau in its south and Indo-Gangetic plain in the north. Kota division comprises of four districts, namely, Kota, Bundi, Baran and Jhalawar. Chambal River passes through a deep gorge in South-East Rajasthan on its northward course to ultimately drain in to Yamuna River at Panchnada in Uttar Pradesh. The average annual rainfall in the area is 850 mm. and the climate is subtropical with temperatures ranging from 45 C. in summer to 7 C. in winter. The soil of the study area is mostly non-calcareous clay or clay-loam.

Sorsan Great Indian Bustard Area is situated on the boundary of Kota and Baran district on the eastern bank of Parban River at a distance of about 65 km from Kota and 35 km from the district headquarter of Baran. An area of approximately 35 sq. km. was declared a Hunting Closed Area in 1986 as per the provisions of Wildlife Protection Act (1972), to protect the Great Indian Bustard habitat. The Hunting Closed Area is surrounded by Amalsara, Takha, Niyana, Manpura, Bilandi and Sorsan villages and agricultural fields. The pebbly upland with outcropping rocks has grasses, Jujube bushes and scantily distributed Khejari Prosopis cineraria trees. The seepage marsh created by Right Main Canal passing on the northern side of the Great Indian Bustard Area, village tanks of Takha, Niyana, Manpura and Sorsan, Parban River and two check dams constructed by the Department of Forest are the sources of water for man, animals and birds. In the beginning the land was owned by private land holders and the revenue department. Later, an area measuring 14 sq. km, falling between Amalsara and Niyana villages was converted in to forest land to provide it with higher level of protection.

The Udpuria Painted Stork Breeding Colony is situated at a distance of 30 km, north-east of Kota. The Udpuria tank has about two hectares submergence area surrounded by the village on two sides and the crop fields on other two sides. The tank had its own catchments but now mostly depends on a feeder canal for water. There is a tiny grove of Babool Acacia nilotica trees in 0.3 hectare area in the east, bordering the submergence area of the tank and there are scattered Bargad Ficus indica, Peepal F. religiosa, Neem Azadirachta indica and Imali Tamarindus indica trees in the village. The Water hyacinth Eichhornia crassipes is choking the tank and only intermittently with the joint efforts of the villagers and the NGOs, it has remained clear of the weed. The total area under observation during the study was about 100 hectares.

This article is a result of the observations of Sorsan Great Indian Bustard Area since 1989 and Udpuria Painted Stork Breeding Colony since 1996. The observations were mainly aimed at studying the avifauna, protection of the scrubland habitat of Great Indian bustard and amelioration measures for man-animal conflict in Sorsan area. The breeding biology of the Painted stork, area's avifauna and community participation in conservation were the study objectives at Udpuria.

The ruralscape in south-east Rajasthan is typically constituted of two or more of these habitats; i.e. human habitation and groves, crop fields, grass/scrubland and wetland. These habitats support a diverse group of birds and together form the basis of the conservation value of ruralscape in its totality.

Observations

The observations were taken on the avifauna of each habitat in both the study areas. Sorsan Great Indian Bustard Area constituted of four habitats; namely, wetland, grass/scrubland, crop fields and village and groves. Udpuria Painted Stork Breeding Colony comprises of three habitats and does not have grassland habitat. The habitat use by the local inhabitants and habitat's ecological value and ecological services rendered by it were also noted. The results for each area are being given in forthcoming paragraphs.

1. Sorsan – Our observations over an extended period of time in this study area showed the presence of three mammalian species, considered endangered and protected under schedule – 1 of Wildlife Protection Act. They are Blackbuck Antilope cervicapra, Chinkara Gazella gazella and Indian wolf Canis lupus. Seventy five bird species are recorded in wetland habitat, 74 in crop fields, 61 in grassland and 46 in the village and groves. The critically endangered and endangered species of birds recorded in this area are; White-rumped vulture Gyps bengalensis, Indian vulture G. indicus, Red-headed vulture Sarcogyps calvus, Egyptian vulture Neophron percnopterus, Great Indian bustard Ardeotis nigriceps, Houbara bustard Chlamydotis undulate and Sarus crane Grus antigone. The birds considered near threatened by the BirdLife International and seen in the area are; Ferruginous duck Aythya nyroca, Painted stork Mycteria leucocephala, Black-headed ibis Threskiornis melanocephalus, Oriental darter Anhinga melanogaster, Pallid harrier Circus macrourus, Black-tailed godwit Limosa limosa and Eurasian curlew Numenius arquata.

The 18 bird species endemic to the south Asian mainland and Sri Lanka, and found in the study area are:

Indian black ibis Pseudibis papillosa, Indian vulture, Indian peafowl Pavo cristatus, Great Indian bustard, Indian courser Cursorius coromandelicus, Plum-headed parakeet Psittacula cyanocephala, Common Hawk-cuckoo Hierococcyx varius, Indian bushlark Mirafra erythroptera, Ashy-crowned Finch-lark Eremopterix griseus, White-browed wagtail Motacilla maderaspatensis, Indian robin Saxicoloides fulicata, Brown Rock-chat Cercomela fusca, Large grey babbler Turdoides malcolmi, Common babbler Turdoides caudatus, Ashy prinia Prinia socialis, White-bellied drongo Dicrurus caerulescens, Brahminy starling Sturnus pagodarum and Indian jungle crow Corvus macrorhynchus (TABLE-1).

The grassland and the wetland are of immense economical and cultural value to the inhabitants of the villages situated around the Great Indian Bustard Area. The grassland is the main source of fodder for the livestock and the villagers plough the marginal grassland area in the close vicinity of the wetlands and take winter crops. The grassland acts as a watershed for Parban River and keeps the soil erosion from the plateau land in check. The wetlands are the source of water, fish and Singhara Trapa sp. for the villagers. The wetlands support wild animals and birds during scorching summer months and provide home to migratory waterbirds in winter.

2. Udpuria – Although the area studied at Udpuria is relatively small but supports a large population of near threatened species, Painted stork and thus qualifies to be an important bird area (IBA) as per the guidelines of BirdLife International. Based on 1% population criterion, it can be said that this area is very important for the survival of over 250 pairs of Painted storks and their juveniles. Some of the other endangered and near threatened bird species found in the area are; White-rumped vulture, Egyptian vulture, Oriental darter and Black-headed ibis.

The endemic species inhabiting this area are; Indian black ibis, Indian peafowl, Ashy-crowned Finch-lark, White-browed wagtail, Indian robin, Brown rock-chat, Common babbler and Brahminy starling (TABLE – 2).

The wetland is found to be of economic and cultural value to the villagers and their livestock, as they depend on it for all their domestic needs of water. It provides nesting habitat to breeding egrets, herons and cormorants in summer and to Painted storks between August and March. These birds breed on the partially submerged Acacia trees growing in the tank bed.

Discussion

Protected areas are considered mainstay of biodiversity conservation around the world but many studies and long term experience demonstrates that reserves alone will not be sufficient to conserve all biodiversity. Future conservation strategies will have to encompass commodity production areas and multiple usage grassland and wetland areas. Off-reserve conservation is critical in the crop fields that were formerly grasslands or marginal forests, before human manipulation altered the natural vegetation, creating artificial grasslands of cereal crops that require some form of repetitious, unnatural disturbance such as cultivation, harvesting, burning or mowing to persist. In our study we have very clearly seen that many marsh and grassland birds like cranes, rails, larks, buntings and sparrows have adopted to cultivated and fallow crop fields and use it as surrogate grassland or marsh. Biodiversity conservation on agricultural land is a major issue worldwide (Ross et al, 2008 [2]).

We once again need to have an in-depth look in to the criterions for high conservation value forests and see their applicability in our context and also see the conservation value of grasslands and wetlands. High Conservation Value Forest (HCVF) needs to fulfill one or more of these following criterions.

1. Forest areas containing, regionally or nationally significant concentrations of biodiversity values, i.e. endemism, endangered species, refugia; and/or large landscape-level forest.

2. Forest areas that contain rare, endangered or threatened ecosystems.

3. Forest areas providing basic services of nature in critical situation, like watershed protection, soil stabilization.

4. Forest areas fundamental to meeting basic need of local communities, like health and sustenance.

5. Forest areas critical to local communities' traditional cultural identity (areas of cultural, religious, ecological or economical significance identified in cooperation with such local communities).

All the above principles can be logically applied to assess the conservation value of grasslands and wetlands. Besides, the grasslands provide goods and services, like food and forage, biodiversity, carbon storage, tourism and recreation. The grasslands also help with pollination of crops by insects, increase soil fertility and check soil erosion, filter and store water, and most importantly provide genetic material for improving food crops.

The loss of wetland habitat in last 60 years is of greatest concern to every environmentalist in India. The time has come to recognize the ecological services rendered by a wetland. It provides home to animals and plants, many of those are of economic value to man. The wildlife gets food, water, and space for living and reproducing, as in case of waterbirds. The aquatic flora can absorb and decompose pollutants in the water. The wetlands supplement the ground water sources and also retain extra water for sometime, thus mitigating the problem of flooding. Semlitsch and Bodie (1998 [6]) questioned the expendability of small wetlands and established the value of wetlands as small as 0.2 hectare in size. According to the authors, "majority of wetlands are small and they are rich in amphibian species and important source of juvenile recruitment. Loss of small wetlands will lead to high nearest-wetland distance impeding the 'rescue' effect on metapopulation level. Reduced connectivity will lead to reduced connectance among remaining species population".

When we look in to the biodiversity value of the Sorsan Great Indian Bustard Area (Sorsan) and Udpuria Painted Stork Breeding Colony (Udpuria) in terms of endangered species and endemic species inhabiting these areas, we find that Sorsan area has three endangered mammalian species and 13 critically endangered, endangered or near threatened species of birds. We found 18 endemic species of birds in this area. The White-rumped vulture, Indian vulture, Red-headed vulture, Egyptian vulture and Great Indian bustard are the birds of national significance and two of them are also endemic to south Asian mainland.

Udpuria has five endangered and eight endemic bird species in a very small area of about 100 hectares. The grassland ecosystems are considered threatened because of its degradation and fragmentation. The loss, degradation and fragmentation of ecosystem leads to lower species diversity, habitat diversity, habitat representativeness, interspersion of habitat types and rating of surrounding habitat and/or landscape (Winning, 1990 [4]). This has happened mainly due to the human induced alteration of ecosystem in spite of its economical, ecological and scenic value. Conversion of grassland for cultivation and overgrazing has resulted in degradation and fragmentation, leading to weed invasion, reduced fodder production, profusion of coarse grasses and reduced land value. It has also resulted in loss of soil moisture and soil erosion, thus affecting the quality of the watershed of adjoining rivers, in this case Parban River. The degradation of grassland has led to degradation of wetland, causing deposition of silt, reduction in carrying capacity and increased turbidity. To restore the ecosystem services provided by the grasslands and wetlands, it is essential to take appropriate conservation measures and incentivize the role played by the local communities. To ensure public participation financial incentives are given and conservation expenses are reimbursed to the landowners in many countries (Claridge and Lindmeyer, 2003 [1]), in our case, the incentive or expenses could be reimbursed to private landowners, Panchayats or Village forest and water management committees. Ecosystem services incentive is given as 'stewardship of ecosystem' whose economic value is often comparable or greater than the value of goods and services that have a market value, like crop, milk or meat.

Two of the major criterions for conservation value of an ecosystem are its fundamental role in providing basic services to local communities and is critical to their cultural and religious identity. In context of our study, it is pertinent to note that the ruralscape in south-east Rajasthan is not complete without its temple groves, ancestor's groves and religious spots where people gather at certain time of the year for specific purpose (Teja Ji ka Thanak). Sorsan has many temples in its vicinity with their groves of old trees, which are protected by local sentiment. The trees like Peepal Ficus religiosa, Bargad F.benghalensis and Amla Emblica officinalis are essential for worship on certain days in a year.

Some of the birds like crows and Indian roller are part of religious ceremonies and are invoked on certain days every year. Sarus crane, Indian peafowl and Red-wattled lapwing are accorded protection by local culture and they are protected by the local communities. Anyone seen directly or indirectly harming the birds or their nests has to pay a penalty and suffer the ire of the community. There is a 'Teja Ji kaThanak', where a fair is held on Teja Dashami every year to treat the cases of serpent bite (by cutting the 'Dassi'- a thread tied by a traditional priest after a snake bite). We see the same thing at Udpuria, where there is a temple grove and a 'Thanak' (place of worship). It is evident from this study that a typical ruralscape in south-east Rajasthan is of immense conservation value as habitat for endemic and endangered birds and animals, its economical value and ecological services provided by its components.

The Way Ahead

The trend so far has been to implement the politically low-risk policies, which have failed to address the underlying issues of conservation. The anthropocentric approach has proven to be counter productive, for it has failed to take in to account the ecosystem services and effectively convey this to the local communities. Essentially the nature with its living and non-living elements is valuable for the web of life, in which interdependence is the cementing material. This message of conservation philosophy needs to go down the line to local communities; in addition to incentives, cost reimbursement and stewardship.

References

[1] A. Claridge, D. Lindermeyer, Wildlife on Farms – How to Conserve Native Animals (CSIRO Publishing, Australia, 2003).

[2] B.C. Ross, D.B. Lindenmayer, M. Crane, D. Michael, C. Macgregor, R. Montague-Drake and J. Fischer, The Combined Effects of Remnant Vegetation and Tree Planting on Farmland Birds. Conservation Biology. 2008, 22 (3), 742-752.

[3] C. H. Sekercioglu, Increasing Awareness of avian Ecological Function, Trends in Ecology and Evolution, 21-8, 2006, 464-471.

[4] G. Winning, A Scheme for Assessment of the Nature Conservation Value of Wetlands. Wetlands (Australia). 9 (1), 1990, 20-27.

[5] J. Vandermeer and I. Perfecto, The Agro-ecosystem: A Need for the Conservation Biologists lens. Conservation Biology, 11, 2003, 591-592.

[6] R.D. Semlitsch and J.R. Bodie, Are small wetlands Expendable? Conservation Biology. 12 (5), 1998, 1129-1133.

[7] S.H. Kevin Peh, N.S. Sodhi, J.D. Jong, C. H. Sekercioglu, C.A.M. Yap, S.L.H. Lim. 2006. Conservation Value of Degraded Habitats for Forest Birds in southern peninsular Malaysia, Diversity and Distribution, 12, 2006, 1-10.

[8] V.I. Kati, C.H. Sekercioglu, Diversity, Ecological Structure and Conservation of the Land bird Community of Dadia Reserve, Greece, Diversity and Distribution, 12, 2006, 620-629.

Chapter-X

Role of Hydropower Dams and Development: Local Perspectives

Ratna Tayeng[3] and Miyo Tayeng[4]*

Abstract

Arunachal Pradesh is today poised as the Power House of India, with plans to build 186 hydro power projects. Consequently, the government of Arunachal Pradesh has signed a memorandum of understanding (MoU) with more than 12 power developers for the development of more than 180 hydropower dams in the state. This has caused lots of anxiety and disquiets among the local people on various counts leading to various anti-dam protests in the state. In this context the present paper attempts to give a broader overview of the local people perceptions and impacts of large dams on the tribal population of Arunachal Pradesh. It also details the challenges that have afflicted the state over the years, namely related to governance and hydropower projects. The paper argues that there must be proper liaison between state government, power developer and local people. They should need to come in one negotiable standard for harness development through mutual cooperation with local people concern. The paper presents the particular case of the Siang River basin where more than 40 hydropower projects are proposed. The work is primarily based on the secondary sources of data. But the primary data have been also done through personal observations, interview with the local activists, Ngos and different student organizations of the region.

Key words: Dams, Development, Environment, Local Perspectives, River

[3] Doctoral Fellow, Department of Anthropology, Rajiv Gandhi University, Itanagar
[4] Doctoral Fellow, Department of Geography, Rajiv Gandhi University, Arunachal Pradesh

Introduction

The present paper is an attempt to give a broader overview of the local people perception of proposed hydro power projects in the Siang River basin of Arunachal Pradesh. As a matter of fact, much has been written on the issue, but still there is a dearth of empirical work on the issue. However, scholars like Ramachadra Guha (2012) and Sanjib Baruah (2012) had given a broader framework of looking the Dam project in the state. Guha (2012) in his article "Dams and the damned: Growth at what cost" warned of the dangers posed by unregulated dam-building in Arunachal Pradesh. He argues that the path of development currently being followed in India is short-sighted, destructive and socially polarizing. And thereby advocated for smaller project as an alternative to large mega-projects, which would be more economically viable, environmentally sustainable and socially inclusive. Sanjib Baruah (2012) in his article "Whose River Is It Anyway? Political Economy of Hydropower in the Eastern Himalayas" focuses on the Lower Subansiri hydropower dam and controversies surrounding the project. He argues that despite the protest, the people of Brahmaputra valley may not have any choice but to learn to live with the risks of mega dams.

Arunachal Pradesh, on the North-eastern tip of India is a land of pristine beauty, abundant with water and forest resources. It would not be wrong to say that in each kilometer you find a river or a rivulet with perennially flowing river water. Most of the rivers origin from the mountains within the state, but few have its sources of origin from the glaciers of the mighty Himalayas (Medha, 2010). Some of the well known rivers are Siang, Subansiri, Kameng, Lohit, Tirap, Dibang etc. of all the rivers, the Siang is the biggest river with its source from the great Himalayas (Nyori, 1993).

Fig.:1 Proposed Dam Projects in Siang River Basin of Arunachal Pradesh

Sl. No	Name of Place	Name of River	Name of Agency	Date of signing MoU	Install capacity (mw)	District
1	Yamne-I	Yamne	Abir Constructions	05 Mar. 2008	60 MW	Upper Siang
2	Yamne-II	Yamne	Abir Construction	05 Mar. 2008	60 MW	Upper Siang
3	Lower Yamne-I	Yamne	M/s Yamne Power	29 Nov. 2008	50 MW	Upper Siang
4	Lower Yamne-II	Yamne	M/s Yamne Power	29 Nov. 2008	40 MW	Upper Siang
5	Palsi	Palsi	Meenakshi Infra	27 Aug. 2010	24 MW	Upper Siang
6	Pango	Sirapteng	Meenakshi Infra	27 Aug. 2010	96 MW	Upper Siang
7	Sipit	Sipit	Aswani Power	29 Nov. 2010	7 MW	Upper Siang
8	Nyikging	Nuyikgong	Aswani Power	29 Nov. 2010	8 MW	Upper Siang
9	Jidu	Yangsang	Meenakshi Power	20-Jul-11	92 MW	Upper Siang
10	Sippi	Ringong	Meenakshi Power	20-Jul-11	96 MW	Upper Siang
11	Tato-I	Siyom	Velcan Energy	30 Jun. 2007	170 MW	West Siang
12	Tato-II	Siyom	Reliance Power	22 Feb. 2006	700MW	West Siang
13	Siyom	Siyom	Reliance Power	22 Feb. 2006	1000MW	West Siang
14	Naying	Siyom	DS Cons. Power	22 Feb. 2006	1000MW	West Siang

15	Pauk	Siyom	Velcan Energy	30 Jun. 2007	120 MW	West Siang
16	Heo	Siyom	Velcan Energy	30 Jun. 2007	210 MW	West Siang
17	Jarong	Siyom	M/s CESC Ltd	25 Nov. 2008	90 MW	West Siang
18	Kaying	Pitgong	Sartda Eco Power	27 Aug. 2010	08MW	West Siang
19	Barpu	Yargyap	Raajratna Energy	27 Dec. 2007	70 MW	West Siang
20	Lower Siang	Siang	Jaypee Power	22 Feb. 2006	2700 MW	East Siang
21	Simang-I	Simang	Adishankar	06 Feb. 2008	67 MW	East Siang
22	Simang-II	Simang	Adishankar	06 Feb. 2008	66 MW	East Siang
23	Simen	Simen	Satyam NEHP	28 Mar. 20 08	21 MW	East Siang
24	Yemsing	Yembung	KVK Energy	02 Mar. 2009	15 MW	East Siang
	Total	13	14	-	6770 MW	3

Historically, the people of the state came into contact with the civilization almost very recently and until then it was ruled by the law of the land. When the British annexed the land they adopted the policy of isolation with less interference from the plain society which is popularly known as the "Inner Line Policy of 1873".

According to the provisions, people from other parts of the country cannot enter the State without the permission of the Government. Moreover, they also cannot own any land nor any fixed assets in this State (Baruah, 2008). Off-course, the sole purpose was to contain the movement of the people into the neighboring plain which were caused problems to the British administration.

Basing on the principle of the inner line, after Indian Independence under the leadership of Prime Minister, Jawaharlal Nehru, a popular policy was adopted "development along the lines of their own genius" (Elwin, 1960). Although the policy still continues to be operational, but in recent years, keeping the need and overall development of the state, lots of dam project is projected on the land. From 2000 to 2012, the state government has signed more than 180 memorandums of understanding (MoU) and memorandums of agreement (MoA) with various companies to harness the potentials for power development of the region. Some of the popular companies are National Hydroelectric Power Corporation (NHPC), North Eastern Electric Power Corporation Limited (NEEPCO), Jindal Steel and Power Limited (JINDAL), Jagran Production Limited (JAPL), Patel Engineering, Sew Energy, Athena Energy, Reliance Power, Jindal Power, Jaiprakash Associates, Abir Infra, Coastal Infra, Navayuga Engineering, Mountain Fall India, Larsen and Toubro Power (L&T Power), Sai Krishnodaya Industries, Meenakshi Power, Velcan Energy and Adishankar Power etc. A majority of them is stuck due to issues ranging from the delayed forest clearance and lack of infrastructure to opposition from local people. Many intellectuals argue that "the central policy of accelerating hydropower development in the state is undesirable[5]". However, the construction of dams is a matter of great concern for the local inhabitants and environmentalists alike. While the local tribes consider dams as an existential threat to their socio-cultural fabric, environmentalists meanwhile have been raising the alarm since the dams would be built on fragile ecological zone prone to frequent earthquakes.

As per the expert knowledge about the regions ecology and geology of the area is not suitable for construction of large dams and hydro projects (Taher and Ahmad, 2007). The hydropower policy of Arunachal Pradesh, however, looks at it differently.

The document states that, "the state provides ideal conditions for the development of hydro power projects...The small rivulets are perennial in nature and therefore provide an ideal condition for developing mini and micro hydel projects[6]."

[5] Kiren Rijiju, MoS, Government of India, posted in a Facebook on 6th May 2014
[6] Hydro Electric Power Policy Arunachal Pradesh, Government of Arunachal Pradesh

Ecological Milieu of Siang River Basin

The present work focused in the central zone of the state within Siang river basin, which covers the three Siang districts namely Upper Siang, East Siang and West Siang district. All these districts are named after the Siang River. The entire area is mountainous and rugged topography and covered with dense forest and rich flora and fauna. The terrain of the area has deep valleys, steep mountains with a complex hill with a varying elevation ranging 50 m in the foothills ascending to about 7000 m.

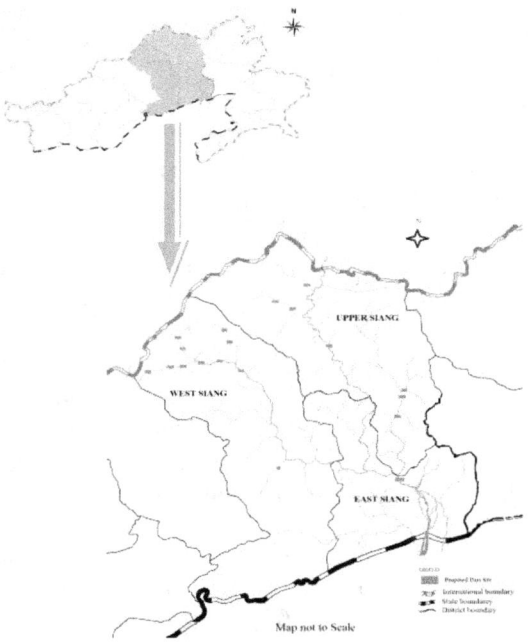

Fig.2: Area of Study

Most of the rivers of Siang basin namely Siang, Siyom and Simang etc., originate in Southern Tibet. Among these rivers, the Siang is the largest and it originates in the Chemayungdung mountain ranges lake in the Mount Kailash range in Southern Tibet. The river Siang enters Arunachal Pradesh near Gelling from where it is known as Siang. The total length of Siang River is 294 km till its point of confluence with

Dibang and Lohit River. After entering India the river traverses approximately 197.0 km to join the Siyom River. From there the length of the river till Assam border is 86.3 km.

The climatic condition of the area is greatly influenced by the Himalayan Mountains. The entire area is located in the south Asian monsoon region, experience humid subtropical climate with hot summer and mild winter. The rainfall of Arunachal is one of the heaviest in the country receive more than 3500 mm in a year and the average annual rainfall of 1000 mm in the higher reaches and 5000 mm in the lower foothill areas. During monsoon season most of the rivers in the area are common in flood, landslides which are hazardous to the environment and human infrastructure. Interestingly, during winter and autumn, when farmers require water for the kharif crop, the dams would store up all the available water for power-generation (Gohain, 2008).

The area is inhabited by indigenous tribal people with distinctive socio-cultural life co-existed from time immemorial. The major tribal people inhabited in this area are Adis and Galos. Apart from this, other tribes such as Mishmis, Membas, and Khambas are also inhabited in the region. These three districts occupy an area of 18,518 square Km with a total population of 24, 6580 as per 2011 census. The people are closely associated with forest and rivers and highly dependent on it. The people still owned community land, forest and rivers in the region7. This diversity of communities comes with unique socio-cultural, agro-ecological and land-holding systems (Vagholikar and Das, 2010). In fact, most of the tribal communities of the state don't considered land and rivers as private property, they are mostly owned collectively by clan members or villagers.

The area is rich in biodiversity and is home to many important populations of various wildlife species. In spite of rich biodiversity, the area is still unexplored region. There are numbers of endangered species of plants and animals dwell in the region. As per the official estimation, 82.26% of the Siang basin is under forest cover (more than 15,000 sq kms), it is rich in orchids (more than 100 species), holds 16 species of rhododendrons, 14 species of Bamboos and 14 species of

---

[7] Interim Report Independent People's Tribunal on Dams in Arunachal Pradesh, February 3, 2008, Itanagar, Arunachal Pradesh, India, pp.8.

canes and overall 27 Rare, Endangered and Threatened (RET) species and 46 endemic plant species. As per the executive summary of the Hirong Hydro Electric Project, "Dam's construction in the state holds possibilities of significant damage on the river ecosystems[8].

Cultural Milieu of Siang River Basin

Water is not only a physical substance, biological necessity or scarce resource, but also an intrinsic part of people's identity, cultures, worldviews and religious perceptions of themselves and the Otherworld or the life thereafter (Baviskar, 2007). Water in its many facets matters for humans, while the social, cultural, ideological and religious roles of water include deep ontological relations and identities ranging from personal perceptions and gender relations, to rainmaking and fertility rites for the benefit of the whole society as well as perceptions of cosmological realms and religious beliefs (Terje, 2009). All views on water relate to its basic functions and significance to life. The entire world seems to recognize the importance of water and its necessity for life. However, water is also respected for many additional reasons in different cultures and religions. There is no doubt about how Siang River plays an intrinsic role in the lives of the people. The people of the Siang river basins largely depend upon the nearby forest and river resources for their daily uses since time immemorial. The water bodies such as rivers, streams, lakes and springs forms an indispensable part in their socio-cultural life.

They have explored all such bodies of water of their area and have given them appropriate names. For instance, The Adis like many of the tribal inhabitants of the state have their own distinct term for water which is popularly known as Asi. They distinguished the water resources available to them according to their size and volume, to them natural springs is known as Hirung or Hikur, river as Korong, rivulets as Kobung, and big river as Hinne (Tapak, 2012). Small streams and rivulets are commonly known by the term kojing Korong. Moreover, many spirits both malevolent and benevolent are believed to dwell in the rivers and their source, in forest and mountains. The galos also have their own distinct term for the water called Aashi similar to Adi. Tomo Riba (2003) provides many insights into the Galos relationship with their natural environment. He explains how the Galo perceive water and relate these natural resources with divinity.

In their local concept Siang River is known by female gender, Ane Siang which means mother. The Siang River is also noted for beautiful scenery, and the tourists from all across the globe do come and visit. Besides that, the people who inhabit herein are also known for vibrant songs and dances. Here, is such one popular folksong on Siang River. The song is originally written by Nakkeng Perme and sung by two Adi folk singers Lomyuk Lego and Yung Tayeng. Here we tried to translate it in English:

> *Ane Siang*
> *Ane saing asi noa*
> *Oh!! Mighty Siang River*
> *Lobo pumu e yago dongkom*
> *Though summer floods may come*
> *Tapam kisa pe ansi la tokyar yeneniya?*
> *Will you keep your flow constantly…as cold as snow?*
> *Bedum situng pe duyar geyeniya?*
> *Will you always stay like a wood in a pathway while guiding out avenues for others?*
> *Ane siang, abu yamne, abu sikang asi nolu*
> *Oh! Mother siang, father yamne and sikang rivers*
> *Ane Siang asi no*
> *Oh! Mother siang*
> *Nokke robe lo duna sine lokne kidar emme sibuk raket em ratmo kane no*
> *Trees that live on your banks are eroded and swept away your by your strong currents Pedong takyot na sedi liying e line bulu, lobo singon em nitap mokan e no*
> *Your mightiness breaks the hard rocks and carries huge logs away during your summer flash floods*
> *Bosi dadi ke tatnam asi e ai no*
> *Your name has been heard by everyone*
> *Borang nommang je tatnam Korong e ai no*
> *Your name has been known by everyone*
> *Sine gebung em botte lenkito to no*
> *Like a small river paves it way to meet its mother drainage*

Dite yamying em tokong gena no, kone yammo em bitkong gena nolu
Crossing through many beautiful mountains and valleys you have showed us your strength and potentiality
Nolum kali dung sine atel pe dakdo pe
We would like to see you all in a unified stand
Nolum kaling dung robung atel lo gido pe
We would like to see you all flowing through the same valley
Korong rongo em lenket mapeka
May your huge flow remain undisturbed for smaller streams and rivers?
Rogic bitting em yitum mapeka
May your flow paves out way and show direction to smaller streams and rivers
Sine banbo em repji bolangka
May you led all small rivers/streams in a unified fashion
Sine Yameng em sangkong gelangka nolu
May you all become the most dashing and energetic leaders

Here, the song expressed the mystic flow of river siang and its scenic beauty. Even in Indian tradition, rivers have always been regarded as divinities. Moreover, the water has been treated as a natural right - a right arising out of human nature, historic conditions, basic needs and notions of justice (Shiva, 2002). According to the people, the River Siang is the source of all life in these hill regions. In their legend, it is the abode of unseen spirits guarded and protected by Asi Uyu, Bumbo-Yiiying, Tusin-rodong and Hili-Hidong (All are water gods). Everything that exists and lives in the water is assigned to be the property of these water spirits. Whenever a person goes out to the jungle or nearby river water, he is obliged to propitiate the presiding deity before carrying out any of his tasks.

In the cosmogony world of the Adis and Galos, every natural resource like forest and river are believed to be the dwelling place of spirits, who guarded and protected it from intrusion of any kind. They inflicted various kinds of disease and sufferings on that person who break away the sacred ethos. For instance, whenever a man leaves for fishing activities his wife is taboo from weaving and knitting clothes of her husband. It is believed that is she does not do that her husband will face difficulties and will return empty.

Although rivers and streams is an economic asset for the people, but they perceived it to be the dwelling place of many unseen spirits. Thus, fishing and allied activities in water is embedded with various socioeconomic and cultural implications. Even though the ground reality around the community has changed or is fast changing with rapid exploitation of the nearby resources, they attempt to guard the essence of their life and are reluctant to resist or lack the necessary attributes for acquisition and intensification of resources use.

Dam as Development: Local Perspective

Fig.3: Women activists at a protest rally against large dams held in Itanagar, the capital of Arunachal Pradesh, in July 2007 (Vagholikar and Das, 2010)

Behold, you highland dwellers
To the neo-colonialism with its ugly hoods
Inundating the paradise with human floods
To cleanse the varied cultural philosophy
Depleting the vast and rich ecology
Wait not for the time opportune
Create not your own fortune
Unite, integrate, and stand up to erupt
Against the anti-Indians, terrorist and corrupt

-Vijay Taram (18 April 2011)8

The people of the region have a great apprehension to loss community land at large scale. They have strong stand that proposed Dam project should be lessened to minimize impact of multipurpose project. As a consequence, several organizations have emerged in the area in opposition to current dam building practices in the region. Most of the local natives hold the view that the proposed dams in the region are posing as a great threat to the local people and it biodiversity. There are organizations like the Forum for Siang Dialogue (FSD), Siang Peoples' Forum (SPF), Mebo Area Bacho Committee (MABC), West Siang Dam Affected Peoples Association (WSDAPA), Lower Siang Project Affected People Action Committee (LSPAPAC) and Lower Siang Dam Project Affected Youth Association (LSDPAYA) active in the region.

Among all the organizations, the most active forum in the region is the Forum for Siang Dialogue (FSD)9 led by Ojing Tasing and Vijay Taram. In an interview with Vijay Taram10 on 23 December 2013, he says: "Dam over the Mighty Siang River is an unjust developmental pursuit. The lush green fields around the villages on the high hills is what we consider our wealth, the pray fishes and shrimps in the hill-streams and rivulets is what we live for our society around and the hunting, trapping and roaming in the wild green-green forest is what we consider our achievements in life.

Our identity is our culture and culture thrives on the nature. Therefore, destruction of nature is impingement to our culture and impingement of culture is cleansing of our identity". Many Adi intellectuals argue that they need development, but not at the cost of destroying their ancestral land, forest and rivers. Ojing Tasing, the chairman of the Siang People Forum says: "No dams on river Siang at the cost of our extinction"[11].

---

[8] Vijay Taram, Posted in a Facebook group-ADI A MAJOR TRIBE on 18 April 2011

[9] The forum was formed in 2001 and since then the Forum is crusading awareness campaign over the impacts of Dam Projects in Siang Valley.

[10] Personal Interview with Vijay Taram on 23 December 2013 at Pasighat, Arunachal Pradesh

[11] SPF Chairman Ojing Tasing said in a joint Press conference here last evening ,the Hindu, December 2, 2010,Tribe fears Arunachal dam will extinct its people

In similar tone, Oni Panyang12, President of Lower Siang Dam Project Affected Youth Association (LSDPAYA) says: "Our land is gifted with rich minerals, resources, and abundant flora and fauna. But today, some hungry politicians are running after our god gifted resources to rob it, declaring these resources as 'the property of nation' disrespecting us who lived in this region for generation".

The issue is clear, the question is right to life of some persons cannot be compromised or bartered just for providing more comforts to many people. Felix Padel (2011) argues that the greatest problem faced in development of tribes is how best to bring the blessing and the advantages of modern science and technology without destroying the rare and precious values of tribal life, not interfering with their ways of life, but helping them to live it. Thus, it is obvious to remark that community people are not against the Dam project, but against the proposed major project.

A young journalist Mr. Ajing Pertin (2011) writes: 'the push by the Centre to accelerate hydropower development in the Siang valley and particularly the 2700MW Lower Siang Hydro Electric Project (LSHEP) of East Siang District of Arunachal Pradesh to counter the Chinese hydro power projects on the Tsangpo has only succeeded in sowing the seeds of major conflicts in the future for the Siang valley. The villagers of Pongging protesting the project near a Jaypee camp had to face violent action by the CRPF and state police in May 25 2010, "the Central Reserve Police Force (CRPF) open fire in Pongging village of Upper Siang"13.

In response to this incident, the apex student organization of the Adis, "AdiSU warns govt of revolt14" and warned to launch "Quit Siang movement15' if their protest against Lower Siang Hydroelectric Project is not looked into.

[12] Personal Interivew with Oni Panyang at Pashighat, on 21 December 2013
[13] Four injured at Pongging as CRPF open fire at protestors, The Arunachal Times, May 27, 2010, P-1
[14] AdiSU nullify outcome of meeting on Dam, the Arunachal Times, 9th September 2010, P-1
[15] Students to launch "Quit Siang movement", The Arunachal Times, June, 07, 2010, P-1

In an interview with Israel Perme16, General Secretary of AdiSU (2010-2012) says: "With a population of more than one lakhs work forces, the Jaypee Groups have to clear vast patches of lands for the humanly dwelling of these workers. These vast clearances of green reserve would certainly create imbalance in eco-system of the whole Siang valley. Dam is not constructed just by erecting a wall across the river with its base through the river-bed. The foundation of dams lies on both ends of the river banks. On both banks of the river deep digging would be undertaken through sophisticated machines not available in India. Digging would lead to the accumulation of huge quantity of earthen waste constituting of mud, gravel, stones, rocks and many more decomposed elements. More, immeasurable quantity of oils and mechanical waste would also accumulate. The improper disposition of the wastages and human carelessness would be the cause factor to the epidemic and pollute the river and water system of the Siang Valley. This would grossly effect depletion of whole bio-diversity of Siang valley, particular and the whole of Arunachal Pradesh in general. This change in the bio-diversity would certainly affect the livelihood of the communities living around Siang Valley. The river system of the valley would start drying and would be polluted immeasurably, the ever green rich vegetations would vanish slowly and slowly, flood and land-slides would be rampant and the vast varieties of flora and fauna would meets its slow end, forever. These processes would engender large displacement of the people inhabiting this beautiful land. The sons of the soil would be alienated from one's own birth place.

The research work done by Tanyang Yaying (2007) on Siyom Hydro Project in the West Siang is worth mentioning, the author writes: "The proposal of 1000mw Siyom hydro project had made the people uncomfortable and forced them to vacate the places occupied by them since time immemorial. As per the EIA report of 2000-01 the total submergence area will be 2854.36 ha, out of 3285 km2 of catchments area actual submerged area is 1891.41 ha. And about 290 families and 1070 population are getting affected by this project. Two villages will submerged under the reservoir of the dam namely Pame and Reying villages comprising of 37 families.

---

[16] Personal Interview with Mr. Isreal Perme, General Secretary of Adi student's Union on 11 June 2010 at Rajiv Gandhi University, Itanagar

The common problems of dam construction of the area are the submergence of suspension bridge over the Siyom River estimated up to 15 numbers. Problems of land slide, soil erosion, adoption of new culture, noise pollution, deforestation, extinction of some plant and animal species are likely to occur as the work on the project progresses. But there are positive aspects of the project also i.e. the increase in power generation, increase in local marketing scope, establishment of new departments, increase in employment potentials, etc" (Page-25-26).

In addition, the history of the developments with respect to dam project on Siang River has not successful enough. The earliest attempt to construct the dam over the river was undertaken by the Brahmaputra Flood Control (BFC), since 1978. The attempt was a complete failure. They had to give away their utopian dreams. After the failure of the BFC, National Hydro Power Cooperation arrived with new plans and policies to construct a series of Dams over Siang River. They too had to double up showing their back to the river. Today, the Jaypee Groups have arrived to complete the task to tame the river. Till date this company was involved in petty construction works only. This company actually survived through availing sub-let works under the National Hydroelectric Power Corporation. Herein lies the greatest question, is this company competent enough to be allowed to undertake Dam Project over the Mighty Siang River.

The perspectives of the various tribes on the Dam projects in Arunachal Pradesh are quite similar. Most of the people across the state are neither against the Dam project nor supporting the Dam project.

According to Rihu Mihu[17], "people living in the proposed Dibang Multipurpose Dam project hold the opinion that the project is very big which is impossible to be accepted since it has great impact on the environment. According to this section of the community they are not against the Dam project, but against the huge 3000MW Dam project. It reveals that they will support the smaller Dam project".

[17] Rihu, Mihu, 2014, Dibang Multipurpose Project - Communities' perception,TheMishmi.com,
http://www.themishmis.com/index.php/resources/paper/32-dibang-multipurpose-project-communities-perception.html

According to Raju Mimi[18], the proposed project will submerge an area of 4009 hectares, and a backwater reservoir of 43 km will be created. The project will acquire 5827.8 hectares of land; of which 5056.50 ha is community forest land classified as Unclassed State Forest (USF).

More recently, Parag Jyoti Saikia[19] (2014) writes: "The impacts of the Dibang multipurpose project are going to severe on the river, people and overall ecology of Dibang river basin. But the sad part is that no proper assessment of these impacts has been done till now. Looking back at the six years since the laying foundation stone for the project we reiterate what Forest Advisory Committee said about the project "ecological, environmental and social costs of diversion of such a vast tract of forest land, which is a major source of livelihood of the tribal population of the State, will far outweigh the benefits likely to accrue from the project".

Lige Sora, a doctoral scholar of Economics (RGU) and former general secretary of Galo Students' Union (GSU) says: few years back, a dam project was proposed at the middle Siang, near Pangin which is at a distance of about 60 Kms south from Aalo town, which was expected to create a great reservoir with an approximated backflow of the river water upto Aalo town. Fortunately, the project was ultimately stopped after we pursued democratic movement in the Galos inhabited areas.

The majority of the lower Siang people holds the opinion against the proposed Mega dam project. According to Okom Megu[20], General Secretary of Lower Siang Project Affected People Action Committee:

"Construction of a Dam in our region would certainly need large human resources. As per the information from a reliable source, the total number of skilled and unskilled labourers only, in the construction site would be approximately of about 30,000/ (Thirty thousand) persons, excluding their family members.

---

[18] Raju Mimi, 2014, The Dibang Multipurpose Project: Resistance of the Idu Mishmi, TheMishmi.com

[19] Parag Jyoti Saikia, Six years after PM Laying the Foundation Stone: No Clearance, No Work for 3000 MW Dibang Dam, SANDRP, South Asia Network on Dams, Rivers and People, Posted on January 31, 2014 by sandrp

[20] Personal Interview with Okom Megu at Pasighat, East Siang, Arunachal Pradesh on 5 May 2010

At an average of 4 persons a family, the total populations to be arriving at the construction site would be approximately of about 1, 20, 000/ (One lakh twenty thousand) persons. This population statistic itself is alarming because the total human population within the radius of 10-15 Kms from the construction site presently is hardly 10,000/ (ten thousand) persons. Leaving it aside, even the total local population of the whole East Siang District would hardly reach 1, 00, 000/ (One lakh) persons. Any thinking person would certainly realize the meaninglessness of the off- repeatedly mentioned policy of Resettlement and Rehabilitation, with these statistical data. A drastic and enormous demographic change is imminent with commencement of construction of the Dam over River Siang. The resultant factor of the population imbalance would be nothing but ethnic cleansing, leading to complete annihilation of the rich culture and traditions of the local populace of the project areas".

Most of the people argue that the 2700MW mega dam will be a decision in haste and advocated for the reduction of the capacity. Apart from that common fear, an argument also put forward in Facebook that apprehend the abolition of Inner Line Permit which will become a necessity. This issue has found space in a number of groups on the social networking site Facebook. Number of Facebook users from the Adi has reacted to the dam project in siang belt. The present General Secretary of Adi Student's Union (AdiSU), Mr. Obuk Gao[21] writes:

My personal view on hydropower development in the State is to go for developing mini/micro or small hydro power projects ranging from few kilowatts to few megawatts. We have huge resources for developing these ranges of power in the State. In fact, if the total potential in these ranges are developed, it might equal the total power that could be produced through mega projects".

He further says that they are ready to take even extreme action if the government continues to pursue big dam projects in the area. In similar line, Behon Jamoh,[22] a young engineer student writes:

---

[21] Obuk Gao, posted in his facebook account on 16 July 2012

[22] Behon jamoh, a young social activist of Adi, posted in his facebook account on 3 November 2013

"Our Arunachal Pradesh is situated in one of most vulnerable tectonic plates classified under Seismic Zone -V. If the Assam earthquake of 1950's is a historic past so as to evoke a faint memory or no memory at all for any Cynical Scientific Great, then the latest Sikkim earthquake where around 500 people were killed, many thousands injured, Ten Thousands of houses lay shattered and many highways and other infrastructures still laying ruined is not a celluloid screening at all. These are the warnings and indications of The Mother Nature for the people to stop irreversible and harmful intervention to the systems and processes of nature which are but supreme. Neither Japanese Engineers & Technocrats could design and develop the human accentuated earthquake & natural disaster proof structure nor there is any human being in this planet who can ever create one. The bottom line is that, the mega dams are destructive and suicidal for the people of Arunachal Pradesh".

Today, it seems that following western materialistic model of development many developing countries give a blind eye to nature, social reality…which has had the effect of divorcing us from nature and social world reality…and if this pace continue…the final darkness is not far (Felix Padel 2009; 313-14). Recently, in the general convention of Bogum Bokang Kebang on 14 & 15th October 2012 held at Pessing, Upper Siang, Arunachal Pradesh, a decision was taken to oppose the Lower Siang Hydroelectric Project (2700 MW) at any cost. In his inaugural speech, the president of ABK, Mr. Kangir Jamoh says that "Ngolu Adi among sok 24 Dam takam solok ke Lower Siang Dam atel petom sim mai oppose dun.

23 Dam sim oppose mang. Seko development dem miiman (We will support the entire small 23 dam projects, but the big dam project is not acceptable, offcourse we all believe in development)

However, it appears that some sections of people are happy with the proposed Dam projects in the region owing the constant power failure. Some of the people say "it is good for development and prosperity of the region". Okom Tamuk, a social worker from Pashighat is of the opinion that: "The pressure groups opposing dam is only behind cash, they will not demand for health centers, engineering college and sports stadiums as these are not going to fill their account. How long we will bag from the central govt. Just blindly opposing Dam will not going to give us anything at the end. We should be practical and see how we can secure our future with the coming of Dam projects".

In an orientation programme titled "legal provisions of Environmental Clearance processes for Mega Dam projects" held at Bahir Jonai (Assam) on June 05, 2014, Vijay Taram, the spokesperson of Forum for Siang Dialogue (FSD) argue that:

"Though many expert claims Arunachal to be capable of generating some 5000 plus MW of power, they deliberately don't tell us the amount of environmental destruction such projects are likely to bring, even if such facts are hidden from us, there are ample of examples in the state to learn from. The Chakmas and Hajong communities of Arunachal, who are unwanted and unwelcome refugees, deprived of basic faculties, did not pop out from nowhere just like that. These communities were displace because of coming up of Kaptai hydropower project, which subsequently led to internal conflict including communal riots forcing them to flee from Chittagong Hill Tracts. Closure home, 2000 MW Subansiri Lower Project is one example. Apart from few contractors who have made huge sums of money, most people continue to live in abject poverty. Another example is those living downstream of the Ranganadi Hydro project. In villages near to Kimin, Sher, people live in continues fear. More so in summers since they never know when the water is going to be released from the dam. The water dramatically dries up in winter and there is deluge in summer. Off course we understand the need of power projects but the question is how big? So far there is no opposition to minor projects which is a clear indication that people do agree to the fact that the state need power to sustain itself".

It is a fact that the comprehensive development approaches towards state in general and Siang Valleys in particular should emphasize on the prosperity of the region, so that the local livelihood, environmental conservation and social justice should be harmonized. The various developments must not seek material wealth only, but wealth that enables people to live justly and sustainably within the capacity of supporting ecosystems.

Hydropower and Development

Hydropower, which uses the energy of flowing water to produce electricity, has always been an important part of human development (Gurbuz, 2006). As hydropower does not consume or pollute the water it uses to generate power, it leaves this vital resource available for other uses such as controlling floods, irrigation, drinking water supply, fishing, tourism etc. At the same time, the revenues generated through electricity sales can finance other infrastructure essential for human welfare[23]. Apart from this, it is also said that the dam site attract tourist resort centre such as view point, water sports etc (Har, 2002). In fact, in a state like Arunachal Pradesh which has a huge water resources and potential, there is no doubt about how hydropower projects can play a significant role in the development of the state. Moreover, the topography of the State also offers very ideal conditions for development of hydro-electric power projects.

Ironically, since independence, national development has been largely equated with economic growth and surplus. All the human and ecological costs were justified in its name (Singh, 1997). Large, centralized industries, irrigation projects have been symbols of such development, which through the process of industrialization promised to set India on the path of modernization and development. One of the inevitable outcomes of this has been massive environmental degradation and 'development induced displacement' (Padel, 2012). As a matter fact, hydro power projects in India have always been regarded as "secular temples of modern India". Proponents of the dam argue that for their own good, the 'backward and savage' adivasis need to be assimilated into the modern mainstream.

If we look closer to society of Arunachal Pradesh, most of the communities are nature-based; largely self sufficient economies of tribal people are sustained and nurtured through their life which is in close proximity to forest, river and mountains. It is on this background, that people's movements have raised several fundamental questions. Who constitutes the nation? Who benefits from projects like large dams? Who has paid the price? Who decides

---

[23] The Role of Hydropower in Sustainable Development, International Hydropower Association (IHA), IHA White paper, February 2003, http://www2.ce.metu.edu.tr/~ce571/links/announcement/LowRes_Hydropower_i n_Sustainable_Development.pdf

and who obeys? Why? Can development that impoverishes communities, particularly the poor and the marginalized and destroys ecological balance for the sake of powerful classes be called development at all? Struggles against the destruction and devastation caused by large dams have challenged the very basis of State's unquestioned power to take control of people's lives and resources.

They have argued that just and sustainable development cannot take place by forcing some people to 'sacrifice' for others (Ibid). People's right to know, to be informed, to participate in the process of shaping their life and future has been the very basis of these struggles.

Conclusion

Arunachal Pradesh is industrially backward state as per the national committee's report on industrial dispersal. However, the problems of development lie not in the lack of natural resources but in the large investments required for infrastructure development. From the point of view of infrastructure development the principal problem in the region is the inadequacy of communication facilities. Arunachal is exceptionally rich in natural resources. It has all the attributes of a national powerhouse and reservoir that could transform the region, ameliorate poverty, and generate national wealth. The gifts of water and biodiversity offer tremendous potential that requires vision, will, and careful planning if they are to be converted into bountiful, renewable resources for sustainable development. However, unregulated waters currently vent their fury in destructive which leads much of social agitation and social unrest in the society.

Therefore, it is essence to address that acceptability of the project to community per se. community are the sole owner of resources their needs and aspiration should be justified. Development for national interest should not harm the tribal community.

For that there must be extensive socio-economic study regarding the particular people who going to lose their land, forest, and rivers. Some sections of the community do against the dam project because for the reason for this was cited as "non-fulfillment of basic environmental conditions and the lack of completion of crucial studies and plans". So, there must be proper liaison between state government, power developer and community people. They should need to come at one negotiable standard to harness development through mutual co-operation with community. It will enhance mutuality of development and communities' aspiration.

References

1. Guha, Ramachadra, Dams and the damned: Growth at what cost, The Telegraph, Saturday, June, 16, 2012, P-1
2. Baruah, Sanjib, Whose River Is It Anyway? Political Economy of Hydropower in the Eastern Himalayas, Economic and Political Weekly, Vol - XLVII No. 29, July 21, 2012
3. Bisht, Medha, Dams in Arunachal Pradesh: Between Development Debates and Strategic Dimensions, Institute for Defense Studies and Analyses, 2010
4. Nyori, Tai, History and Culture of the Adis, New Delhi, Omsons Publications, 1993
5. Baruah, Sanjib, Territoriality, Indigeneity and Rights in the North-east India, Economic & Political Weekly, March 22, 2008, Pp-15-17
6. Elwin, Verrier, A Philosophy for NEFA, Itanagar, Directorate of Research, Government of Arunachal Pradesh, Itanagar, 2006 (1960)
7. Taher M and Ahmad P, Geography of North East India, Guwahati, Mani Manik Prakash, pp.28, 2007
8. Gohain, Hiren, Big Dams, Big Floods: On Predatory Development, Economic & Political Weekly, July 26, 2008
9. Vagholikar, N. and Das, P.J., Damming Northeast India. Kalpavriksh, New Delhi, Aaranyak and Action Aid India, 2010
10. Baviskar, Amita, In the belly of the river. Tribal conflicts over development in the Narmada Valley, Delhi, Oxford University Press, 1995
11. Oestigaard, Terje (ed.),Water, Culture and Identity: Comparing Past and Present Traditionsin the Nile Basin Region, University of Bergen, BRIC Press, 2009
12. Tapak, Tanong, Perception and Utilization of Water Resources: A Study among the Adis of Arunachal Pradesh, Mphil Dissertation, Arunachal Institute of Tribal Studies, Rajiv Gandhi University, 2012
13. Riba, Tomo, The Tribes and their Changing Environment, New Delhi, Himalayan Publisher, 2003
14. Shiva, Vandana, Water Wars: Privatization, Pollution and Profit, London, Pluto Press, 2002

15. Padel, Felix, Sacrificing People: Invasions of a Tribal Landscape, New Delhi, Orient Blackswan, 2011
16. Pertin, Ajing, Hydropower from Siang – a cost to pay?, Echo of Arunachal, 16 June 2011, p-1
17. Tanyang Yaying, Problems and Prospects of Siyom Hydro-Project of Payum Circle, West Siang, Arunachal Pradesh, MA dissertation, Department of Geography, Rajiv Gandhi University, 2007
18. Gurbuz, The Role of Hydropower in Sustainable Development, European Water, 13/14: 63-70, 2006, P-65
19. Har D. D et al How Dams Vary and Why It Matters for the Emerging Science of Dam Removal, August 2002 / V ol. 52 No. 8, 2002
20. Singh, S., Taming the waters. The political economy of large dams in India, Delhi, Oxford University Press,1997

Chapter-XI

The Post Mortem of IPCC on Climate Change

P.B. Reddy and G.R. Gangle[*]

Abstract

The issue of climate change had become the top of the international political agenda due to Hurricane Katrina, Al Gore's An Inconvenient Truth, publication of the IPCC AR4 in 2007, and award of the Nobel Peace Prize to Al Gore and the IPCC. The IPCC of United Nations Environment Programme (UNEP) mainly assesses the effects and actions of climate change by collecting scientific, technical and socio-economic information. The AR5 of IPCC provides an updated knowledge of different aspects of climate change. Like past reports it again also claims and predicts the human induced global warming.

But the credibility of the IPCC has been the subject of much debate. Because despite a 7%rise in carbon dioxide percentage in last 15 years the observed global warming was insignificant. Beside the average temperatures of the world have not shown any statistically significant increase since 1997. Now they understood and admit that the computer predictions for the effects of carbon emissions on global warming have been proved to be mistaken. They also admitted that the forecast of computers may not have taken enough notice of natural variability in the climate, therefore multiplied the effect of increased carbon emissions on world temperatures.

It has also been found that IPCC officials violated standard rules of procedure and altered the data in such a way as to justify an acceptable political agenda. Therefore, in this critical research review we are going to highlight the flaws and politics involved in finalization of climate change report.

Keywords: IPCC, climate change, politics, green house gases.

---

[*] *Associate Professor, PG Department of Zoology, Government PG College, Ratlam, Madhya Pardesh*

Introduction

Global warming refers to the increase of global average temperature. But to many politicians and the corporate people, the term carries the allegation that mankind is responsible for that warming [1], [2].The issue of climate change is complex global and is linked with many global issues like poverty, economic development, population growth, sustainable development and resource management. Therefore, solutions have to come from all disciplines and fields of research and development. Since 1992 earth summit a number of treaties were launched but so far nothing has been achieved. In the last three decades, concerns regarding human induced climate change have moved from uncertain scientific inquiries to the forefront of science, politics, policy and practices at many levels including corporate [3]. The sources of funding for both supporting and opposing mainstream scientific positions have been questioned by both sides. There are debates about the best policy responses to the science, their cost-effectiveness and their urgency. Climate scientists have reported officially to censor or suppress their work and hide scientific data, with directives not to discuss the subject in public communications. Legal cases regarding global warming, its effects, and measures to reduce it, have already reached American courts.

Sustainability, population control, and redistributive-based social justice were offered as moral justifications for the one-world governance needed to solve one-world problems. In order to solve the global problems the U.N. global bureaucrats built the Intergovernmental Panel on Climate Change (IPCC) and (Environmental Protection agency) EPA as the instruments by which life-sustaining carbon dioxide would be found as the most dangerous threat to the world [4]. As the well fabricated global-warming disaster runs out of main stream, the greenies (IPCC) have begun in search of new theaters to continue their campaign to bring about the end of Western industrial civilization. Now the latest target is agriculture. This campaign is big and well coordinated. Around 500 activist organizations in the U.S. are going to spend up to $5 billion targeting the agriculture sector (for methane emissions) of developing countries [5].

The IPCC is a Nobel Prize-winning group of highly reputed scientists from all over the world. Since IPCC inception, it has been releasing climate reports every five to seven years and was awarded the Nobel Peace Prize in 2007. But late it was found that the' Inconvenient Truths," of Al Gore is not so truthful. Al Gore and IPCC tried to make climate change as global issue and as a big disaster on the global temperature history. These risk experts (greenies) and their companies have harvested huge financial rewards by profitably defining and pricing risk, and then getting the public to pay insurance premiums to protect itself from the hypothetical risk. The greater the overvalued risk, the greater the corporate insurance profit. Businesses profit from proclaiming that they are "green." Renewable is the key word for obtaining government donations. Scientific validity in these matters is an essential, but not adequate response to change the public's emotional concerns for "clean air," "clean energy," and a "healthy environment for themselves and their children [6].

The recent IPCC report has truly dumped to the level of funny logics. It is quite surprising to see that the IPCC has to go through in order to keep the international climate agenda going. The credibility of the IPCC has been the topic of much debate, as it has been suggested that IPCC officials violated standard rules of procedure in finalizing their reports. The allegation is that IPCC findings have been altered in such a way as to justify a planned political agenda that global warming is a real and legitimate threat. It has also been alleged that the conclusions of the IPCC Summary are not supported by the scientific evidence. The fact is that there is no consensus matching among the scientific world about the human induced global warming. Even after many years the IPCC still doesn't get the correct answer for melting of glaciers from the Little Ice Age for several hundred years. Warming and cooling has been going on for millions of years, long before CO_2 has no role in global warming. Therefore, in this paper we tried to highlight the few controversies and flaws surrounding the climate change and IPCC's hockey stick graphs [7].

Methodology

This research work is mainly based on the secondary data. The secondary data was collected from reports released by the IPCC, journals, proceedings, news, blogs of eminent climate scientists and media clips.

Information was also gathered from various subject experts from university and colleges. The reports of the various British and Europe metrological centers were also used as source of information. Information was also obtained on from web sites and articles addressing climate issues. Selected references to the articles reviewed can be found in the Appendices of the working document. In addition, many press releases have been reviewed on a regular basis.

Results and Discussion

The intention of the IPCC since it was founded in 1988 has always been to balance political and scientific input. Results from the above data clearly indicate that he IPCC has clearly been playing clever politics with flawed climate science. The recent AR5 of IPCC states with 97% confidence that humans are the main cause of the current global warming [1], [2]. The statement that 97% of scientists believe that climate change is a man-made, urgent problem is a fiction. Even the so called consensus comes from a handful of surveys and abstract counting exercises that have been contradicted by more reliable research [8] [9], [10], [11], [12]. There is no scientific basis for the claim that 97% of scientists believe that man made climate change is a dangerous problem. The fact is that heated negotiations among IPCC scientists and diplomats led to important deletion of figures and text from the influential 'Summary for Policy-makers of AR5 [13] [14].

The scientists openly manipulated the world's most influential climate records of US surface temperature records. The effect of this has been to downgrade earlier temperatures and to amplify those from recent decades, to give the impression that the Earth has been warming up much more than is justified by the actual data[15] [16]. When we compare the currently published temperature graphs with those of tampered data of IPCC, it show that the US has actually been cooling since the Thirties, whereas the tampered data of IPCC shows warming at a rate equivalent to more than 3 degrees centigrade per century. This use of terminology is also unscientific. It has been used improperly to create a false impression of increasing statistical certainty through the most recent IPCC assessment reports [17].

Shifts in opinion

Since its creation of the IPCC in 1988, has been sounding the alarm about human induced global warming [2], [13].

The fact is that the earth has warmed just 0.5 degrees over the past 50 years. And Met Office records show that for the past 16 years temperatures have paused and, if anything, are going down.

There have been dramatic shifts in public opinion on climate change over the last few years. In the USA, public opinion polling showed a steady increase in both awareness and concern about climate change, peaking in 2008. The Yale public opinion study showed that in 2008, 71% of Americans thought that climate change was happening and 57% that this was caused by human activities. But this number decreased to 47% in 2010 and this change was accompanied by a belief that there was more disagreement amongst scientists about climate change. The 'consensus' of opinion is that the Earth's climate sensitivity is quite high, and so warming of about 0.25 deg. C to 0.5 deg. C (about 0.5 deg. F to 0.9 deg. F) every 10 years can be expected for as long as mankind continues to use fossil fuels. NASA claims that climate sensitivity is very high, and that we have already put too much extra CO_2 in the atmosphere. Most probably this is why he and Al Gore are campaigning for a halt on the construction of any more coal fired power plants in the U.S [18].

Our findings reveal that The Earth has not warmed at all in the past 15-20 years.

Climate models of IPCC are severely flawed and have not predicted the pause in warming over the past 15-20 years.

IPCC claims that the planet will be free of ice by the summer of 2020, and we would be ice-free right now as recently as 2007.

The Arctic ice sheet is healthier than it's been in the past five years and is over 50 per cent above last year's ice total.

The Antarctic ice sheet has actually grown over the past 33 years and is now near an all-time record high.

The current warming is temporary and it was due to solar cycle but not due to the green house gases.

The Pacific Ocean has recently entered its cool cycle which will last for at least the next couple decades. The Atlantic will follow in a few years time. The last time the two oceans were cool was in the 70s where fears of a "mini ice age" made the cover of Time magazine among other major publications.

Storms, Cyclones, Floods, hurricanes, tornadoes, droughts and other extremes are part of nature. It was observed that numbers of Tornado are at a record low this year and the hurricane season is practically non-existent.

The frustrating is the fact that politics is fully rushed into the fight of "climate science". In AR 5 the IPCC has not mentioned the reasons for paused global warming or the recovering ice caps or the faulty climate models. It is all because of pressure from the U.S. government, corporate leaders and other major political players around the globe.

They are up against a wall because the public is becoming increasingly aware that their horrible predictions are not coming true and any sign of further weakness would completely derail the climate change movement.

The hockey stick debate

The data and methods used by IPCC in reconstructions of the temperature record of the past 1000 years have been disputed. [19]. The U.S. National Academy of science assessed the validity of temperature reconstructions and hockey stick graphs and they concluded that temperature of the 20th Century were warmer than any comparable period in the last 400 years. In November 2009 a large number of emails were exchanged among climate scientists to hide and decline the facts of climate change at the University of East Anglia Climatic Research Unit (CRU). These emails revealed about how climate scientists 'fabricated' evidence to manipulate measurements to make them fit better with the IPCC theories [20].

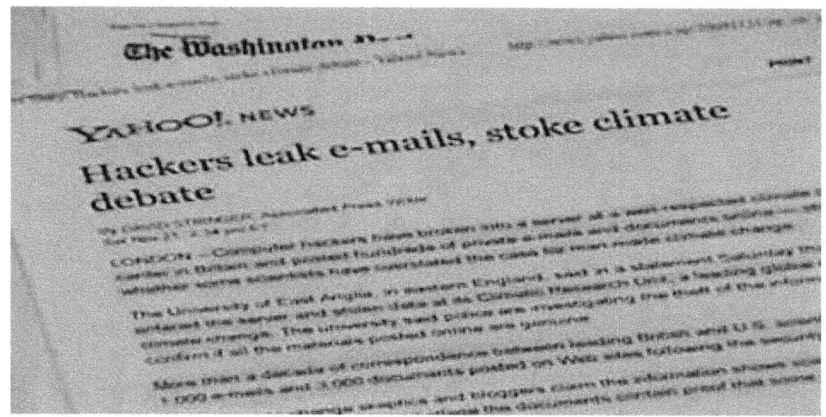

Fig.1 Leaked e mails from scientists

At the same time 'climate gate found many errors in AR4 of IPCC which has become a big controversy. It mainly focused on two areas. The first one is that the glaciers in the Himalayas would melt by 2035 and another on the source of figures on the rate of drying in the Amazon basin. In the case of the Himalaya figure, this was very obviously wrong had been mistakenly taken from a report that had not undergone the proper scientific review process. The IPCC acknowledged this error and issued an apology in January 2010 [17].

Greenhouse gases

At present carbon dioxide accounts for about 390 ppm and contributes 9-26% of the green house gases. [21]. In Paleozoic era the Earth had an atmospheric CO^2 concentration estimated at 4400ppm (or 0.44% of the atmosphere), while also having evidence of some glaciations. A study suggests that the elevated CO^2 levels and the glaciations are not synchronous [22].

It is clear from the above research that climate models are only able to simulate the temperature record of the past century when GHG forcing is included [23]. Recently it was also observed that CO^2 has no link with rising global temperature. However one argument against global warming says that rising levels of CO^2 and other greenhouse gases (GHGs) do not correlate with global warming [21]. Whereas it is generally approved that variations before the industrial age are mostly timed by astronomical forcing [24]. Analysis of carbon isotopes in atmospheric CO 2 shows that it is not a response to rising temperatures [25]. Now the IPCC is claiming that it is not CO2 but Methane is main culprit for Global warming and blaming developing countries for the same which traps heat 21 times more than CO2. IPCC also claiming that wet paddy cultivation from developing countries release methane emissions around 38 million tonnes per year [26] but it was disapproved by Indian scientist, A.P. Mitra [27] Late Dr.Mitra also found that it is only 4-6 million tonnes per year which is very much less to trap the heat. This is important since methane is a more lethal greenhouse gas than carbon dioxide. According to a report by Evans (2005) water vapor holds over 10 times the heat in the environment than CO2 which accounts for only .04 percent of the atmosphere [28].

Solar Variation

The IPCC consensus position is that solar radiation may have increased by 0.12 W/m^2 since 1750, compared to 1.6 W/m^2 for the net anthropogenic forcing. According to the TAR of IPCC the combined change in radioactive forcing of the solar variation and volcanic aerosols, is estimated to be negative for the past two or four decades. The AR4 makes no direct assertions on the recent role of solar forcing, but the previous statement is consistent with the AR4.The reduced trend in radioactive forcing (between 1998 and 2012) is primarily due to volcanic eruptions and the timing of the downward phase of the 11-year solar cycle. This statement marks the first time the IPCC has acknowledged that solar factors may play an important role in climate variability. This is a critically important acknowledgment to the views of the many independent scientists who have concluded that solar effects play a bigger role in controlling climate than does CO^2 [29], [30], [31].

The huge published literature shows that recent warming is not only unusual, but more intense warming has occurred many times in the past centuries. [32]. The misrepresentation of data from IPCC is also not reasonable. In Fig. 1, the IPCC report claims to show warming of 0.5°C since 1980, but measured temperature show no warming since last 17 years and satellite temperature data shows the August 13 temperature only 0.12°C (0.21°F) above the 1908 temperature [33]. IPCC shows a decadal warming of 0.6°C (1°F) since 1980 but the temperature over the past decade has actually cooled, not warmed.

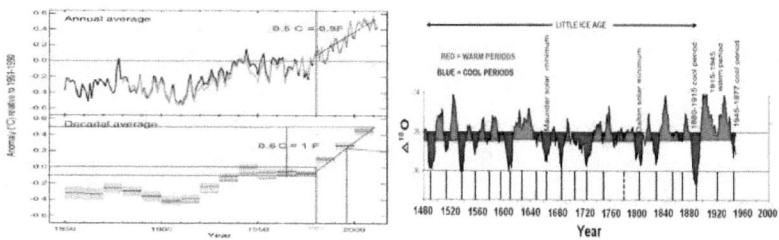

Fig 1. IPCC graph of temperatures. Fig. 2. Measured surface temperatures for the past decade (modified from Monckton, 2013).

Melting of Glaciers

The ice sheet from Antarctica is not melting but growing. Some part may be melting from West Antarctic Peninsula, which contains less than 10% of Antarctic ice. Even the temperature records at the South ole show no warming since records began in 1957[34], [35], [36].Some melting has occurred in Greenland during the 1978-1998 warming, but that is not at all unusual. Temperatures in Greenland were warmer in the 1930s than during the recent warming.

Arctic sea also ice expanded by 60% in 2013 and Antarctic sea ice has increased by about 1 million km2 (but IPCC makes no mention of this). The total extent of global sea ice has not diminished in recent decades. The statement that Northern Hemisphere snow cover has "continued to decrease in extent is false (despite the IPCC claim of 'high confidence' is false. Snow extent in the Northern Hemisphere shows no decline since 1967 and five of the six snowiest winters have occurred since 2003 (Fig. 3), [37].

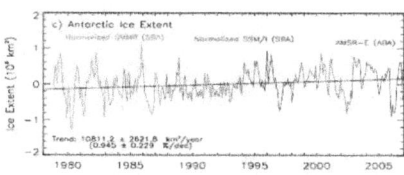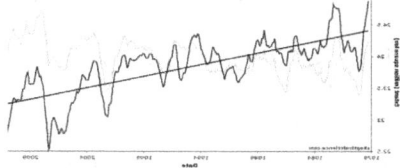

Sea level Scam

Sea level rise over the past century has varied from 1-3mm/yr, averaging 1.7mm/yr (7 inches/yr) from 1900-2000 (Fig.4.) Sea level rose at a fairly constant rate from 1993 to about 2005 but the rate of rise has flattened out since then (Fig. 5). It is obvious from these curves is that sea level is continuing to rise at a rate of about 7 inches per century, and there is no evidence of accelerating sea level rise. Nor is there any basis for blaming it on CO_2 because sea level has been rising on for 150 years, long before CO_2 levels began to rise after 1945[38].

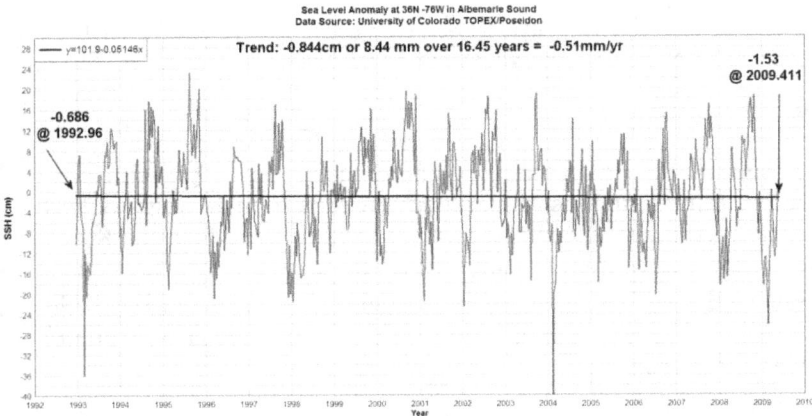

Figure 5. Past sea level rise. Figure 5. Sea levels rise from 1993-2010.

Conclusions

Here we highlighted only a few flaws of the highly biased, misrepresentations of material in the 2013 IPCC report. Sadly enough, recent allegations that the IPCC, the lead scientific body and supposed to be responsible for providing information regarding global warming science and policy, has misrepresented its findings in order to support the interest of Western corporate lobby. It is observed that the IPCC has no formal process or criteria for selecting authors and "the selection criteria seemed random to many respondents. Government officials appoint scientists from their countries and "do not always nominate the best scientists. Among those who or because of political considerations are given more weight than scientific qualifications who agree with the alarmist perspective favored by politicians. They were written by scientists chosen by politicians rather than on the basis of merit. Many of them were reviewing their own work and were free to ignore the questions and comments of people with whom they disagree. Billions of money in subsidies to solar and wind may have been wasted. Trillions of dollars of personal income may have been wasted worldwide in campaigns to "fix" a problem that didn't really exist. We feel that now Climate science has become politically motivated science funded by governments, based on assumptions, lies and faulty computer modeling. We also feel strongly that human induced global warming do not exists. These are earth's normal cycles. Their computer models didn't account for current warming reductions and water vapor changes. IPCC conclusions are flawed.

We aren't overloading the atmosphere. Manmade CO_2 isn't causing run-away global warming. As seen by the examples above, it isn't science at all but it is rigid, political, propaganda. It will take months if not years to expose the absolute lies and twists that IPCC AR5 report contains. Unfortunately and amazingly this propaganda is never uncovered by the main stream media who are also actually a major part of this scientific scandal. This debate has become much complicated mainly due to the corruption of the scientific process. Controversies over the science behind global warming, potential impacts, as well as ways of mitigation are all topics of disagreement, with scientists and nonscientists. Finally we feel that a potential environmental threat of such extent cannot be misrepresented nor misunderstood. Furthermore we also felt that the scientific method cannot be compromised in an effort to support the position of a specific individual's or group's ideology. In light of the uncertainties surrounding this topic, we would go further and argue that policymakers should wait for more information before they make a policy.

References

1. Lovejoy, Shaun; Chipello, Chris, McGill University. Retrieved 17 April 2014.
2. Lovejoy, S, Scaling fluctuation analysis and statistical hypothesis testing of anthropogenic warming". Climate Dynamics. Retrieved 17 April 2014.
3. Public Support for Climate and Energy Policies, Yale Project on Climate Change Communication, 2012.
4. http://www.forbes.com/sites/markhendrickson/2014/04/04/the-un-epa-and-the-latest-climate-change-folly/
5. Craig, M.C. Robert, S. Fred Singer and Willie Soon, Scientific Critique of IPCC's 2013 'Summary for Policymakers', http://climatechangereconsidered.org/abouttheipcc/ 2013.
6. Greg Foyster, The question greenees are afraid to discuss. http://www.abc.net.au/news/2014-07-01/foyster-the-question-2014.
7. Anthony Watts, Two scathing reviews by scholars working with the IPCC show why the organization is hopelessly corrupted by politics. http://wattsupwiththat.com/2014/04/26/two-scathing-reviews,2014.
8. America's Climate Choices: Panel on Advancing the Science of Climate Change; National Research Council, Advancing the Science of Climate Change. Washington, D.C.: The National Academies Press. pp. 1 & 21–22.ISBN 0-309-14588-0. Retrieved 19 February 2014.
9. Dr. Roy W., Spencer, The Great Global Warming Blunder. Encounter Books. 2010, ISBN 1-59403-373-0.
10. Carter, Professor Robert M, Climate: The Counter Consensus. 2010, 191–210.
11. New York Global Warming Conference Considers 'Manhattan Declaration' – by Heartland Institute staff – The Heartland Institute". Heartland.org. 4 March 2008. Retrieved 29 August 2010.

12. Crichton, Michael, Lecture at CalTech: "Aliens Cause Global Warming"". Archived from the original on 10 January 2006. Retrieved 14 April 2007. Monbiot, George, The climate denial industry seeks to dupe the public. It's working". The Hindu. Retrieved 3rd September 2010.

13. Joseph Bast, Controversy Arises Over Lists of Scientists Whose Research Contradicts Man-Made Global Warming Scares – News Releases". Heartland.org. Retrieved 29 August 2010.

14. Chameides, Bill. "Climategate Redux." Scientific American, 30 August 2010. Retrieved 17 August 2011.

15. "Closing the Climate gate." Nature. 18 November 2010. Retrieved 17 August 2011.

16. Gillis, Justin, Global Temperatures Highest in 4,000 Years, Study Says - NYTimes.com, New York Times, retrieved 10 March 2013.

17. J.B. Robert, Jason Carmichael and J. Craig Jenkins, Shifting public opinion on climate change: an empirical assessment of factors influencing concern over climate change in the U.S., 2002–2010. Climatic Change. DOI 10.1007/s10584-012-0403-y. Springer Science Business Media B.V. 2012.

18. Olive Heffernan, The decay of Hockey stick. http://blogs.nature.com/climatefeedback/2007/05/the_decay_of_the_hockey_stick.html. 2007

19. Chameides, Bill, Climate gate Redux, Scientific American, and Retrived 4March, 2012.

20. Idso, C. D.; K. E. Idso. "Carbon Dioxide and Global Warming — Where We Stand on the Issue". CO2science. Archived from the original on 10 April 2007. Retrieved 13 April 2007.

21. Gorder, Pam Frost, (25 October 2006), Appalachian Mountains, carbon dioxide caused long-ago global cooling". Ohio State University Research news. Retrieved 13 April 2007.

22. Crowley, Thomas J and Baum, Steven K, Reconciling Late Ordovician (440 Ma) glaciation with very high (14X) CO2 levels". Journal of Geophysical Research 100 (D1):1995, 1093 1102. Bibcode: 1995JGR...100.1093C.doi:10.1029/94JD02521.
23. Weart, Spencer, Past Cycles: Ice Age Speculations". In Weart, Spencer. The Discovery of Global Warming. American Institute of Physics. ISBN 978-0-674-01157-1. Retrieved 14 April 2007.
24. "More Notes on Global Warming". Physics Today, Archived from the original on 11 August 2007. Retrieved 10 September 2007.
25. IPCC Fourth Assessment Report, Table 2.14, Chap. 2, p. 212
26. A.P. Mitra, CH4, CO and o3 for India and neighboring regions.2006.http://www.htap.org/meetings/200 6/2006_06/files/presentations/Day%202/Mitra. pdf.
27. Evans, Kimberly Masters, "The greenhouse effect and climate change".The environment: a revolution in attitudes. Detroit: Thomson Gale. 2005. ISBN 0-7876-9082-1
28. Muscheler, Raimund; Joos, Fortunat; Müller, Simon A.; Snowball, Ian, How unusual is today's solar activity? Arising from: Nature, 2004, 431, 1084–1087" Nature436 (7050):E3E4. Bibcode: 2005.Natur.436E.
3M. doi:10.1038/nature04045.PMID 16049429.
29. Leidig, Michael; Nikkhah, Roya, The truth about global warming – it's the Sun that's to blame". London: The Daily Telegraph. Retrieved 12 April 2007.
30. Solanki, Sami K., Usoskin, Ilya G, Kromer, Bernd, Schüssler, Manfred, and Beer, Jürg, Unusual activity of the Sun during recent decades compared to the previous 11,000 years". Nature 431 (7012): 1084 7. Bibcode: 2004Natur. 431.1084S. doi: 10.1038/nature 02995. PMID 1551014.

31. Easterbrook, Don J. 'Global Warming' is Over: Geologic Oceanographic and Solar Evidence for Global Cooling in the Coming Decades, International Conference on Climate Change, New York, 2009.

32. Spencer, Roy W.; Braswell, William D, Balance". Remote Sensing, 2011. 3 (8): 1603–1613. Bibcode: 2011 RemS....3.1603S. doi:10.3390/rs3081603.

33. P.T.Doran, J.C. Priscu and W.B. Lyons, Antarctic climate cooling and terrestrial ecosystem response". Nature 415 (6871): 517–20.doi:10.1038/nature710. PMID11793010. Archived from the original on 11 December 2004.

34. Crichton, Michael, State of Fear. HarperCollins, New York. p. 109.ISBN 0-06-621413-0. First Edition,2004

35. Michael Crichton, The Case for Skepticism in Global Warming". Michael Crichton The official site. Retrieved 13 April 2013. Speech at the National Press Club, Washington, D.C. (restored from archived copy)

36. Peter Doran ,"Cold, Hard Facts". The New York Times. Retrieved 13 August 2013.http://www.forbes. com/sites/ larrybell/2013/09/24/alarmists-are-in-way-over-their-heads-on-rising-ocean-claims/

Chapter-XII

Climate Change to trigger Bangla exodus in Assam: A Critical Review on the Climate Induce Migration and Environment and Demographic situation of Assam

Sailajananda Saikia* Bishmita Medhi

Abstract

In an admission that is likely to have serious ramifications for the infiltration-hit North Eastern States, Bangladesh Prime Minister Sheikh Hasina warned of 30 million Bangladeshis becoming 'climate migrants' due to global warming. Here the question of migration is directly related to Assam to a large extern. Assam is part of a region of Northeast India known as the "Seven Sister States," contiguous states that share at least one border with another nation and have correspondingly diverse cultures and ethnicities. Climate changes in Bangladesh, with its low-lying geography, dense population, and large subsistence agriculture base, create push factors for migration into Assam. Climate change alters habitats so that the carrying capacity of lands can no longer maintain the indigenous population. Bangladesh is currently experiencing this change, forcing locals to migrate to resource-rich locations. Unfortunately, there are few unsettled locales left on earth, so these migrants inevitably come into contact with local populations. Through this paper an attempt will be made to look into the consequence of global warming and its impact on socio- economic situation on Assam. Moreover, attempt will also be made on the impact on environment, its biodiversity, ethnic tension and demographic transition in the region.

Keywords: Climatic change; global warming; Bangladesh; migration; socio-economic; biodiversity; Assam

*Assistant Professor, Dept. of Geography, M.C.College, Barpeta, Assam

Introduction

Mass migration due to climate change may have negative consequences including escalating humanitarian crisis, rapid urbanization and associated slum growth and stalled development. This may require national governments and international organizations to plan for the relocation and resettlement and protection of affected population inside their country as well as immigration from other countries. This paper brings together the important issue of climate change and its impacts on population movement from Bangladesh to Assam, India.

Bangladesh, the world's most densely populated country, is also environmentally one of the most vulnerable regions due to its geographical and spatial location (Ministry of Environment and Forests 2002). With a population of over 133 million people in a small area and a population density of more than 1,209 persons per sq.km, and 75% of the population lives in rural areas, Bangladesh is a very densely populated country (World Bank, 2002). Higher population density increases vulnerability to climate change because more people are exposed to risk and opportunities for migration within a country are limited. The country is composed largely of low lying areas lands less than sea-level above sea level. About 80% land is floodplain. It is also frequently visited by extreme climatic events, causing damage to life property and economy.

Bangladesh is a disaster-prone country. Almost every year, the country experiences disasters of one kind or another—such as tropical cyclones, storm surges, coastal erosion, floods, and droughts—causing heavy loss of life and property and jeopardizing the development activities. Bangladesh, one the least developed nations of the world, may also be one of the most vulnerable to climate change. The widespread flood in 1988 which submerged about two-thirds of the country, and the storm surge of April 1991 which resulted in the deaths of nearly 140,000 coastal inhabitants, are recent reminders of the degree to which the people of Bangladesh are subject to present-day variations in climate. The possibility of changes in climate and sea-level rise must be considered seriously in the context of the future development of Bangladesh.

Illegal migration from Bangladesh into Assam should be viewed against the backdrop of past history, present realities and future designs. Migration into Assam has been taking place from the dawn of history. However, after the British annexed Assam, large scale population movement from the South (Bengal, East Pakistan and now Bangladesh) has been an ongoing phenomenon for over a century. Initially, this movement was for economic reasons only but with the approach of Independence, it started developing both communal and political overtones. After Independence, it acquired an international dimension and it now poses a grave threat to our national security. Illegal migration from Assam has been taking place primarily for economic reasons. Bangladesh is the world's most densely populated country with a population density of 969 per square kilometre. The growth rate of population in that country is 2.2 per cent and its population is growing at the rate of 2.8 million per year. Each year nearly one third of Bangladesh gets inundated by floods, displacing 19 million people. 70 million people constituting 60 per cent of the population live below the poverty line. The per capita income in Bangladesh is 170 dollars per year, which is much lower than the per capita income in India. The border between India and Bangladesh is very porous. In these circumstances, the continued large scale population movement from Bangladesh to India is inevitable, unless effective measures are taken to counter it.

Impact of Climatic Change and Bangladesh

Climate change and sea level rise are now a reality. The recent finding of the fourth assessment report of the world scientific community, represented by the intergovernmental panel on climate change (IPCC), demonstrates that human activities are responsible for global warming and global climate change and sea level rise (UNDP, 2007).

Various human activities are making the world hot to hotter where the ultimate result is global warming, i.e. climate change. Anthropogenic causes responsible for global warming are expected to continue to contribute to an increase in global-mean sea level rise during this century and beyond (Church et al., 2001, IPCC; 2007).

It is commonly accepted that the global average surface air temperatures have risen by 0.74°C (0.56 0 C to 0.92 °C) over the last 100 year from 1906 to 2005. Eleven of last twelve years (1995 –2006) rank among the 12 warmest years in the instrumental record of global surface temperature (since 1850) (IPCC, 2007).Rising temperature in the atmosphere causes sea level rise and affects low lying coastal area sand deltas of the world. In 1990, Intergovernmental Panel on Climate Change (IPCC) estimates that with a business-as-usual scenario of greenhouse gas emission, the world would be 3.3°C warmer by the end of the next century, with a range of uncertainty of 2.2° to 4.9°C (Warrick et al., 1993).

The major environmental effects of sea level rise include the loss of habitats and biodiversity due to inundation, shoreline retreat, increased coastal flooding, landslide and erosion during storm surges and rainstorms, and the intrusion of salt water into aquifers, estuaries, and wetlands (Titus et al., 1991). Sea level rise will increase the vulnerability of coastal populations and ecosystems via permanent inundation of low-lying regions, inland extension of episodic flooding, increased beach erosion and salinity intrusion of aquifers (Mclean et al., 2001).

Bangladesh is a disaster prone country. Bangladesh's geographical vulnerability lies in the fact that it is an exceedingly flat, low lying, alluvial plain covered by over 230 rivers and rivulets with approximately 710 kilometers of exposed coastline along the Bay of Bengal. As a result of its geography, Bangladesh is frequently suffers from devastating floods, cyclones and storm surge, tornadoes, riverbank erosion and drought as well as constituting a very high-risk location for devastating seismic activity (Sarwar, 2005).

Ahmed and Alam (1999) reported that the average increase in temperature in Bangladesh would be 1.3°C and 2.6°C by the year 2030 and 2075 respectively with respect to the base year 1990. Two estimates of potential future SLR for Bangladesh are 0.30-1.5 m and 0.30-0.50 m for 2050 (DoE, 1993). Analysis of meteorological data from 1977 to 1998 clearly shows annual sea level rise at the rate of 7.88 mm, 6 mm and 4 mm respectively in Cox's Bazar, Chardanga at Hatiya and Hiron point in Sundarban (Shamsuddoha and Chowdhury, 2007).

Sea level rise has various impacts on Bangladesh. Its potential threats are coming even strongly in the future. Sea level rise will cause river bank erosion, salinity intrusion, flood, damage to infrastructures, crop failure, destruction of fisheries, loss of biodiversity etc. along this coast. World Bank (2000) projection showed 10 cm, 25 cm and 1 m rise in sea level by2020, 2050 and 2100 which will affect 2%, 4% and 17.5% of the total land mass respectively.

Climate change scenarios for Bangladesh

There are various estimates of temperature rise in Bangladesh. Ahmed and Alam (1999) reported that the average increase in temperature in Bangladesh would be 1.3°C and 2.6°C by the year 2030 and 2075 respectively with respect to the base year 1990. The seasonal variation of temperature will be more in winter 1.3°C than in summer 0.7°C for 2030 and2.1°C for winter and 1.7°C for summer for 2075.

Using the 1961-1990 baseline data for Bangladesh it was shown that annual mean maximum temperature will increase by 0.40°C and 0.73°C by the years 2050 and 2100 respectively. The mean minimum temperature will correspondingly rise by 0.04°C and 0.08°C. But the mean annual temperature will increase by 0.22°C and 0.41°C respectively (Karmakar and Shrestha, 2000).

In 2030, precipitation will increase slightly in winter and moderately in summer. But, in 2075, evaporation would be much higher in winter. There would be more precipitation during the monsoon period and precipitation would decrease in winter. This means that increased rainfall would lead to more severe flood situation in summer, and low precipitation and higher temperature in winter will cause more drought like conditions in winter. On the other hand, in 2075, the change will be very pronounced in monsoon while there would not be any noticeable precipitation in winter (Ahmed and Alam, 1999).

In a study, Karmakar and Shrestha (2000) predict that annual total rainfall over Bangladesh is likely to increase by 295.94 mm and 542.55 mm by 2050 and 2100 respectively. Global warming will increase the intensity of south-west monsoon (SWM) which will, in turn, bring about catastrophic ravages like erosion, land sides and floods and have far reaching consequences on agriculture, habitat, economy, etc.

Climate change scenario used in Bangladesh National Adaptation Programme of Action (NAPA)

Year	Temperature change (°C) Mean (standard deviation)			Precipitation change (°C) Mean (standard deviation)		
	Annual	Winter	Monsoon	Annual	Winter	Monsoon
2030	1.0	1.1	0.8	5	-2	6
2050	1.4	1.6	1.1	6	-5	8
2100	2.4	2.7	1.9	10	-10	12

(Source: NAPA: cited in UNDP, 2007)

Sea level rise (SLR) scenarios for Bangladesh

Bangladesh is highly vulnerable to sea level rise, as it is a densely populated coastal country of smooth relief comprising broad and narrow ridges and depressions (Brammer et al., 1993).

Various scenarios have been predicted about SLR in Bangladesh. Two estimates of potential future SLR for Bangladesh are 0.30 to 1.5 m and 0.30 to 0.50 m for 2050 (DoE, 1993).Several factors such as non-uniform rise in temperature, accelerated rise in temperature, geological subsidence and sedimentation may influence this rate .

A study by Singh et al. (2000) shows that mean tidal level at Hiron Point (21°48' N, 89°28 E),Char Changa (22°08'N, 91°06'E) and Cox's Bazar (21°26'N, 91°59'E) is showing an increase of 4.0 mm yr -1, 6.0 mm yr -1and 7.8 mm yr -1 respectively, which is much higher than the global rate. The higher rate has been attributed to subsidence. An increasing tendency in SLR from west to east along the coast has also been found.

Using tidal gauge records, researchers at the SAARC Meteorology Research Centre (SMRC) in Dhaka, Bangladesh found an increasing east-west trend of 4 mm to 7.8 mm year −1 rise in sea level for the Sundarbans from 1977 to 1998 (Alam, 2003; SMRC, 2003), which is greater than the average global SLR estimate during the same period.

Sea level rise (SLR) scenarios in Bangladesh and its possible impacts

Impact on	Projected		
	2020	2050	2100
Sea Level Rise	10 cm	25 cm	1 m (high end estimate)
Land below SLR	2%	4%	17.5%
Storm surge	-	Storms surge goes from 7.1 to 8.6 m with 0.3 m SLR	Storms surge goes from 7.4 to 9.1 m with 0.3 m SLR
Flooding	20% increase in inundation.	Increase flooding in Meghna and Ganga floodplain.	Both inundation area and flood intensity will increase tremendously.
Agriculture	Inundate 0.2 million metric tons of production; <1% of current total	0.3m SLR inundate 0.5 Mmt. Of production; 2% of current total.	Devastating flood may cause crop failure for any year.
Ecosystem	Inundates 15% of the Sundarbans.	Inundates 40% of the Sundarbans.	The entire Sundarbans would be lost.
Salinity	Increase	Increase	Increase

Source: World Bank, 2000.

In the Ganges-Brahmaputra-Meghna basin as a whole the increase in rainfall in the monsoon is predicted to be larger from around 4-8% by the 2020s and 9-10% by the 2050s, while winter rainfall is expected to reduce by 4-5% by 2050 (Tanner et al, 2007). The combined total catchments of these rivers from where rainfall drains into these rivers totals about 1.74 million km² and the amount of water coming through Bangladesh varies from less than 5000 cubic metres per second in the driest period (March-April) to 80,000-140,000 m³/s in late August to early September.

Therefore higher rainfall outside of Bangladesh in the monsoon is likely to lead to more frequent and severe floods from swollen rivers, while less rain in the winter will mean less water in rivers in the dry season affecting river fed irrigation, industry, fisheries, and travel by launch/ferries and increase salinity around the coast (Alam, 2004).

As only 7% the catchment of these major rivers lies inside Bangladesh, it is also vulnerable to extraction for irrigation and hydroelectric schemes further upstream. The Ganges/Padma River is particularly affected and in India, barrages control all of the tributaries to the Ganges and divert roughly 60% of river flow to large scale irrigation. India also controls the flow of the Ganges into Bangladesh with over 30 upstream water diversions and the 5th largest dam in the world; the Farraka Barrage only 18 km from the Bangladeshi border was shown to reduce the average monthly flow by 86%. As Indi's „garland of rivers" project aims to build many more dams as well as seek to interlink rivers and divert water from the Ganges and Brahmaputra Rivers to its drier southern states. Despite the 1996 Ganges Water Sharing Treaty with Bangladesh the amount of water entering the smaller, less powerful Bangladesh is expected to be further reduced due to climate change and accentuated by India's irrigation and electricity generation plans (Wong et al, 2007). This is likely to increase political tensions between the countries and may lead to conflict at least diplomatically.

Ganges/Padma, Brahmaputra/Jamuna and Megna Basins (Mirza, 2002).

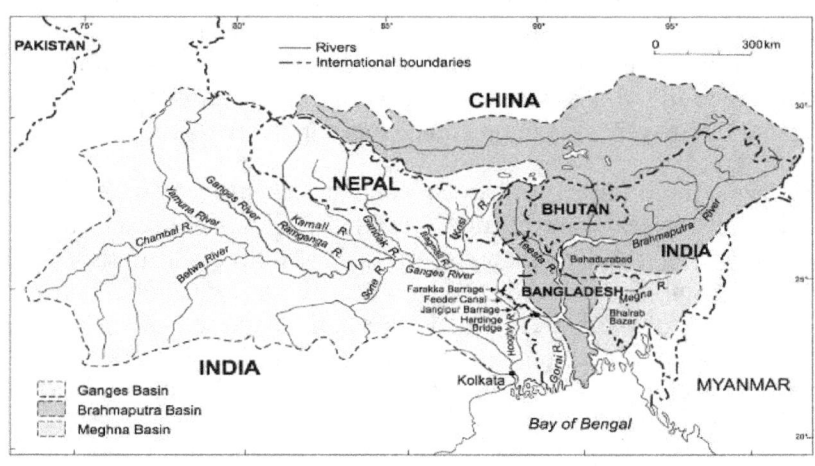

185

Impact of Migration on Assam

Illegal migration from Bangladesh into Assam has been a major political, economic, social and security issue for Assamese society, so much so that it evoked the non-violent, highly visible, Assam Agitation (1979-1985) spearheaded by the All Assam Students Union (AASU). That agitation resulted in the Assam Accord of 1985 which stated that anybody settled in Assam from Bangladesh after March 25, 1971 is not a citizen, but an illegal migrant. This provision of the Accord has not been implemented and has therefore failed to change the nature of Bangladeshi immigration into Assam, now termed as a "silent invasion" with the majority of the infiltration taking place through the Dhubri district in lower Assam bordering West Bengal, the districts of Cachar and Karimganj in Assam bordering Bangladesh and the 443 km Bangladesh-Meghalaya border. Assam shares a highly porous 262 kilometre border with Bangladesh with portions of it left completely unchecked due to the difficult nature of the terrain unchecked global warming could cause unprecedented climate change induced migration to infiltration-hit northeastern Indian state, warns Bangladesh Prime Minister Sheikh Hasina. "Global assessments indicate that natural disasters in our region would increase in frequency and intensity," the Bangladesh prime minister told the Bay of Bengal Initiative for Multi-Sectoral Technical and Economic Cooperation (BIMSTEC) summit 2014.

The issue of illegal migration from Bangladesh has been plaguing northeastern India for long. In 2005, the Supreme Court of India, in a judgment referring to the then Governor Lt Gen (Retd) SK Sinha's report, maintained that the impact of the "aggression," represented by large-scale illegal migrants from Bangladesh, had made the life of the people of Assam "wholly insecure and the panic generated thereby had created fear-psychosis" among other states in the region.

Assam faces more direct effects of climate change as well. In September of last year, more than 1.4 million people were displaced by flooding along the Brahmaputra River in 18 of 27 districts of Assam, and 6 million were displaced in July. Unfortunately, "the frequency and extent of these floods is set to increase," write the authors. Changing rainfall patterns also mean more erosion, creating the risk of deadly landslides like those that struck Western India earlier this summer, and unexpected droughts.

An additional population dynamic at work in Assam is urbanization. Rapid, unplanned urbanization puts pressure on water and other resources. This rural-to-urban movement can be temporary or permanent, depending on the severity of push factors, further complicating Assam's ability to plan for infrastructure challenges.

To know the demographical contours of what has been called the melting pot of Assam, one has to go at least to the colonial times, and the impact of the politics of those time on the present political and demographic scenario in Assam. Migration has always been a reality in Assam. Throughout history people from various places have migrated to Assam, and the melting pot of Assam has assimilated them since time immemorial. However, these migrations were during the time when the concept of nation-states and citizenship were not well-defined, and hence there was no definition of the legality and illegality of such migration. However, after 1947, when the British left India, we had our own policy of immigration, citizenship and voting rights. Hence, the legal definition of the word "foreigner" comes into effect from 1947.

Assam shares an international border with Bangladesh and has been plagued with the problem of illegal immigration by Bangladeshi Muslims for the past four decades. The Governor of Assam, in a secret communiqué to the Central Government in 2005, revealed that "upto 6000 Bangladeshis enter Assam every day." According to conservative estimates, India is host to around ten million illegal Bangladeshi immigrants. Assam itself is inhabited by around five million illegal immigrants. The magnitude of this influx can only be assessed from the fact that the period between 1971 and 1991 witnessed the growth of Muslim population in Assam by 77.42 per cent as compared to a Hindu growth of 41.89 per cent. The population explosion has subsequently stabilized but even then, the decadal growth of 1991-2001 at 29.3 per cent for Muslims remained abnormally high as compared to a Hindu growth at 14.9 per cent.

Dhubri, which shares a long riverine border with Bangladesh, is an example of how illegal infiltration into the State continues unabated. As per provisional census details for the period 2001-2011, the decadal population growth for Dhubri at 24.4 per cent was distinctly higher when compared to the population growth of Assam at 16.9 percent for the same period.

With the Brahmaputra River providing convenient entry points, the district is being virtually overrun by Bangladeshi infiltrators.

Future Impact of Migration in Assam

Reliable estimates of the number of illegal Bangladeshis living in Assam in the 1970s and 80s are not available. There seems to be a mystery about the number of Bangladeshi foreigners in Assam.

Political shortsightedness has resulted in a situation where most Indian cities are getting burdened with these illegal Bangladeshi immigrants. The immigrants who have started shifting to greener urban pastures, which offer greater economic opportunities. However, it is in Assam that the conflict between the Indians and illegal Bangladeshi Muslims is growing. Emotions have been running high ever since the migrants started obtaining squatters rights on the lands which they were initially employed to till.

With the demography being dramatically altered by their steady influx, illegal immigrants have started wielding enormous political power in Assam. Muslims have become the majority in 11 out 27 districts in the State and the dominant factor in determining electoral fortunes in 54 out of 126 constituencies in the local Assembly. A stage has been reached where no party can expect to attain political dominance without support from the Bangladeshi Muslims. The large scale migration from Bangladesh has significantly altered demographics in India's northeastern states, leading to social, economic, and political tensions between tribals and Bangladeshi Muslim settlers.

For instance, in Assam, Muslims make up approximately 33% of Assam's population, and 11 out of 27 districts in the state now contain Muslim majorities. Bodo leaders in Assam assert that Bangladeshi Muslims are using their growing power to impose their culture and religion in the area.

It is this conversion of the illegal migrants into a political force, which has made the indigenous population apprehensive of losing its identity and culture. This unfettered illegal migration has ominous implications for national security and socio-economic stability. Intelligence inputs indicate that the Inter Service Intelligence Agency (ISI) of Pakistan is utilizing these migrants as conduits to ferry in terrorists and arms into India. Counterfeit Indian currency with its origins in Bangladesh has flooded border areas, crippling the economy in these parts.

Conclusion and Policy Recommendations

Climate change is likely to expose hundreds of millions of people to increasing environmental risks displacing a large number of people and forcing them to migrate. There is an emerging view that these people should be recognized as climate refugees by international laws and proper institutional arrangements should be made to address their problems.

The illegal Bangladeshi migrants issue tends to dominate the political, economic, social, and security discourses in Assam with residents of the state expressing concern of being taken over demographically by this silent invasion. The lack of data on migration adds to a sense of being 'under siege' by outsiders as no one is sure as to the number of migrants visibly infiltrating all walks of life in Assam. The issue has political resonance as there is a general understanding in Assam that most of the local political parties depend on the votes of these illegal migrants for their hold on power.

The social impact of Bangladeshi migrants on Assamese society is mostly to do with culture and lifestyles. The social fear is that the Assamese way of life will get subverted once the migrants dominate the state. A strong impact is also envisioned in the spheres of language and religion. Assam, being a Hindu majority state, fears that it will become Muslim-dominated due to the influx of illegal migrants.

This has also resulted in unnecessary tensions between Assamese Hindus and Assamese Muslims who have made Assam their home for centuries. Pegged at over 20 million in India these migrants – mostly Muslims from Bangladesh – have been permanently settling down in Assam which has impacted the state's demography reducing the ethnic people of Assam into a minority in many areas, declining land availability and employment and increasing the crime rate.

Issue of illegal immigration in northeast region is becoming a serious concern and it has been a herculean task due to lack of political consensus on the subject. The problem of immigration is far more complex in view of the ethnic ties that the migrants share with the native population. As a result, to campaign against immigrants on the other hand is not an easy task and it tends to divide people on communal lines. Almost 80 percent of Bangladesh's population lives in the rural areas, of which 53 percent are classified as poor by the World Bank. While the country's population is growing, producing a bigger labor force, the land base is shrinking resulting in decline in cultivated areas at a rate of 1 percent per year.

The country is facing serious issues with living space due to alarming population growth. As per 2011estimates, the population density of Bangladesh is 964 per sq km, one of the highest in the world. This poverty stricken population illegally migrates to India to work as farm labor, industrial labor, construction workers etc. These migrant settlers constitute a majority in many parts of Assam bordering Bangladesh, reducing local tribes to a minority. For instance Dhubri, on the Indo-Bangladesh border and point of entry for Bangladeshis, has Bengali-speaking Muslims rising from 70.45 per cent in 1991 to 76 per cent according to the 2011 Census, in contrast to a marginal growth of the indigenous Assamese-speaking Muslims.

The Central Indian Government and State Government in Assam must take all necessary steps to fully rehabilitate the victims of the recent riots and ensure the safety of all communities in the state going forward. India must protect the social, economic, and political rights of the vulnerable tribal population in Assam and comprehensively address the underlying issue of illegal immigration from Bangladesh. The Indian Government should encourage the Government of Bangladesh to implement strong measures to curtail the flow of illegal immigrants, militants, and drugs from its side of the Indo-Bangladesh border in order to prevent further destabilization of the region. While it is perhaps wise to refrain from overstating the negative implications of the impact of illegal Bangladeshi migration on Assam's overall health since every migrant is not necessarily bad, it is good to have a check on who is the crossing the border, when he or she is crossing and for what purpose as that ensures better security against future crimes. This will also instill a sense of security in India's border populations who fear domination by a migrant population especially in matters related to politics.

Reference

1. Adnan, S. (1991) Floods, 'People and the Environment'. Grassroots: An Alternative Development Journal, 1 (1), pp.27-47.
2. Ahmed, A.U. 2006. Bangladesh Climate Change Impacts and Vulnerability: A Synthesis. Dhaka: Climate Change Cell, Bangladesh Department of Environment.
3. Adnan, S. (with M. Ghani, S. Uddin, S. Khandaker, A. Dewan, S. Zaker, A. Suflyan, S. Manic, A. Hossain, and S. Akhter) (1991) Floods, People and the Environment: Institutional Aspects of Flood Protection Programmes in Bangladesh, 1990. Research and Advisory Services, Dhaka.
4. Baruah, S. (1999). India against Itself, University of Pennsylvania, Philadelphia.
5. Bhuyan, A.C. and S. De (eds), (1999). Political History of Assam, Vol III, Publication Board of Assam.
6. Bora, N.B. (2009). Assamese Response to Regionalism, Mittal Publications, New Delhi.
7. Borkataky, M.C. (2013). "The Kakrajhar Violence: a Lebensrum Theory", The Sentinel, Guwahati, 24th April Issue.
8. Borooah, V.K. (2013). "The Killing Fields of Assam: Myth and Reality of Its Muslim Immigration", Economic and Political Weekly, 26th January Issue, vol. XLVIII No.4.
9. Christian Aid, 2007. Adapting to inevitable changes in the climate. Climate Change: Policy and Approach. (A Global Advocacy Briefing). London: Christian Aid. 8.
10. Gogoi, J. (2005). "The Migration Problem in Assam: An Analysis" in Alokesh Barua (ed), India's North-East: Developmental Issues in a Historical Perspective, Manohar Centre De Sciences Humaines, New Delhi.
11. Goswami, A., A. Saikia & H. Goswami (2003). Population Growth in Assam 1951-1991 with Focus on Migration, Akansha Publishing House, New Delhi.
12. Hazarika, S. (2000). Rites of Passage, Penguin, London.

13. Jenkins, A. 2006. The Bangladesh Integrated Planning for Sustainable Water Management (IPSWAM) Programme, and Climate Change. Dhaka: IPSWAM, Bangladesh Water Development Board.
14. Kumar, B.B. (ed). (2006). Illegal Migration from Bangladesh, Concept Publishing Corporation, New Delhi.
15. Leslie, N.G. (1945). "On the Use of Matrices in Certain Population Mathematics", Biometrika, vol 33, pp. 183-212.
16. Mahanta, N.G. (2013). Confronting the State: ULFA's Quest for Sovereignty, SAGE Publications India Pvt. Ltd., New Delhi.
17. Misra, V. (2008). Periphery Strikes Back, IIAS, Simla.
18. Moon, P. (ed). (1978). Wavell: The Viceroy's Journal, Oxford University Press, London.
19. Mullen, C.S. (1931). Census of Assam 1931.
20. Nath B.K., D.C. Nath and B. Bhattachaya (2012). "Undocumented Migration in the State of Assam in North East India: Estimates since 1971 to 2001", Asian Journal of Applied Sciences, vol. 5, pp.164-173.
21. Ravi, R.N. (2012). "Assam Accord, a Pernicious Deception", Article in The Statesman, 23 September 2012 issue.
22. Sarmah, B. (2012). "Assam's Indigenous Fear Based on Reality" Editorial Article in The Sentinel Assam, 10 August 2010 issue.
23. Sinha, S.K. (1998). Report on Illegal Migration to Assam, submitted to the President of India by the Governor of Assam, 8 November 1998.
24. Singh, M. (1990). Assam, Politics of Migration & Quest for Identity, Anita Publications, Jaipur.
25. Stern, N. 2006. Report of the Stern Review: The Economics of Climate Change. HM Treasury: London. Satterthwaite, D. 2006. Climate change and cities. (Sustainable Development Opinion). London: International Institute for Environment and Development (IIED).

Chapter-XIII

Concept of Sustainable Development: Evolving Framework for Sustainable Development in India

Sandhya Gihar & Sanjeev Bhardwaj[*]

Abstract

The environment itself is a system of systems that, from the viewpoint of human existence and development, is a part of the superior system of systems, the human system. Basic human system assets are human lives, health and security; environment; property and public welfare; infrastructures and technologies, in particular those that belong to the critical ones. The sustainability assessment in general sense is the formalized process for identification, prediction and assessment of potential impact of arbitrary inputs including the variants for society sustainable development. Over 190 countries agreed the conclusions document of the Rio+20 Summit, The Future We Want. It emphasized the importance of making progress towards sustainable development globally and set out principles and processes to help achieve that goal. India witnessed uncontrollably planned growth and development in past time which created compound situations as a result of which, it transpired conspicuously evident that country's economic development can no longer be envisaged in complete fragmentation from socio-cultural progression and ecological protection. This paper aims at discussing some of the important issues to carve out concept of sustainable development in India needed to evolve framework for sustainable development in India keeping in view of recommendations put forth by Rio Earth Summit in 2012 where over 190 countries agreed the conclusions document of the Rio+20 Summit regarding the future we wish to shape for ourselves, emphasizing the significance of sustainable development throughout the globe.

Key Words: Climate Change, Environmental Protection, Evolving Framework, Recommendations Laid Down In Rio De Janeiro, Sustainable Development

---

[*]Associate Professors, M M College of Education, MM University Campus, Mullana, Ambala, Haryana

Introduction

The next fifty years will witness complex human and environmental interaction and result in extremely compound situation like Global Population explosion by 2050 will mount to 2 to 4 billion as compared to recent times [1], eutrophication of environmen [2], higher rates of 15 out of 24 categories of physician-diagnosed diseases, including cardiovascular diseases, stress and anxiety and higher rates of mortality in younger and older adults [3], about 5.8°C rise in global temperatures [4]. Eroding of Biodiversity by monoculture in both plants and animals, soil water air pollution, soil erosion, unsustainable water consumption, Inefficient energy conversion, antibiotic resistance [5] other impacts on agriculture, forestry, rural communities, biodiversity and amenities such as traditional landscapes [6] .

The investigation of complex environmental systems that are affected by human action is considered a major scientific challenge in general and keeping in view the sustainable development in particular. This challenge has to overcome both the gap between natural and social sciences and to master modeling on different scales. Thus, there is a need for integrating knowledge from natural and social sciences. Human-environment systems (HES) are defined as the interaction of human systems with corresponding environmental or technological systems [7]. The environment itself is a system of systems that, from the viewpoint of human existence and development, is a part of the superior system of systems, the human system. From the given fact that it is evidently impossible to elevate the environment existence and return to original state under the interests connected with human existence and development, but, simultaneously, it is impossible to damage the environment irresponsibly, because it creates the medium necessary for human existence itself. Therefore, we have to introduce the compromises that respect human needs and environment into the practice, based on our knowledge and experience. Their impact and benefits are monitored in the way that allows carrying out the corrective measures if they seem to be necessary. Based on recent cognition, sustainability (sustainable development), is not only related to the environment, but also to the entire human system and it basic assets (i.e. public assets) on which the human lives are dependent. Basic human system assets are human lives, health and security; environment; property and public welfare; infrastructures and technologies, in particular those that belong to the critical ones (2). The sustainability assessment in general sense is the formalized process for identification, prediction and assessment of potential impact of arbitrary inputs including the variants for society sustainable development (e.g. legal rules, ordinances, regulations, political intent, plan, program, and project [8]. Over 190 countries agreed the conclusions document of the Rio+20 Summit, The Future We Want. It emphasized the importance of making progress towards sustainable development globally and set out principles and processes to help achieve that goal. The 49-page document reaffirmed previous international commitments (the Rio Principles and Agenda 21 agreed at the original Earth Summit in 1992 and the Johannesburg Plan for Implementation agreed at the 'Rio+10' Summit in Johannesburg in 2002) and set out renewed global priorities [9]. Since Rio, there have been extensive efforts to operationalize sustainable development by governments, international organizations, local authorities, business, citizen groups and individuals. Agenda-21 remains a powerful document that provides long-term vision for balancing economic and social needs with the capacity of the earth's resources and ecosystems. Twenty years post Rio, the goals of Agenda 21 have not been fully realized and there is universal agreement that efforts must be redoubled to enhance sustainable development that is equitable as well as ecological[10]. It is therefore present paper aims at making an attempt to find out the conceptual framework in regard to programmes and policies employed by India to meet sustainable development in order to keep pace with economic, ecological and social progress inclusively.

Concept of Sustainable Development

Concept of Sustainable development, emerged as a result of the requirements to balance Socio-economic development with special emphasis on protection of Environment and natural resources. There have been made many attempts to frame statements and principles by several nations but no concise definition widely accepted has been rendered which could have been globally accepted. The reason lies in the fact, that it has been left on the individual efforts of institutions and environmentalists to frame the definition and as a result of which it became more a concept of debate than a definition of precision. Despite of this all some attempts have been made to define the term sustainable development in view of drawing the concept and ideology behind. According to Cruz [11] sustainable development is related to find out a balance between economic development and environmental protection also between the requirements in present time and in future time. It is therefore there exists a dire need to collaborate socio-cultural, techno-scientific, economic and ecological areas to work together to reach growth and developmental aims in recent time with a vision for tomorrow. Further, sustainable urban development pertains to employ social-economic progression keeping in view issues related to ecological protection during Industrialization, urbanization in the influence of globalization. Sustainable development may be defined as the development that meets the needs of the present without compromising the ability of future generations to meet their own needs [12]. Research into environmental and natural-resource issues is concerned with extending our understanding of how the world works and of how we can better manage our interaction with that world. As local, regional and global communities have become more aware of environmental degradation and the complexity and fragility of coupled natural-social systems, there has been an increasing focus on issues of sustainability.

UNESCO [13] emphasizes that human security and poverty alleviation are inconceivable without sustainable development. This requires that environmental, social and cultural as well as economic aspects of sustainable development be taken together, and that the interactions and interfaces between them be better understood. Activities relating to sustainable development are found in many parts of UNESCO's programme, and it is possible to group these activities in several different ways. UNESCO's activities have been presented under five main thematic headings:

Educating for sustainability
Including both formal and non-formal education, alternative delivery systems to reach the unreached, and training and capacity-building in fields related to sustainable development.

Science for sustainable development
Including the promotion of multi- and inter-disciplinary approaches involving the natural as well as social and human sciences to the wise use of natural resources and to the improved understanding of human-environment relationships.

Ethical principles and guidelines

For sustainable development, including the promotion of principles, policies and ethical norms to guide scientific and technological development that is sustainable.

Integrating culture

Cultural diversity and the world heritage as key dimensions in activities aimed at sustainable development.

Efforts to promote sustainable development received a major boost as the World Summit on Sustainable Development drew inferences bearing significant commitments to work in directions of eradicating poverty and to take steps to stop global environmental degradation. The Summit envisages that sustainable development could turn as a reality through a path that reduces poverty while protecting the environment, a path that works for all peoples, rich and poor, in present and in future too. The Governments of various nations agreed to, an impressive range of concrete commitments and future actions to cause a difference in people's lives, throughout the globe. Apart from eradication of poverty and environmental protection varied level of commitment were made to increase access to clean water and proper sanitation, to increase access to energy services, to improve health conditions and agriculture, particularly in drylands, and to better protect the world's biodiversity and ecosystems. The major outcome document, the Plan of Implementation, contains targets and timetables to spur action on a wide range of issues, including halving the proportion of people who lack access to clean water or proper sanitation, restoring depleted fisheries, reducing biodiversity loss, and, using and producing chemicals in ways that do not harm human health and the environment mostly by 2020. In addition, for the first time countries committed to increase the use of renewable energy. Further, the Summit generated concrete partnership initiatives by and between governments, citizen groups and businesses, rather than concluding with only the words of an agreed document to employ additional resources and expertise for meeting significant results, across the globe.

Further, the development which could be consistently reaping out the benefits may be referred as sustainable. It means that there must be nothing inherent in the process or activity concerned, or in the circumstances in which it takes place, that would limit the time it can endure. This is clear in the most commonly cited definition of sustainable development as "development that satisfies the needs of the present without compromising the ability of the future to meet their own needs" [14]. It also means that it must be worthwhile; it must meet the social and economic objectives just noted. To characterize an activity as sustainable, or to refer to sustainability, is to predict the future – an activity that is risky at best. It follows then that sustainability is inevitably an uncertain characteristic, and that the best we can do is to choose activities that careful analysis tells us are likely to be sustainable. There are many grounds for such choices as well as for rejecting activities that are clearly unsustainable. To summarize then, sustainable development is the complex of activities that can be expected to improve the human condition in such a manner that the improvement can be maintained [15]. Further the emerging question is that how intra- and inter-generational equity issues are linked, compliment and conflict with each other. This is a wider, relatively unaddressed arena, which requires to be traced in the future. A frank and open discussion of the links, complementarities and conflicts will also go some way in addressing the criticism of vagueness laid against the concept of sustainable human development [16].

Like other development approaches, sustainable development is all about an improvement in the human condition, yet unlike many of the others it does not emphasise human growth or production. The difference rests on the underlying philosophy that what is done now to improve the quality of life of people should not degrade the environment and resources such that future generations are put at a disadvantage. In other words we (the present) should not cheat the future; improving lives now should not be at the price of degrading the quality of life of future generations. At the same time, the sustainable element does not imply stasis. Human societies cannot remain static, and the aspirations that comprise a part of 'needs' constantly shift [17]. Some of the nations like Australia defined ecologically sustainable development as using, conserving and enhancing the community's resources so that ecological processes, on which life depends, are maintained, and the total quality of life, now and in the future, can be increased [18]. In New South Wales the varied levels of principles were provided to find a common definition of sustainability for use across the public sector. These may be depicted as:

Sustainability in the NSW public sector means addressing the needs of current and future generations through the integration of social justice, economic prosperity and environmental protection in ways that are transparent, accountable and fiscally responsible. In NSW foundation principles have been depicted as Inter-generational equity, Sustainable communities, Economic prosperity, and ecologically sustainable development, full pricing, Bio-diversity and the Precautionary principle. The process principles described were like Sustainable practice, Stewardship, Shared responsibility, Participation and the local-global principle.

Environmental Protection, Climate Change and Conditions Needed For Sustainable Development

From the system viewpoint, the sustainable system has attributes as productivity, resilience, adaptability and vulnerability, and therefore, sometimes it is not easy to find a suitable reference state or conditions. The reference point of sustainability is a demanded future state (scenarios, techniques and foresight).The reference points are, on the one hand, inputs and, on the other hand, outputs of system processes (ecological trace, product life times etc.).Therefore it may be assumed that the context given in Figure 1. Since these attributes are mutually tied up, in the relation to the existence of system, the sustainability is on the peak. The decision making on system adaptive capacity is defined by the relation given in the decision matrix in Fig-1[19].

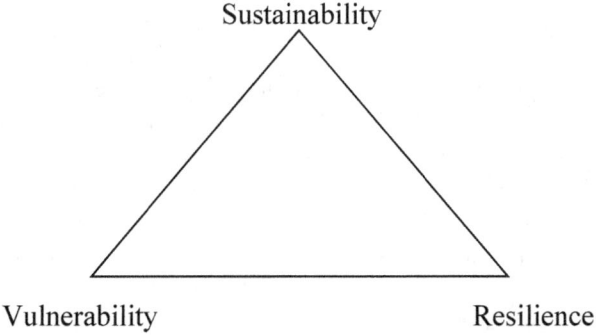

Fig. 1 Relation among sustainability, vulnerability and resilience [19].

Sustainability is often misinterpreted as the goal that we all strive for. In fact, sustainability is not an achievable final state, since it is rather the basic characteristics of a dynamically developed system. Thus, sustainability is permanent adaptation to changing conditions. This adaptive property is natural to all ecosystems. It is only a question of education to introduce the adaptive procedures to the public administration decision-making on human, i.e. socio-ecologic-technical system [19]. Further, according to Climate Action Tracker [20] global average temperatures will increase by about 3.5°C by 2100. Throughout the globe in general and in Asia in particular, more frequent and severe extreme weather, combined with ever growing numbers of people and assets in exposed coastal areas and floodplains, will lead to massive economic losses by 2030 [21]. Whereas by the same time the global needs will enhance at least 50 percent for food, 45 percent in regard to energy needs and 30 percent in case of water needs [22].

Sustainable Development in India, in Light of Recommendations Laid Down in Rio de Janeiro

Since Rio De Janeiro, there extensive strivings have been made to meet the sustainable development by governments, international organizations, local authorities, business, citizen groups and individuals in light of Agenda [21] which carries a position of powerful document. In addition this document renders long-term vision to integrate and balance socio-economic and ecological requirements in order to potentially apply the natuaral resources and ecosystems judiciously. Twenty years post Rio, the goals of Agenda [21] have not been fully realized and there is universal agreement that efforts must be redoubled to enhance sustainable development that is equitable as well as ecological. The Constitution of India and relevant amendments that have been incorporated over the years, reinforce the policy and legal basis of sustainable development in India. The Preamble, which lays down the 'basic features' and remains the 'soul' of the Constitution promises to all Indian citizens justice encompassing the social, economic and political, equality of status and opportunity and the dignity of the individual.

The pillars of sustainable development are embedded in the fundamental rights guaranteed by the Constitution, which lay down the framework for social justice in India.

In addition to the state mandate to ensure social and economic justice, the Directive Principles also enjoins a duty upon the state to protect and improve the environment and safeguard the forests and wildlife. The National Environmental Policy of 2006 articulates the spirit of 'sustainable development'; it states that only such development is sustainable, which respects ecological constraints and the imperatives of social justice. The NEP highlights the consensus around the sustainable development concept through three foundational aspirations: first, that human beings should enjoy a decent quality of life; second, that human beings should become capable of recognizing the finiteness of the biosphere; and third, that neither the aspiration of a good life, nor the recognition of the limits of the biophysical world should preclude the search for greater justice in the world. The NEP 2006 also asserts that the most viable basis of environmental conservation is to ensure that people gain better livelihoods from the act of conservation of natural resources than from environmental degradation [23].

India's engagement with the environment predates the Brundtland Report [24] as evident in several policiesand Acts. The National Environment Policy of 2006 acts as a key policy document that lays down the principles for sustainable development. Following major areas can be detailed with reference to efforts made by Indian programmes and policies to meet the Rio objectives [25].

Forestry

The National Forest Policy (NFP), 1988 made environmental stability and maintenance of ecological balance as its principal aim, whereas in 1990, the central government outlined a Joint Forest Management (JFM) framework for creating a people's movement through involvement of village committees for the protection, regeneration and development of degraded forest lands. The National Afforestation and Eco-development Board (NAEB) set up in 1992 focuses on afforestation in forest and adjoining lands. A National Forestry Action Programme was launched in 1999, which was a comprehensive strategy and long-term work plan formulated for the next twenty years to address the issues underlying the major problems of the forestry sector in line with NFP.

A National Afforestation Programme (NAfP) was launched in 2002, which involves plantation in degraded forests of the country. In February 2011, India's Prime Minister approved the National Mission for a Green India, which aims to double India's afforested areas by 2020 and the objective to enable forests to absorb 50–60 million tones of CO_2 annually, offsetting about six percent of India's annual emissions. The National Biodiversity Action Plan was formulated in 2008 that entails integration of in situ, on farm and ex-situ conservation along with other measures to augment the natural resource base [26].

Biodiversity

India ranks among the top ten species-rich nations with high endemism and socio-cultural diversity and uniqueness. The enactment of Biological Diversity Act 2002 has facilitated the establishment of dedicated institutions like National Biodiversity Authority at the national level and the State Biodiversity Boards at state level. The National Biodiversity Action Plan was formulated in 2008 that entails integration of in situ, on farm and ex-situ conservation along with other measures to augment the natural resource base [27].

Pollution Control

National Ambient Air Quality Standards (NAAQS) were notified in the year 1982, duly revised in 1994 and further in November 2009 for 12 pollutants, which include sulphur dioxide (SO_2), nitrogen dioxide (NO_2), particulate matter having size less than 10 micron (PM10), particulate matter having size less than 2.5 micron (PM2.5), ozone, lead, carbon monoxide (CO), arsenic, nickel, benzene, ammonia, and benzopyrene. India started adopting European equivalent emission and fuel regulations for four-wheeled light-duty and for heavy-duty vehicles since 2000. Introduction of mass transport, such as the metro and CNG buses in cities is yet another initiative to address air quality concerns. The government has notified emission and effluent standards relevant for 102 categories of processes and industries, which include the 17 categories of highly polluting industries under the Environment (Protection) Act of 1986 [28].

Water and its Management

The National Ganga River Basin Authority (NGRBA) was constituted on 20 February 2009 under Section 3(3) of the Environment (Protection) Act, 1986. In June 2011, Government of India signed an agreement with the World Bank for $1 billion towards long-term support for cleaning the Ganga River. Drought Prone Areas Programme—DPAP (started in 1973–1974), Desert Development Programme—DDP (started in 1977–1978) and Integrated Wasteland Development Programme— IWDP (started in 1989–1990) to be implemented under Land Degradation Common Guidelines on Watershed Development, 2008 [29].

Land Degradation

Natural factors, such as high storm intensity, soil characteristics and climatic conditions, the land management practices and other social factors contributed to land degradation.Some of the major schemes are National Watershed Development Project for Rainfed Areas (NWDPRA); Soil Conservation in the Catchments of River Valley Project (RVP) and Flood Prone River (FPR); Reclamation and Development of Alkali and Acid Soil (RADAS), Watershed Development Project in Shifting Cultivation Areas (WDPSCA); Drought Prone Area Programme (DPAP); Integrated Wasteland Development Programme (IWDP); and National Afforestation and Eco–Development Project (NAEP). Apart from these programmes, the Ministry of Environment and Forests has recently notified the Wetlands (Conservation and Management) Rules, 2010 in order to ensure that there is no further degradation of wetlands [30].

Climate Change

Government has been actively engaged in initiatives that address the issue of global climate change. Twenty four initiatives have been put in place by the Government of India that address climate science and research, policy development and implementation, international cooperation and forest issues. The most significant of these is the National Action Plan on Climate Change (NAPCC) announced in June 2008, which links development and climate change frontally. Eight missions of NAPCC that focus on solar energy, energy efficiency, sustainable habitat, water, sustaining the Himalayan eco-system, Green India, sustainable agriculture and strategic knowledge for climate care are being implemented by the nodal ministries to address vulnerability to climate change and enhance capacity at central and state levels.

Clean Energy

According to MoEF[31] there have been policies and programmes targeted towards promotion of energy efficiency and renewable energy, which not only address environmental sustainability concerns, but also are able to promote sustainability of economic growth. Some of the specific policies include:

Electricity from renewable

The Electricity Act, 2003, requires State Electricity Regulatory Commissions to specify a percentage of electricity that the electricity distribution companies must procure from renewable sources.

Enhancing efficiency of power plants

New plants are being encouraged to adopt more efficient and clean coal technologies, and some plants under construction have adopted the more-efficient supercritical technology for power generation.

Introduction of labeling programme for appliances

An energy labeling programme for appliances was launched in 2006, and comparative star-based labeling has been introduced for fluorescent tube lights, air conditioners, and distribution transformers.

Energy Conservation Building Code

An Energy Conservation Building Code (ECBC) was launched in May 2007, which addresses the design of new, large commercial buildings to optimize the building's energy demand. A National Rating System—GRIHA (Green Rating for Integrated Habitat Assessment) has been developed, which is suitable for all types of buildings in different climatic zones of the country. All new government buildings would henceforth mandatorily conform to 3 star or 4 star GRIHA ratings. Recently, the Clean Energy Fund has been created, which is based on a cess on coal at the rate of INR 50 ($ 1) per metric tone imposed on domestic and imported coal [32].

Energy audits of large industrial consumers

In March 2007, the conduct of energy audits was made mandatory in large energy-consuming units in selected industrial sectors.

Solar and wind Power

The Jawaharlal Nehru Solar Mission envisages establishing India as a global leader in solar energy. It sets an ambitious target of 20,000 MW of solar power by the year 2022. To promote generation of wind energy, generation based incentives are provided. Perform Achieve and Trade (PAT), as a certification scheme of energy savings that could be traded, has been introduced by the Bureau of Energy Efficiency [33].

Economic	Social
New Industrial Policy, 1991 Pharmaceuticals Policy, 2002 Marketing Assistance Scheme for SME Export Promotion Capital Goods Scheme National Mineral Policy, 2008 New Exploration and Licensing Policy National Telecom Policy, 2011 National Electricity Policy, 2005	National Housing and Habitat Policy, 1998 Pradhan Mantri Gramodaya Yojna, 2000 National Policy for Empowerment of Women, 2001 Sarva Shiksha Abhiyaan, 2003 National Policy for Urban Street Vendors, 2004 National Rural Health Mission, 2005 National Food Security Mission, 2007 National Rehabilitation and Resettlement Policy, 2007 Debt Waiver and Debt Relief Scheme, 2008 National Mission on Education, 2009
Environment	Social equity (economic and social)

National Forestry Action Programme, 1999	Rural Infrastructure Development Fund, 1995
National Afforestation Programme, 2002	Annapurna Scheme, 2000–2001
National Mission for a Green India, 2011	Rashtriya Krishi Vikas Yojana, 2007
Auto Fuel Policy, 2002	Indira Gandhi National Old Age Pension Scheme, 2007
Mission Clean Ganga Initiative	Indira Gandhi National Widow Pension Scheme, 2009
National Forest Policy	
Socio-ecological (environment and social)	Green economy (economic and environment)
National Agricultural Policy, 2002	Technological Upgradation Fund Schemes, 1999
National Urban Sanitation Policy, 2008	Fodder and Feed Development Scheme, 2005
Integrated Watershed Management Programme, 2009	Integrated Energy Policy of 2008 Perform, Achieve and Trade (PAT)
Sustainable development (social, environment and economic)	
Mahatma Gandhi National Rural Employment Guarantee Scheme, 2005	
National Urban Transport Policy, 2006	
National Environmental Policy, 2006	
National Urban Housing and Habitat Policy, 2007	
National Action Plan on Climate Change, 2008	
National Disaster Management Policy, 2009	
National Rural Livelihood Mission, 2009	

Table Showing Key Policies and Programmes Relevant to Sustainable Development

Conclusion

Present paper aimed at finding the framework generated and further evolved by Indian efforts in order to meet sustainable development as a prominent concept, inclusively. It became quite evident that after Earth Summit in 1992, India came up with numerous policies, schemes and programmes relating to economic growth, social progress and environmental conservation to meet the objectives of sustainable development.

In order to lay strong foundations for the same several programmes and policies are evolving in recent time in order to create a framework in post Rio phase. Further, in post Rio stage, environmental principles, like precautionary principle, polluter pays principle, public trust law doctrine, inter-generational equity and absolute liability transpired as part of Article 21 (Right to Life) in a number of judicial pronouncements by the Supreme Court, now quite accepted in India. As accordance with sustainable developmental requirements Programmes and schemes have been revisited and restructured as and when needed. Government of India commenced and implemented stringently several key programmes and policies in socio-economic, social equity, socio-ecological and environmental protection legislations areas in order to meet the aims to build green economy and sustainable development by integrating social,economic and environmental issues not in isolation but as an inclusive concept one affecting the other. Present paper establishes firmly that India started taking good decisions, in order to reach out the society's developmental requirements, since it is indispensible to carry on the economic development of India on the one hand, and to sustain it in long run the environmental protection on the other. Further, on the basis of present findings it may be pointed out that though India showed commendable beginning yet the efforts taken are still inadequate and insufficient in alarming situation of increasing population, reducing economic growth in 2010-13 and complex socio-educational conditions. It is therefore it could be inferred through evolved framework of sustainable development that in spite of the prominent endeavours long way of challenges are ahead to effectively dealt and address with the issues like eradication of poverty and sustainable economic and ecological development to keep the pace for standing in the list of developed nations by 2020.

References

1. Cohen J. E, Human population: The next half century. Science, Vol. 302, 2003, 1172.
2. Galloway J.N, Acidification of the world: natural and anthropogenic, Water, Air, and Soil Pollution, Vol. 130, 2001, 17-24.
3. Kuo. F,E, Parks and Other Green Environments: Essential Components of a Healthy Human Habitat, Executive Research Summary National Recreation and Park Association Ashburn, (2010) Retrieved from: http://arris.ca/~arris2/ARCHIVE/Parks%20and%20O ther%20Greens.pdf
4. Houghton, J.T., Y. Ding, D.J. Griggs, M. Noguer, P.J. van der Linden, X. Dai, K. Maskell, C.A. Johnson, editors. Climate change 2001: the scientific basis. Contribution of Working Group I to the Third Assessment Report of the Intergovernmental Panel on Climate Change. Cambridge University Press, Cambridge and New York. 2001, 881.
5. Horrigan, L. Lawrence,R.S., and Walker,P, How Sustainable Agriculture Can Address the Environmental and Human Health Harms of Industrial Agriculture, Research Review, Environmental Health Perspectives, 110(5), 2002, 445-456
6. Nicholls, L, Birds of a feather? UNDP and Action Aid Implementation of Sustainable Human Development", Development in Practice, 9(4), 1999, 396-409.
7. Watson, R. T., Noble, I.R., Bolin B., Ravindranath N.H., Verardo D.J. & Dokken D.J. (Eds.) Land Use, Land-Use Change And Forestry. A Special Report of the Intergovernmental Panel on Climate Change (IPCC), (Cambridge: Cambridge University Press, 2000).
8. Scholz, R.W., and Binder, C.R, Principles of Human-Environment Systems(HES) Research, The International Environmental Modelling and Software Society,University of Osnabrück, Germany, 2004 Retrieved from: http://www.uns.ethz.ch/people/formerhead/scholzr/pu bl/UNS_A116.pdf

9. Rusko, M and Procházkova, D, Solution to the Problems of the Sustainable Development Management , Faculty of Materials Science and Technology in Trnava, Slovak University of Technology in Bratislava, Research Papers No-31, 2011, 77-84.

10. House of Commons Environmental Audit Committee, 2013. Retrieved from: http://www.publications.parliament.uk/pa/cm201314/ cmselect/cmenvaud/191/191.pdf

11. Ministry of Environment and Forests Government of India, Sustainable Development in India: Stocktaking in the run up to Rio+20 New Delhi, 2011 Retrieved from: www.moef.nic.in

12. Cruz, R.V., H. Harasawa, M. Lal, S. Wu, Y.Anokhin, B. Punsalmaa, Y. Honda, M. Jafari, C. Li and N. Hu Ninh : Asia. Climate Change: Impacts, Adaptation and Vulnerability. Contribution of Working Group II to The Fourth Assessment Report the Intergovernmental Panel on Climate Change, M.L.Parry, O.F. Canziani, J.P. Palutikof, P.J. van der Linden and C.E. Hanson Eds, (Cambridge University Press, Cambridge, 2007) U.K. 469-506.

13. Brundtland Commission or World Commission on Environment and Development. Our Common Future. (1987). http://www.un-documents.net/wced-ocf.htm

14. UNESCO (2003). Sustainable development an evolving concept. http://www.unesco.org/education

15. World Commission on Environment and Development (Our Common Future, Oxford: Oxford University Press.1987).

16. Munro, D, (Sustainability: Rhetoric or reality? In A Sustainable World: Defining and measuring Sustainable Development. Earthscan, 1995).

17. Nicholls, L, Birds of a Feather? UNDP and Aid Implementation of Sustainable Human Development, Development in Practice, 9 (4), 1999, 396-409.

18. Bell, S & Morse, S, (Measuring Sustainability. Earthscan, 2003)

19. Council of Australian Governments, National Strategy for Ecologically Sustainable Development. 1992 http://www.environment.gov.au/esd/national/nsesd/strategy/index.html
20. Prochazkova, D, Research Reports to Ministry of Agriculture project 1R56002 Auxiliary Multi-Criteria System for Decision-making Supporting the Sustainable development of Land and Human Seats. 2007 Praha: MZe ČR, 2005-2007, 1023.
21. Climate Action Tracker, 2012. Retrieved from: http://www.climateactiontracker.org
22. Brundtland Commission or World Commission on Environment and Development. Our Common Future. (1987). http://www.un-documents.net/wced-ocf.htm
23. Intergovernmental Panel on Climate Change, Special Report, Managing the Risks of Extreme Events and Disasters to Advance Climate Change Adaption, 2012.
24. World Commission on Environment and Development (Our Common Future, Oxford: Oxford University Press.1987).
25. Same as [12].
26. World Commission on Environment and Development (Our Common Future, Oxford: Oxford University Press.1987). http://www.arlis.org/docs/vol1 /69415913/ fraserj_edited_final_dec_17.pdf
27. Intergovernmental Panel on Climate Change (2012). Special Report, Managing the Risks of Extreme Events and Disasters to Advance Climate Change Adaption.
28. Peduzzi, P., Chatenoux, B., Dao, H., De Bono, A., Herold, C., Kossin, J., Mouton, F., Nordbeck, O. (2011). 'Global Trends in Tropical Cyclone Risk' in Nature, Climate, Change, 2012.
29. UNEP (2002). GEO-3: Global Environmental Outlook Report 3. UNEP: United Nations Environment Programme

Chapter-XIV

Important Aspects Associated with Catastrophic Decline of Vultures in the Indian Subcontinent

Sanjay Kumar Narang, Kiran Chauhan & M.L. Thakur*

Abstract

Eight, out of nine species of vultures found in India have been facing problem of existence and therefore declared as threatened. During the 1980s Indian White-backed Vulture was thought likely to be the commonest large bird of prey in the world but the era of abundant Gyps vultures in the Indian subcontinent came to a sudden end in the 1990s which was firstly documented in Keoladeo National Park, Bharatpur in eastern Rajasthan. Veterinary use of the non-steroidal anti-inflammatory drug, diclofenac in livestock is the main, cause of the population declines. Other reasons believed to be responsible for the decline are loss of nesting habitat, decreased breeding efficiency, infectious diseases, general environmental pollution etc. Vultures are exposed to toxic levels of diclofenac when they feed on carcasses of livestock which have died within a few days of treatment, and which contain residues of the drug. Vultures provide very important ecological, social and cultural services especially in India by scavenging on animal carcasses of animals and thereby helping keep the environment clean, and the disposal of dead bodies as per the religious practices of the Parsi community. Vultures are the primary removers of carrion in India and Africa. Removal of a major scavenger from the ecosystem will affect the equilibrium between populations of other scavenging species and/or result in increase in putrefying carcasses. The provision of supplementary food is a well established tool in the conservation of vulture species. General public involvement and supplementary feeding tried in different parts of the world could be successful in conservation of vultures in India.

Key words: Vultures, Population Decline, Diclofenac, Supplementary Feeding, Indian subcontinent, Conservation measures

Associate Professors, Govt. College Mandi-175 001 (HP), India

Introduction

Eight, out of nine species of vultures found in India have been facing problem of existence and therefore declared as threatened. Of these, four species endemic to South Asia, the Indian White-backed Vulture Gyps bengalensis, Long-billed Vulture Gyps indicus, Slender-billed Vulture Gyps tenuirostris and Red-headed Vulture Sarcogyps calvus are at high risk of global extinction and are listed as critically endangered because of rapid population declines within the last decade in the Indian subcontinent. Moreover, Egyptian Vulture Neophron percnopterus has been categorised as endangered, and Cinereous Vulture Aegypius monachus, Himalayan Griffon Gyps himalayensis and Bearded Vulture Gypeatus barbatus have been placed under near threatened category (Prakash et al. 2003; Green et al. 2004; IUCN 2014).

Although Gyps vulture populations were probably declining slowly in many parts of the world during the 20th century, a very different situation existed in the India subcontinent. In the subcontinent, large populations of Indian White-backed Vulture and Long-billed Vulture remained until the 1990s. Large numbers of Slender-billed Vulture, which was not distinguished as a separate species from Long-billed Vulture until recently (Rasmussen and Parry 2001), were also found in the northeastern parts of the subcontinent (Ali and Ripley 1983; Prakash et al. 2007). During the 1980s Indian White-backed Vulture was thought likely to be the commonest large bird of prey in the world (Houston 1985). In India, Gyps vulture densities were so high in some areas that they were considered a hazard to aircraft (Grubh et al. 1990). This abundance was undoubtedly due to a plentiful food supply, in the form of the carcasses of domesticated ungulates (Pain et al. 2008). The era of abundant Gyps vultures in the Indian subcontinent came to a sudden end in the 1990s. This was firstly documented in Keoladeo National Park, Bharatpur in eastern Rajasthan (Prakash 1999; Prakash et al. 2003). Subsequently, this population crash was documented throughout the Indian subcontinent (Prakash et al. 2003, 2005 a & b, 2007; Gilbert et al. 2004, 2006; Green et al. 2004; Pain et al. 2008). In the initial stages of investigations, some infectious disease was thought to be the likely cause of population decline (Cunningham et al. 2003). But it took a little to discover the veterinary use of the non-steroidal anti-inflammatory drug (NSAID) diclofenac in livestock as the main, and perhaps the only, cause of the population declines (Oaks et al. 2004; Shultz et al. 2004; Green et al. 2004, 2007). Other environmental changes have also produced adverse effects on the population of vultures as well. Food shortages, caused by the burial or burning of carcasses to reduce the nuisance and health risks have also contributed to their decline. Other reasons believed to be responsible for the decline are loss of nesting habitat, decreased breeding efficiency, infectious diseases, general environmental pollution etc. (Pain et al. 2003, 2008; Oaks et al. 2004; Shultz et al. 2004; Johnson et al. 2006; Green et al. 2007; Prakash et al. 2007).

Vultures are exposed to toxic levels of diclofenac when they feed on carcasses of livestock which have died within a few days of treatment, and which contain residues of the drug (Oaks et al. 2004). Likewise, due to this chemical, vultures suffer from a disease called gout. Vultures that consume sufficient tissue from such carcasses die from the effects of diclofenac induced kidney failure. Shultz et al. (2004) found that a high proportion of Indian White-backed Vulture and Long-billed Vultures found dead in the wild had severe visceral gout, consistent with diclofenac poisoning being the main or sole cause of the population declines. Simulation modeling has indicated that less than 1% of the livestock carcasses available to vultures need to contain levels of diclofenac lethal to vultures to cause the recorded rates of decline across the country (Green et al. 2004). Green et al. (2006) reported that though concentration of diclofenac across all the edible tissues of investigated carcasses was hazardous to the vultures, but the concentration in intestine, kidney and liver had the highest levels which could be the reason for differential rate of population decline in different species of vultures keeping in view the differential foraging behaviour of vulture species found in the Indian subcontinent.

The minimum decline in Indian White-backed vulture numbers in India during the period 1992-2003 was 99.7% and 97.4% for Long-billed/Slender-billed. This corresponds with a minimum estimated rate of decline of 34% per year for White-backed Vultures and 27% per year for the Long-billed/Slender-billed group. In the most recent census, there is evidence that the rate of declines may be increasing with a measured 81% decline between 2002 and 2003 in White-backed vultures, a 59% decline in Long-billed vultures, and a 47% decline for Slender-billed vultures (MoEF 2006).

Vultures are classified into two groups: Old World vultures and New World vultures. World list of living species of Vultures stand at 23, comprising of seven species of New World and 16 Old World species. The similarities between the two different groups are due to convergent evolution. The Old World vultures found in Africa, Asia, and Europe belong to the family Accipitridae, which also includes eagles, kites, buzzards, and hawks. Old World vultures find carcasses exclusively by sight. The New World vultures and condors found in warm and temperate areas of the Americas are not closely related to the superficially similar Accipitridae, but belong in the family Cathartidae, which was once considered to be related to the storks. However, recent DNA evidence suggests that they should be included among the Accipitriformes, along with other birds of prey. However, they are still not directly related to the other vultures. Several species have a good sense of smell, unusual for raptors, and are able to smell the dead they focus upon from great heights, up to a mile away (BirdLife International 2011, Wikipedia 2011).

Both groups (Old World and New World) of vultures have certain characteristics in common-for example a hooked bill, naked or downy head, food-holding crop, therefore, they illustrate the phenomenon of convergent evolution very well (Houston 2001). In addition, within the Old World vultures, there are at least three different evolutionary lines (Seibold and Helbig 1995). Finally, within this group of birds there is a smaller group of five species of super vultures, all of which are called griffons. They exhibit a whole set of adaptations to a life scavenging on the carcasses of large animals (Houston 1983). Vultures are also renowned for congregating in large numbers at a carcass. A dead elephant can attract 1000 birds at a time and for several days, and even a small Impala can bring in up to 250 (Yohannes and Bekele 1998). Some vultures are among the world's largest flying birds, for example the Cinereous Vulture is said to weigh up to 12.5 kg, and the Lappetfaced Vulture has a wingspan up to 2.9 m. The adult Cape Griffon would probably have a weight of about 9 kg and a wingspan of about 2.5 m and is a considerable flying object. In addition, the griffons are renowned for flying together at their colonies and in particular in thermals over open country. In the latter they would usually be outnumbered by the common White-backed Vultures (av. weight about 5 kg).

A thermal of around 100 circling vultures is an awesome sight-but not for an aeroplane pilot in Africa. When foraging, vultures would perhaps usually fly along at about 300 m above ground level and at gliding speeds of up to 96 kph. At times they will fly or soar at very much higher altitudes than 300 m, even up to 11000 m a.g.l., though they have rarely (if ever) been seen by pilots at these phenomenal altitudes. Here, the partial pressure of oxygen is very low, and the cold is very intense, but vultures-at least the Ruppell's Griffon can cope with these well. Among other adaptations, this griffon is so far unique in having four haemoglobins in its blood, with strong affinities for oxygen (Mundy 1982).

A detailed account of vultures in Africa has been published (Mundy et al. 1992), but a little is known about Asia or Europe, or for North and South America (Kiff 2000, Satheesan 2000, Schlee 2000). The distributions of each species of Old World vulture shows that four species are found on all three continents, but of these only two i.e. Eurasian Griffon and Egyptian Vulture are strongly migratory. In the former, mostly the juveniles migrate to North Africa and Ethiopia, and even Kenya (Clark 2001), and presumably return in the following spring, while in the latter all ages migrate. As far as is known, all migratory routes are on a north-south axis (Yosef and Alon 1997). All the European vultures are also represented in Asia, and indeed into the Indian subcontinent. But it is not known whether there is any connection or gene flow between India and Europe in these species, and certainly no east-west (or vice versa) movements or migrations have been discovered. In addition, the detailed distributions of vultures from western Pakistan through Afghanistan and Iran to Iraq and Saudi Arabia are not yet known (Mundy 1982). Two South Asian Gyps species, Oriental White-backed Vulture and Slender-billed Vulture, were widespread and generally common in Southeast Asia (Cambodia, Vietnam, Laos, Thailand, Malaysia) at the beginning of the 20th century, but by the end of that century only a few small relict populations remained, primarily in Cambodia (Pain et al. 2003). Populations remain in Myanmar, but their numbers and status remain uncertain. Whilst factors like persecution may have played a role in the Southeast Asian declines, their main cause is believed to be food shortage. Overhunting resulted in a collapse in the populations of wild ungulates throughout the region (Srikosamatara and Suteethorn 1995, Duckworth et al. 1999, Hilton-Taylor 2000), and current livestock husbandry practices appear not to provide a sufficiently large food supply to support large populations (Pain et al. 2003).

Table Showing Old World Vultures and their Conservation Status (Family: Accipitridae)

S. No.	Species	Conservation Status
1.	Turkey Vulture Cathartes aura (Linnaeus, 1758)	LC
2.	Lesser Yellow-headed Vulture Cathartes burrovianus Cassin, 1845	LC
3.	Greater Yellow-headed Vulture Cathartes melambrotus Wetmore, 1964	LC
4.	Black Vulture Coragyps atratus (Bechstein, 1783)	LC
5.	King Vulture Sarcoramphus papa (Linnaeus, 1758)	LC
6.	California Condor Gymnogyps californianus (Shaw, 1797)	CR
7.	Andean Condor Vultur gryphus Linnaeus, 1758	NT

(Source: BirdLife International, 2014)

S. No.	Species	Conservation Status
1.	Palm-nut Vulture Gypohierax angolensis (Gmelin, 1788)	LC
2.	Lammergeier Gypaetus barbatus (Linnaeus, 1758)	NT
3.	Egyptian Vulture Neophron percnopterus (Linnaeus, 1758)	EN
4.	Hooded Vulture Necrosyrtes monachus (Temminck, 1823)	EN
5.	White-backed Vulture Gyps africanus Salvadori, 1865	NT
6.	White-rumped Vulture Gyps bengalensis (Gmelin, 1788)	CR
7.	Indian Vulture Gyps indicus (Scopoli, 1786)	CR

8.	Slender-billed Vulture Gyps tenuirostris Gray, 1844	CR
9.	Rueppell's Vulture Gyps rueppellii (Brehm, 1852)	NT
10.	Himalayan Vulture Gyps himalayensis Hume, 1869	NT
11.	Griffon Vulture Gyps fulvus (Hablizl, 1783)	LC
12.	Cape Vulture Gyps coprotheres (Forster, 1798)	VU
13.	Red-headed Vulture Sarcogyps calvus (Scopoli, 1786)	CR
14.	White-headed Vulture Trigonoceps occipitalis (Burchell, 1824)	VU
15.	Cinereous Vulture Aegypius monachus (Linnaeus, 1766)	NT
16.	Lappet-faced Vulture Torgos tracheliotos (Forster, 1791)	VU

LC= Least Concern
EN= Endangered
CR= Critical
NT= Near Threatened
VU= Vulnerable

Social Perspectives

Vultures are scavenging birds, feeding mostly on the carcasses of dead animals. They seldom attack healthy animals, but may kill the wounded or sick. When a carcass has too thick a hide for its beak to open, it waits for a larger scavenger to eat first. They do not carry food to their young in their claws, but disgorge it from the crop. These birds are of great value as scavengers, especially in hot regions. Vulture stomach acid is exceptionally corrosive, allowing them to safely digest putrid carcasses infected with Botulinum toxin, hog cholera, and anthrax bacteria that would be lethal to other scavengers. This also enables them to use their reeking, corrosive vomit as a defensive projectile when threatened. Vultures urinate straight down their legs, the uric acid kills bacteria accumulated from walking through carcasses, and also acts as evaporative cooling (Wikipedia 2011). Vultures provide very important ecological, social and cultural services especially in India by scavenging on animal carcasses of animals and thereby helping keep the environment clean, and the disposal of dead bodies as per the religious practices of the Parsi community. Vultures are the primary removers of carrion in India and Africa. Removal of a major scavenger from the ecosystem will affect the equilibrium between populations of other scavenging species and/or result in increase in putrefying carcasses. In the absence of carcass disposing mechanisms, vulture declines may lead to an increase in the number of putrefying animal carcasses in the country side. In some areas the population of feral dogs, being the main scavenging species in the absence of vultures, has been observed to have increased. Both increases in putrefying carcasses and changes in the scavenger populations have associated disease risks for wildlife, livestock and humans. In the absence of any alternative mode of disposal of animal carcasses, they continue to be disposed off in the open, and with increasing numbers of feral dogs, there is increased risk of spread of rabies, and livestock borne diseases like anthrax (Prakash et al. 2003). The decline in vultures has also affected the traditional custom of the Parsis of placing their dead in the 'Towers of Silence' for vultures to feed upon (Anonymous 2006).

Supplementary Feeding and Community Involvement

The provision of supplementary food is a well established tool in the conservation of vulture species (Mundy et al. 1992). This practice is used to provide a safe food source in the areas where carcasses are commonly baited with poison. Rapid and extensive decline of vultures in the Indian subcontinent has been attributed to the toxic effects of diclofenac, a pharmaceutical used in the treatment of livestock, to which vultures are exposed while feeding on the carcasses of treated animals (Gilbert et al. 2007). Supplementary feeding has been shown to increase the survival of Cape Vultures Gyps caprotheres in South Africa (Piper et al. 1999), has been employed during successful reintroduction programmes (Sarrazin et al. 1994; Terrasse et al. 1994) and has facilitated the recolonization of abandoned breeding sites (Mundy et al. 1992). This method has been used to provide alternative source of diclofenac free (uncontaminated) food (Susic and Pavokovic 2003; Gilbert et al. 2007). General public involvement and supplementary feeding tried in different parts of the world could be successful in conservation of vultures India. Food provisioning near a colony of Oriental White-backed Vulture in Pakistan during the 2003-

04 breeding season illustrated that the provision of clean food appeared to be able to reduce, but not eliminate, mortality from diclofenac (Gilbert et al. 2007). There was also considerable seasonal variation in the extent to which vultures used the diversionary food, with the vulture restaurant visited on, only 16% of days and by a relatively small number of birds at the end of the breeding season compared with 74% of days by a far larger number of birds earlier in the season. There were significant declines in mortality when vultures were fed clean food, but no reduction in the rate at which numbers of breeding pairs (active nests) declined at the colony in the year following the diversionary feeding (298 nests in 2002-03, 203 nests in 2003-04 and 118 nests in 2004-05, AVPP 2007). These results show that, whilst food provisioning may be of some benefit, it did not prevent the population from declining. Whilst the impact of year-long food provisioning remains untested, it is likely to have a greater impact on vulture survival in areas where alternative food is scarce, in colonies where a high proportion of birds tend to be sedentary, and where local diclofenac use is minimal or non-existent (Pain et al. 2008).

Conservation Measures

Keeping in view the level of endangerment mainly due to their population crash, three captive breeding and rescue centers for vultures, one in Haryana, second in West Bengal and third in Assam have been setup in India. Four more are planned, in an attempt to create reservoirs of birds to be re-introduced once the environment is clear of diclofenac.

Identification and monitoring of the locations and number of remaining individuals of vultures in the wild would be effective measure for conservation. Most efficient way to protect these threatened birds would be in-situ approach of conservation. Therefore, protection of nesting and feeding habitat is very essential.

More scientific investigations based on logical data, gathered through standard protocols are required. Information on terrain type, altitude, relief etc.; height, type, density and status of vegetation; nearby human settlements, source of water and food, mortality rate of cattle in nearby villages, socio-cultural practices of disposal of carcasses; vulture species type and richness, population dynamics, habitat-use pattern, breeding ecology and breeding success; human/animal interference needs to be generated. Breeding colonies of vultures should be continuously monitored for any changes in the population size. These records, in the long run would help in the formulation of area/locality based, viable vulture conservation strategies.

Measurement of the amount of diclofenac in carcasses available to vultures in different parts of the state and country should be done to elucidate the level of diclofenac exposure to remaining populations of vultures. In addition, data base on faecal glucocorticoid levels should be investigated, as it has competency in assessment of physiological stress and induction of ovulation in different bird species. Molecular characterization of threatened vultures should be done for molecular identification of different races of vultures and for enlisting some important resistant genes.

Some previous studies have indicated that different species of vultures in Kangra valley get attracted towards easily-available food at some cowsheds therefore these cowsheds can play a key role in providing diclofenac free and continuously available food. Lastly, public support programmes are the most important aspects of any effective conservation and management plan. Therefore, local people should be engaged in the whole process of conservation and management of vultures.

References

1. Ali, S. and Ripley, S.D., 1983. Handbook of the Birds of India and Pakistan. Oxford University Press, New Delhi.
2. Anonymous, 2006. Action Plan for Vulture Conservation in India. New Delhi: Ministry of Environment & Forests (Government of India), 28 pp.
3. BirdLife International 2011. IUCN Red List of birds. www.birdlife.org
4. Clark, W.S. 2001. First record of European Griffon Gyps fulvus for Kenya. Bull. Afr. Bird Club 8 (1): 59-60.
5. Cunningham, A.A., Prakash, V., Pain, D.J., Ghalsasi, G.R., Wells, A.H., Kolte, G.N., Nighot, P., Goudar, M.S., Kshirgar, S. and Rahmani, A. 2003. Indian vultures: victims of a disease epidemic? Animal Conservation 6: 189-197.
6. Duckworth, J.W.; Salter, R.E. and Khounboline, K. 1999. Wildlife in Lao PDR: 1999 status report. IUCN-The World Conservation Union/Wildlife Conservation Society/Centre for Protected Areas and Watershed Management, Vientiane.
7. Gilbert, M., Watson, R.T., Ahmed, S., Asim, M. and Johnson, J.A. 2007. Vulture restaurants and their role in reducing diclofenac exposure in Asian vultures. Bird Conservation International 17: 63-77.
8. Gilbert, M., Oaks, J.L., Virani, M.Z., Watson, R.T., Ahmed, S., Chaudhry, M.J.I., Arshad, M., Mahmood, S., Ali, A., Khattak, R.M. and Khan, A.A., 2004. The status and decline of vultures in the provinces of Punjab and Sind, Pakistan: a 2003 update. In: Raptors Worldwide (Eds. R.C. Chancellor and B.U. Meyburg). Proc. of the 6th world conference on birds of prey and owls, Berlin and Budapest. pp. 221-234.
9. Gilbert, M., Watson, R.T., Virani, M.Z., Oaks, J.L., Ahmed, S., Chaudhary, M.J.I., Arshad, M., Mahmood, S., Ali, A., Khattak, R.M. and Khan, A.A., 2006. Rapid population declines and mortality clusters in three Oriental white-backed vulture Gyps bengalensis colonies in Pakistan due to diclofenac poisoning. Oryx 40: 388-399.

10. Green, R.E., Newton, I., Shultz, S., Cunningham, A.A., Gilbert, M., Pain, D.J. and Prakash, V., 2004. Diclofenac poisoning as a cause of vulture population declines across the Indian subcontinent. Journal of Applied Ecology 41: 793-800.

11. Green, R.E., Taggart, M.A., Das, D., Pain, D.J., Kumar, C.S., Cunningham, A.A. and Cuthbert, R., 2006. Collapse of Asian vulture populations: risk of mortality from residues of the veterinary drug diclofenac in carcasses of treated cattle. Journal of Applied Ecology 43: 949-956.

12. Green, R.E., Taggart, M.A., Senacha, K.R., Pain, D.J., Jhala, Y. and Cuthbert, R., 2007. Rate of decline of the Oriental White-backed Vulture Gyps bengalensis population in India estimated from measurements of diclofenac in carcasses of domesticated ungulates. PloS One 2 (8) e 686.

13. Grubh, R.B., Narayan, G. and Satheesan, S.M., 1990. Conservation of vultures in (developing) India. In: Conservation in developing countries (Eds: J.C. Daniel & J.S. Serrao). Bombay Natural History Society and Oxford University Press, Bombay. 360-363 pp.

14. Hilton-Taylor, C. 2000. IUCN Red List of Threatened Species. IUCN/SSC, Gland, Switzerland, & Cambridge, UK.

15. Houston, D. 1983. The adaptive radiation of the griffon vultures. In: Vulture biology and management (Eds. S.R. Wilbur & J.A. Jackson). University of California Press, Berkeley. pp. 135-152.

16. Houston, D., 1985. Indian White-backed Vulture Gyps bengalensis. In: Conservation studies on raptors (Eds. I. Newton and R.D. Chancellor). International Council for Bird Preservation, Cambridge, Technical Publication No. 5. pp. 465-466.

17. Houston, D. 2001. Vultures & Condors. Colin Baxter Photography, Grantown-on-Spey, Scotland.

18. IUCN, 2007. IUCN Red List of threatened species (http://www.iucnredlist.org. downloaded on 3/12/2007).

19. IUCN, 2014. IUCN Red List of threatened species (http://www.iucnredlist.org. downloaded on 20/09/2014).

20. Johnson, J.A., Lerner, H.R.L., Rasmussen, P.C. and Mindell, D.P., 2006. Systematics within Gyps vultures: a clade at risk. BMC Evolutionary Biology 6: 65.
21. Kiff, L.F. 2000. The current status of North American vultures, In: Raptors at risk, (Eds. R.D. Chancellor & B.U. Meyburg). World Working Group on Birds of Prey and Hancock House, Berlin and Surrey, Canada. pp 175-189.
22. MoEF 2006. Action plan for vulture conservation in India. Ministry of Environment and Forests, Government of India, New Delhi.
23. Mundy, P.J. 1982. The Comparative Biology of Southern African Vultures. Vulture Study Group, Johannesburg, RSA.
24. Mundy, P., Butchart, D., Ledger, J. and Piper, S. 1992. The Vultures of Africa. Acorn Books, Russel Friedman Books and Vulture Study Group, Johannesburg.
25. Oaks, J.L., Gilbert, M., Virani, M.Z., Watson, R.T., Meteyer, C.U., Rideout, B., Shivaprasad, H.L., Ahmed, S., Chaudhry, M.J.I., Arshad, M., Mahmood, S., Ali, A. and Khan, A.A., 2004. Diclofenac residues as the cause of vulture population decline in Pakistan. Nature 427: 630-633.
26. Pain, D.J., Bowden, C.G.R., Cunningham, A.A., Cuthbert, R., Das, D., Gilbert, M., Jakati, R.D., Jhala, Y.D., Khan, A.A., Naidoo, V., Oaks, J.L., Parry-Jones, J., Prakash, V., Rahmani, A., Ranade, S.P., Baral, H.S., Senacha, K.R., Saravanan, S., Shah, N., Swan, G., Swarup, D., Taggart, M.A., Watson, R.T., Virani, M.Z., Wolter, K. and Green, R.E., 2008. The race to prevent the extinction of south Asian vultures. BirdLife International, United Kingdom.
27. Pain, D.J., Cunningham, A.A., Donald, P.F., Duckworth, J.W., Houston, D.C., Katzner, T., Parry-Jones, J., Poole, C., Prakash, V., Round P. and Timmins, R., 2003. Causes and effects of temporospatial declines of Gyps vultures in Asia. Conservation Biology 17 (3): 661-671.
28. Piper, S.E., Boshoff, A.E. and Scott, H.A.1999. Modelling survival rates in the Cape Griffon Gyps coprotheres, with emphasison the effects of suppl ementary feeding. Bird Study 46 (Suppl.): S230-238.

29. Prakash, V., Pain, D.J., Cunningham, A.A., Donald, P.F., Prakash, N., Verma, A., Gargi, R., Sivakumar, S. and Rahmani, A.R., 2003. Catastrophic collapse of Indian White-backed Gyps bengalensis and Longbilled Gyps indicus Vulture populations. Biological Conservation 109: 381-390.

30. Prakash, V., Pain, D.J., Cunningham, A.A., Donald, P.F., Prakash, N., Verma, A., Gargi, R., Sivakumar, S. and Rahmani, A.R., 2005 a. Corrigendum to 'Catastrophic collapse of Indian White-backed Gyps bengalensis and Long-billed Gyps indicus Vulture populations'. Biological Conservation 124: 559.

31. Prakash, V., Green, R.E., Rahmani, A.R., Pain, D.J., Virani, M.Z., Khan, A.A., Baral, H.S., Jhala, Y.V., Naoroji, R., Shah, N., Bowden, C.G.R., Choudhury, B.C., Narayan, G. and Gautam, P., 2005 b. Evidence to support that diclofenac caused catastrophic vulture population decline. Current Science 88: 2.

32. Prakash, V., Green, R.E., Pain, D.J., Ranade, S.P., Saravanan, S., Prakash, N., Venkitachalam, R., Cuthbert, R., Rahmani, A.R. and Cunningham, A.A., 2007. Recent changes in populations of resident Gyps vultures in India. Journal of Bombay Natural History Society 104: 129-135.

33. Prakash, V., 1999. Status of vultures in Keoladeo National Park, Bharatpur, Rajasthan, with special reference to population crash in Gyps species. Journal of Bombay Natural History Society 96: 365-378.

34. Rasmussen, P.C. and Parry, S.J., 2001. The taxonomic status of the 'Long-billed Vulture Gyps indicus. Vulture News 44: 18-21.

35. Sarrazin, F., Bagnolini, C., Pinna, J.L., Danchin, E. and Clobert, J. 1994. High survival of Griffon vultures (Gyps fulvus fulvus) in areintroduced population. Auk 111: 853-862.

36. Satheesan, S.M. 2000. Vultures in Asia. In: Raptors at risk (Eds. R.D. Chancellor & B.U. Meyburg). World Working Group on Birds of Prey and Hancock House, Berlin and Surrey, Canada. 165-174 pp.

37. Schlee, M.A. 2000. The status of vultures in Latin America. In: Raptors at risk (Eds. R.D. Chancellor & B.E. Meyburg). World Working Group on Birds of Prey and Hancock House, Berlin and Surrey (Canada). pp. 191-206.

38. Seibold, I. and Helbig, A.J. 1995. Evolutionary history of New and Old World vultures inferred from nucleotide sequences of the mitochondrial cytochrome b gene. Phil. Trans. R. Soc. Lond. B 350: 163-178.

39. Shultz, S., Baral, H.S., Charman, S., Cunningham, A.A., Das, D., Ghalsasi, D.R., Goudar, M.S., Green, R.E., Jones, A., Nighot, P., Pain, D.J. and Prakash, V. 2004. Diclofenac poisoning is widespread in declining vulture populations across the Indian subcontinent. Proceedings of the Royal Society of London B (Supplement) 271 (Suppl 6): S 458–S 460.

40. Srikosamatara, S. and Suteethorn, V. 1995. Populations of Gaur and Banteng and their management in Thailand. Nat. Hist. Bull. Siam Soc. 43: 55-83.

41. Susic, G. and Pavokovic, G. 2003. Poisoning and unexplained high Griffon Vulture Gyps fulvus mortality in Croatia. Vulture News 48: 58-59.

42. Terrasse, M., Bagnolini, C., Bonnet, J., Pinna,J.L. and Sarrazin, F.1994. Reintroduction of the Griffon Gyps fulvus in the Massif Central, France. Raptors conservation today. WWGBP/The Pica Press, Berlin, pp. 479-491.

43. Wikipedia, 2011. Vulture, (www.en.wikipedia.org/wiki/Vulture, downloaded on 26/12/2011).

44. Yohannes, E. And Bekele, A. 1998. Behavioural responses of vultures to aircraft at Bole Airport in Addis Ababa, Ethiopia. Vulture News 39: 20-24.

45. Yosef, R. and Alon, D. 1997. Do immature Palearctic Egyptian Vultures Neophron percnopterus remain in Africa during the northern summer? Vogelwelt 118: 285-289.

Chapter-XV

Riparian Zone of Kulsi River: A Landscape Ecology Study in Pre-Monsoon Season

Shah Nawaz Jelil1, Mridul Bora1 & Prasanta Kumar Saikia*

Abstract

Kulsi, a southern tributary of Brahmaputra harbours the endangered Ganges River Dolphin. Its riparian zones were surveyed to document the condition of these areas as well as record different wildlife using these areas with the anthropogenic stress on the riparian zones was also recorded. The whole river was fragmented into three sample sites. The study reveals drying up of the riparian zones of the river in the Pre-monsoon season. Study also revealed that all three sample sites had distinctive riparian structure and geomorphology. A parallel study indicated the presence of only 5 dolphins in the river, whereas Wakid & Braulik (2009) reported 29 individual dolphins. Hence climate change studies with respect to degradation of habitats are an immediate need in the study area. This is the first riparian zone study carried out in Kulsi and this paper will act as a database for future studies to be carried out. The nature of riparian zones may be surveyed in the future and could be compared with these results and implications of climate change could be readily deduced.

Keywords: Landscape Ecology, Riparian Zone, Kulsi River, Ganges River Dolphin

*Animal Ecology and Wildlife Biology, Department of Zoology, Gauhati University, Guwahati, Assam, India

Introduction

Riparian Zones are one of the most dynamic portions of the landscape (Swanson et al. 1988). Frequent disturbance events in riparian zones create complex mosaics of landforms and associated biological communities that often are more heterogenous and diverse than those associated with upslope landscapes. The linear nature of lotic ecosystems enhances the importance of riparian zones in landscape ecology. River valleys connect montane headwaters with lowland terrains, provided avenues for the transfer of water, nutrients, sediment, particulate organic matter and organisms. These fluxes are not solely in a downstream direction. Nutrients, sediments, and organic matter move laterally and are deposited onto floodplains, as well as being transported off the land into the stream. Riparian zones are important routes for the dispersal of plants and animals, both upstream and downstream, and provide corridors for migratory species 4. Riparian zone study is comparatively new in Assam and the riparian areas of river Kulsi had never been assessed before. Kulsi is an important southern tributary of the Brahmaputra providing life to various living beings including man. Previous research on Kulsi concentrated on Ganges river dolphin population, fish diversity estimation, hydrology, etc. This landscape ecology approach to assess the status of the river is the first and foremost.

Materials and Methods

Study Area

Kulsi River, a southern tributary of river Brahmaputra origins from the state of Meghalaya (25°38′ N, 91°38′ E) in India. After travelling about 12 km from its origin, the river enters Kamrup district of Assam at Umkiam and is known as Kulsi from this point 8. It meets Brahmaputra in Goalpara district of Assam in Nagarbera at Jaljoli. The river is 76 km in length from Kulsi town to the Brahmaputra confluence, Kulsi harbor ichthyofaunae, which are diverse, the diversity is attributed due to the climatic conditions, physiography, topography as well as its drainage system. A total of 63 fish species belonging to 8 orders and 21 families are present along with 6 exotic fishes 3.

Kulsi which supports a rich and varied semi-aquatic macrophytes distributed along its bank exhibits a heterogenous assemblage. Plenty rainfall, high humidity, moderate and high temperature influences primarily the profuse development of semi-aquatic macrphytes, Ipomea cornea fistulosa during the monsoon and early autumnal period in Kulsi 6. There are 25 villages abounding Kulsi. These people depend on the river water for bathing, washing, cattle bathing, recreation and other purposes. Roy (2000) observed that 70% of the total population abounding the river use the river for above mentioned purposes and subsequently pollute the river.

Data Collection

The whole river was fragmented into three sample sites viz. sample 1: Kukurmara, sample 2: Samaria and sample 3: Nagarbera. The study was carried out from mid-April to June 2014. All surveys were done either in foot or traditional wooden canoes. Day long surveys were carried out in all the three sites. Data such as channel width (narrow/wide), nearby confluences, meanders, weather, bank type (sandy/muddy/hard ground), and human activities in the river were recorded and filled into field datasheets. Photos were also taken for comparison among the sample sites later. Moreover, line transects following (Bibby et al. 1992) along the riparian zones were followed. Birds were identified using field guide books of Ali and Ripley, (1987) and Grimmet et al. (2000). Opportunistic sightings of Ganges River Dolphin were also recorded.

Data Analysis

Based on the morphology, all the three sites were analysed and compared. For bird diversity, Shannon-Weiner Index was used to see which site harboured most avian fauna using the Species Diversity and Richness Software 3.02. ANOVA was carried out to see if there are significant differences among the sample sites with the help of SPSS 16.

Results

All three sample sites differed in basic morphology. Sample 1: Kukurmara had a hard ground river bank and also muddy at some places. The river slope was gentle almost 45%. No vegetation was seen in the toe zone, bank zone, overbank zone and transition zone.

On the upland zone, there were woodland trees. Away from this upland zone, grasslands were observed on both the sides of the river in Kukurmara which supported grassland birds. In Sample 2: Samaria, the river bank type was muddy. The river slope was more slant than sample 1. Similarly, no vegetation was observed in the lower lying zones, only in the upland zone, trees were seen. In sample 3: small shrubs and succulent vegetation was observed in the toe zone, bank zone, overbank zone and the transition zone. River bank type was muddy. In sample 2 and sample 3, bank erosion was clearly visible. Various human activities on the river were recorded (Table 1).

A total of 23 birds belonging to 18 families were recorded in the study area (Table 2). Sample 1 showed the highest diversity (H=2.992) out of the three sample sites. ANOVA test carried out showed that there were significant difference (P=0.000) among the samples. Post Hoc test revealed that sample 1 and sample 2 showed significant difference (P=0.000), sample 1 and sample 3 also showed significant difference (P=0.000). Only sample 2 and sample 3 showed no significant difference (P=0.630).

Out of the three sample sites surveyed, Sample Site 1 showed the presence of river dolphins. The threats to dolphins and to the ecosystem in general included sand mining, habitat degradation, uncontrolled fishing with fishing gears such as katal and hook fishing, unregulated motor boats running in the confluence of Kulsi and Brahmaputra, drying up of wetlands in this season and bank erosion in all the sample sites.

Table 1: Showing channel width, bank type, nearby confluences and human activities observed during the field study period

Sample No.	Sample Name	Channel width	Bank type	Nearby confluence	Human activities
1	Kukurmara	Narrow	Hard ground and Muddy	Botha and Kulsi	Sand mining, washing, fishing
2	Samaria	Narrow	Muddy	Boko and Kulsi	Boats running
3	Nagarbera	Wide	Muddy	Kulsi and Brahmaputra	Washing, bathing, swimming, motor boats running

Table 2: Checklist of avifauna of Kulsi River during the Study Period

Sr. No.	Family	Common Name	Scientific Name	IUCN status
1	Sturnidae	Jungle myna	Acridotheras fuscus	LC
2		Common myna	Acridotheras tristis	LC
3		Asian pied starling	Gracupica contra	LC
4	Ardeidae	Cattle egret	Bubulcus ibis	LC
5		Median egret	Mesophoyx intermedia	LC
6	Pycnonotidae	Red Vented Bulbul	Pycnonotus cafer	LC
7	Muscicapidae	Oriental Magpie Robin	Copsychus saularis	LC
8	Dicruridae	Black Drongo	Dicrurus macrocercus	LC
9	Columbidae	Yellow Footed Green Pigeon	Treron phoenicoptera	LC
10	Cerylidae	Pied Kingfisher	Cerlye rudis	LC
11	Picidae	Fulvous Breasted Kingfisher	Dendrocopos macei	LC
12	Megalaimidae	Blue Throated Barbet	Megalaima asiatica	LC
13	Motacillidae	White Wagtail	Motacilla alba	LC
14	Passeridae	Tree Sparrow	Passer montanus	LC

15	Ciconiidae	Black Necked Stork	Ephippiorhynchus asiaticus	NT
16		Open Bill Stork	Anastomus oscitans	LC
17	Accripitridae	Black Kite	Milvus migrans	LC
18	Phalacrocoracidae	Little Cormorant	Microcarbo niger	LC
19		Indian Cormorant	Phalacrocorax fusciollis	LC
20	Halcyonidae	White Breasted Kingfisher	Halcyon smyrnensis	LC
21	Oriolidae	Black Headed Oriole	Oriolus larvatus	LC
22	Paridae	Great Tit	Parus major	LC
23	Corvidae	Rufous Treepie	Dendrocitta vagabunda	LC

Discussion

Kulsi, a life giving river is rich in its riparian zone vegetation and bird diversity. 23 species of birds were found in the Pre-monsoon season, which suggests that the year proceeds, more and more species will be recorded. Also it is rich in riparian zone morphology diversity; all three sites differed from each other in its riparian structure.

Kukurmara, the sample 1 showed the highest number of birds among all the sample sites. Also, dolphins were only sighted in Kukurmara, whereas study carried out in monsoon and retreating monsoon earlier revealed that all the sites harboured dolphins. The local disappearance is owing to the changed season. The ecosystem degradation was clearly observed especially river bank erosion and uncontrolled sand mining activities in the Kulsi river. The present study revealed that riparian zones play an important role in the functioning of both the terrestrial and aquatic system.

References

1. Ali, S and Ripley, S. D. (1987): A Compact Handbook of the Birds of India and Pakistan, Second Edition. Oxford University Press, Delhi, 737 pp.
2. Bibby, C. J., Burgress, N. D. and Hall, D. A. (1992): Bird Census Techniques: Academic press, London, New York, San Diego, Boston, 248 pp.
3. Goswami, C. and Ali, S. (2012): Ichthyofaunal Diversity of Kulsi River; Prime Habitat of Dolphin. Biological Forum- An International Journal 4(2): 38-44.
4. Gregory, S. V., Swanson, F. J. McKee, W. A. and Cummins, K. W. (1991): An Ecosystem Perspective of Riparian Zones. Bioscience 41 (8) Pg. 540
5. Grimmet, R., Inskipp, C. and Inskipp (2000): The Pocket Guide to the birds of the Indian Subcontinent. Oxford University Press, Delhi, 888 pp.
6. Roy, S. (2000): Studies on the Ecology of the Gangetic River Dolphin Pltanista gangetica gangetica (Roxburgh, 1801) in the Kulsi river of Assam. PhD Thesis. Gauhati University.
7. Swanson, F. J., Kratz, T. K., Caine, N. and Woodmansee, R. G. (1988): Landform effects on ecosystem patterns and processes. Bioscience 38: 92-98.
8. Wakid, A. and Braulik, G. (2009): Protection of endangered Ganges River dolphin in Brahmaputra River. Final Technical Report submitted to IUCN-Sir Peter Scott Fund, 44 pp.

Chapter XVI

An Appraisal of Environmental Legislation in India

Shailesh Yadav*

Abstract

The environment has become the first casualty in the tussle between rapid urban growth and fast paced industrialisation in the country. In its aspirations to reach global standards the nation's environmental assets are being sacrificed at the altar of economic development. With the nation's geographical space being gradually taken over by the forces of urbanisation and the air becoming a cocktail of various kinds of toxins, environmental assets like clean air, potable water, lush green fields, and unspoilt virgin forests are becoming things of the distant past. However where the planet is heading if we continue in our destructive ways have been realised and efforts are under way to make the wrongs right again. One of the effective tools that have the capacity to deliver on ensuring a better environment has been found to be in the legal discourse. The global community at large as well as the national agencies like the governments at the states and the centre has realised the utility of legal jurisprudence in ensuring that the natural assets are provided with the much needed protection and conservation.

This paper shall look into the legal and institutional systems that have been put in place to meet the emerging challenges against the environment of the country and also examine the extent to which these institutional and legal frameworks have been successful in delivering the nation from its environmental problems.

Keywords: Environmental Law, Sustainable Development, Human Rights, Right to Life, Judiciary

*Department of Geography, University of Rajasthan, Jaipur, India

Introduction

The first imprint of mankind on earth has not been earlier than the Cenozoic. When the human life initiated, the earth did not see major conflicts with nature. Man was as much at home with his natural settings as the other living species. However as the times changed and man gradually shifted his sight from the simple life to the modern living, man's relations with the natural world changed forever.

The dawn of the Industrial Revolution in the 18th century ushered in an era where nothing would be the same as before. Man's aspirations had reached new heights where the desirable life was seen equivalent to fast-paced industrialization, rapid urbanization and transformation of the natural landscape into concrete spaces. The diffusion of such 'so-called' modern aspirations ensured that the human species not only lost its touch with the natural environment, but at the same time indulged in actions that went a long way towards harming the carrying capacity of the environment.

The destruction has pervaded into almost all aspects of the natural environment. No part of the natural world today is safe from the disparaging anthropological influence, so much so that the human race itself has come face to face with the possibility of destruction.

The realizations that the endowments from nature are not unlimited and there is a need to protect the environment were always a part of human culture, at least in the oriental world. It was understood that the term "environment" includes water, air and land and the inter-relationship which exists among and between water, air and land and human beings, other living creatures, plants, micro-organisms and property[24].

After the destructive human influence on the environment was acknowledged in the open, the ideas from the olden days have seen a revival. The idea of Sustainable Development, popularized since 1983, which saw the unveiling of Our Common Future, has come to represent the requisite criterion defining almost all current human activities. The concept of Sustainable Development has revolutionized the way in which the importance of environment is perceived today.

---

[24] Section 2(a), Environment (Protection) Act, 1986.

The idea, 'Development that meets the needs of the present without compromising the ability of the future generations to meet their own needs', has managed successfully to drag the focus back towards sustainability from destructive 'developmental practices'.

The concerns for the environmental factors reached a new crescendo, especially after the 1960s. This is also the period when Environmental Legislation came into its own [1]. The heightened concerns for the environment began to be reflected in a number of domestic and international legal documents reflecting the serious concerns regarding the changing quality of the environment [2]. The importance to protect the quality of the air, the water, the forests, the wildlife and the ecosystems was felt urgently and sincerely.

This paper attempts to analyze the legal and institutional systems that have been put in place to meet the emerging challenges against the environment of the country. The attempt shall also be to examine the extent to which these institutional and legal frameworks have been successful in delivering the nation from its environmental problems.

The Genesis of Environmental Legislation

Prior to 1980s international legal alternatives looking into the welfare of the environment were few and far stretched. The few existing bilateral and multilateral agreements were mostly in place to assert a nation's sovereign rights on its natural resources rather than to address problems like pollution, quality deterioration, overexploitation and other environmental problems. A few exceptional legislations of the time pertaining to the environment were the Convention for the Protection of Birds Useful to Agriculture (1902), US-UK Boundary Waters Treaty (1909), the Convention for the Protection of Migratory Birds in the United States and Canada (1916), London Convention on Preservation of Fauna and Flora in their Natural State (1933) and the more notable convention regarding the establishment of the International Whaling Commission (1946). As can be observed, the countries that set precedents in adopting international environmental legislations were mostly from the developed world.

From the 1950s to the 1970s there were heightened concerns regarding fallouts from nuclear disasters and marine pollution from oil spills, which also saw negotiations at the international level. Soon other nations, both developed as well as developing followed suit that led to environmental law becoming an essential facet of international legal issues. The modern era of international environmental legislation was ushered in with the United Nations Stockholm Conference on the Human Environment (1972). This convention was a landmark amongst the many important conventions that saw the light of the day during this period. The Convention on Wetlands of International Importance, Ramsar, Iran (1971), Convention concerning the Protection of the World Cultural and Natural Heritage, Paris (1972), the Convention on International Trade in Endangered Species of Wild Fauna and Flora, Washington (1973), and the Convention on the Conservation of Migratory Species of Wild Animals (Bonn Convention, 1979) were some conventions of immense importance to be formulated during this period.

The 1980s was a watershed decade for international environmental law and policy-making. This period represents the shift in concerns from asserting sovereign rights over natural resources to the common environmental concerns that were being voiced on the global platform. The global community by this time had begun to recon the importance of marrying economic concerns with environmental issues and move away from only monitoring the environmental changes towards actual conservation of the natural resources.

The stage for the paradigm shift was being set up by conventions like the Convention for the Protection of the Ozone Layer, Vienna (1985), Protocol on Substances that Deplete the Ozone Layer, Montreal (1987), and the Convention on the Control of Trans boundary Movements of Hazardous Wastes and their Disposal, Basel (1989) which culminated into the United Nations Conference on Environment and Development, Rio de Janeiro (1992). The notable outcomes of this Earth Summit were the setting up of the United Nations Framework Convention on Climate Change (1992), that set the ground for Kyoto Protocol of 1997, and the Convention on Biological Diversity (1992), both of which were legally binding.

A Temporal Analysis of Environmental Legislation in the Country

While delving into the Indian scenario it can be observed that Indian concerns for the protection of the environment are not far removed from the concerns of the global community. In fact respect for nature and the need for its conservation has been imbibed into Indian culture from the ancient times. Vasudev Kutumbakam (the whole world is one family), the idea contained in the Maha Upanishads, can be interpreted to mean that all life on earth should be respected and this idea can be used to address the global concerns regarding the environment [3].

The Atharva Veda more explicitly states in Bhumi Suktathat the earth is the provider of life and the welfare of humankind is intertwined with a living and thriving earth. Apart from the Vedas and Upanishads, the Puranas and the other holy texts of the time also extol the needs of a healthy environment in maintaining prosperity on earth [4].

The ancient civilization of Harappa and Mohenjo-Daro, the Arthashastra of Kautiliya of Mauryan times, the Ashoka 5th Pillar Edict, the Jain philosophy of ahimsa, all acknowledged the importance of the various facets of the environment.

However environmental jurisprudence came to India only with the coming of the British. Although they were initiated to address the narrow British needs, nonetheless the British were the first in the country to formulate laws pertaining to the forests, wildlife, air and water. Some of the examples of laws made by the British to safeguard the environment were Shore Nuisance (Bombay and Kolaba) Act of 1853, Lord Dalhousie's Forest Charter of 1855, and Forest Act of 1865 [5]. Under the Indian Penal Code the British made it punishable to pollute fresh water sources and also brought in laws pertaining to air pollution in the form of Bengal Smoke Nuisance Act of 1905 and the Bombay Smoke Nuisance Act of 1912.

When the British rule came to an end in 1947, the Constitution of free India came into force. However the founding fathers were most distressed with the poverty, the inequality, and the illiteracy that the country inherited from the British. Hence the founding fathers dedicated that the bulk of the constitution towards addressing these problems. In other words, 'the post-independence India was concerned with equity and growth and the environmental concerns were added only as a third dimension' [6].

Hence environment related rights were conspicuously absent from the original version of the Constitution of India, which was prominently dominated by business and property rights. Consequently, environmental jurisprudence was an unknown appellation for the Indian judiciary. However Article 21[25] of the Indian Constitution, that makes the 'Right to Life' a Fundamental Right for every being within the territory of the Indian Union, has enough scope of progressive interpretations that allowed the Indian courts to acknowledge that the right to a clean and healthy environment forms an integral part of right to life. In the case of Francis Coralie vs. the Administrator, Union Territory of Delhi and others[26] the Hon. Supreme Court of India observed, "We think that the Right to Life includes the right to live with human dignity and all that goes along with it.... The magnitude and content of the components of this right would depend upon the extent of development of the country, but it must, in any view of the matter, include the right to the basic necessities of life. This now includes the right to clean and hygienic environment and above all, the right to live with basic dignity."Moreover, Article 47[27] entitled to a clean and healthy environment becomes a necessity.

Explicit concerns regarding the environment had begun to surface post-1972 after Mrs Indira Gandhi delivered her historic speech at the United Nations Conference on the Human Environment held in Stockholm. Her speech outlined the difficulties of most developing countries in addressing both economic as well as environmental concerns at the same time when she said, "We do not wish to impoverish the environment any further and yet we cannot for a moment forget the grim poverty of large numbers of people. Are not poverty and need the greatest polluters? For instance, unless we are in a position to provide employment and purchasing power for the daily necessities of the tribal people and those who live in or around our jungles, we cannot prevent them from combing the forest for food and

---

[25]Protection of life and personal liberty -No person shall be deprived of his life or personal liberty except according to procedure established by law.

[26]Francis Coralie Mullin v. Administrator, Union Territory of Delhi and others (1981) 1 SCC 608

[27]Duty of the State to raise the level of nutrition and the standard of living and to improve public health- The State shall regard the raising of the level of nutrition and the standard of living of its people and the improvement of public health as among its primary duties and, in particular, the State shall endeavor to bring about prohibition of the consumption except for medicinal purposes of intoxicating drinks and of drugs which are injurious to health.

livelihood; from poaching and from despoiling the vegetation. When they themselves feel deprived, how can we urge preservation of animals? How can we speak to those who live in villages and in slums about keeping the oceans, the rivers and the air clean when their own lives are contaminated at the source? The environment cannot be improved in conditions of poverty. Nor can poverty be eradicated without the use of science and technology."

Her concerns paved the way for the 42nd Amendment Act (1976) that made caring for the environment an integral part of the constitution. Articles 48-A28 of Directive Principles of State Policy and 51-A (g)29 of Fundamental Duties have been imposed on both the state and its citizens. Such acknowledgements were clear indications to the changing perceptions about the importance of environmental protection [5].

Indian Judiciary as an Environmental Crusader

The judicial institutions too have displayed in both words and action that environmental legislation is a matter of serious consideration for them. In its efforts to protect and restore the environment, the Supreme Court and the Indian Judiciary in general have adopted several means to put across their concerns about the environment. The Judiciary has relied on the public trust doctrine, precautionary principle, *polluter pays* principle, the doctrine of strict and absolute liability, the exemplary damages principle, the pollution fine principle and inter-generational equity principle, public participation in decision-making apart from the existing law of the land. Another guiding principle has been that of adopting a model of sustainable development.

The Legal Remedies

Recognition of Public Trust doctrine for the protection of natural

---

[28]Article 48-A reads as: Protection and improvement of environment and safeguarding of forests and wild life-the state shall endeavor to protect and improve the environment and to safeguard the forest and wild life of the country.

[29]Article 51A(g) reads as: Fundamental Duties- It shall be the duty of every citizen of India- (g) to and improve the natural environment including forests, lakes, rivers and wild life, and to have compassion for living creatures.

resources is judicial innovation of Indian judiciary, this principle underlies that the state has a certain obligation to protect and preserve resources, which are for public use. This doctrine was invoked by court in the case of M.C. Mehta V. Kamal Nath30 and articulated that "a disturbance of the basic environment elements, namely air, water and soil which are necessary for "life" would be hazardous to "life" within the meaning of article 21 of the constitution" It is pertinent to mention here that in Narmada Bachao Andolan V. UOI31 court held that a mere change in environment does not violate article 21 though the ratio presented in two cases were different. But looking into the facts and circumstances of each case individually legal proposition were rightly marked.

Precautionary Principle determines whether developmental process is sustainable or not. It underlies principle 1532 of the Rio declaration. This is the principle which enables and ensures that a substance and activity posing a threat to the environment is prevented from adversely affecting it, even if there is no conclusive scientific proof linking that particular substance or activity to the environmental damage.

In AP Pollution Control Board v. Nayudu33 the Indian Supreme Court applied the precautionary principle in considering a petition against the development of certain hazardous industries. The Court held that "It is necessary that the party attempting to preserve the status quo by maintaining a less-polluted state should not carry the burden of proof and the party who wants to alter it, must bear this burden."

---

[30]M.C. Mehta v Kamal Nath, Supreme Court of India, Judgment of 12 May 2000, (2000) 6 SCC 213.

[31]Narmada Bachao Andolan v Union of India, Supreme Court of India, Judgment of 18 October 2000, (2000) 10 SCC 664

[32]Principle 15 of Rio Declaration on Environment and Development, In order to protect the environment, the precautionary approach shall be widely applied by States according to their capabilities. Where there are threats of serious or irreversible damage, lack of full scientific certainty shall not be used as a reason for postponing cost-effective measures to prevent environmental degradation.

[33]*A.P. Pollution Control Board v Prof. M.V. Nayadu (Retd.) &Ors,* Supreme Court of India, Judgment of 27 January 1999, (1999) 2 SCC 718,730-731 and *A.P. Pollution Control Board*

Polluter pay principle as incorporated by Supreme Court of India exposes polluter to two fold liabilities, namely compensation to the victims of pollution and ecological restoration. Hence it includes both environmental costs as well as direct cost to people or property. Polluter pay principle finds prominent place in principle 1634of the Rio declaration. Supreme Court of India recognised this principle in Indian Council for Enviro-Legal Actions v Union of India35 and Vellore Citizens' Welfare Forum v Union of India36 cases.

Another principle has been that of adopting a model of sustainable development that is "the development that meets the needs of the present without compromising the ability of future to meet their own needs". The consistent position adopted by the courts as enunciated in one of its judgments37 has been that there can neither be development at the cost of the environment or environment at the cost of development.

The option of filing of Public Interest Litigation with the Indian courts provides for another legal recourse that has helped the environmental cause immensely. It has allowed the concerned parties to bring the attention of the judiciary to issues where the citizens' right to a healthy environment was being violated. One such earliest documented case is that of the Doon Valley Case (Rural Litigation Entitlement Kendra Dehradun vs. State of U.P.)38[7]. Imprudent developmental initiatives, large-scale limestone quarrying and unchecked deforestation of the region had begun to jeopardize the ecological balance of the region. A writ petition by the Rural Litigation Entitlement Kendra to the Hon. Supreme Court elicited a verdict that stated, "Preservation of the environment and keeping the

---

v *Prof. M.V. Nayudu (Retd.) &Ors.*, Supreme Court of India, Judgment of 1 December 2000, (2001) 2 SCC 62, 84-85

[34]Principle 16 of Rio Declaration on Environment and Development promote the internalization of environmental costs and the use of economic instruments, taking into account the approach that the polluter should, in principle, bear the cost of pollution, with due regard to the public interest and without distorting international trade and investment.

[35]Indian Council for Enviro Legal Action v Union of India, Supreme Court of India, Judgment of 13 February 1996, (1996) 3 SCC 212, 252

[36]Vellore Citizens' Welfare Forum v Union of India, Supreme Court of India, Judgment of 28 August 1996, (1996) 5 SCC 647

[37]Goa Foundation v Diksha Holdings Pvt. Ltd., Supreme Court of India, Judgment of 10 November 2000, (2001) 2 SCC 97

[38]Rural Litigation & Entitlement Kendra Vs. State of U.P [1988] INSC 254 (30 August 1988)

ecological balance unaffected is a task which not only Governments, but also every citizen must undertake. It is a social obligation and let us remind every Indian citizen that it is his fundamental duty as enshrined in Article 51- A (g) of the Constitution."

The immense natural wealth of the country and the need to safeguard them has many a times raised the question of having law courts dedicated solely to the environmental cause. The Hon. Supreme Court has observed in more than one occasion, the need for environmental courts. In cases like M.C Mehta vs. Union of India case (1986) and Indian Council for Enviro-Legal Action vs. Union of India (1996) the Supreme Court stated that cases pertaining to the environment require expertise in data handling and assessing and expert knowledge of the subject for which special courts are a necessity. The Supreme Court went as far as to state that environmental courts with special civil and criminal jurisdiction need to be established that can dispose cases pertaining to the environment in a prompt manner.

The Law Commission's 186th Report entitled 'Proposal To Constitute Environmental Courts'(2003) also suggested, "…these Courts must be established to reduce the pressure and burden on the High Courts and Supreme Court. These Courts will be Courts of fact and law, exercising all powers of a civil court in its original jurisdiction."

Finally in the year 2009 the Indian Parliament introduced the National Green Tribunal Bill which was passed as the National Green Tribunal Act, 2010. The Tribunal is dedicated to the protection of the ecological and the environmental resources of the nation and also looks into the matters that concern the wellbeing of those affected or displaced by various projects. National Green Tribunal Act is a path breaking legislation which is unique in many ways. It will provide a new dimension to environment adjudication by curtailing delays and imparting objectivity. The Tribunal, given its composition and jurisdiction, including wide powers to settle environment dispute and providing relief, compensation including restitution of environment, is envisaged to be a specialized environmental adjudicatory body having both original as well as appellate jurisdiction [8].

In a significant judgement on 18th July, 2014 the National Green Tribunal (NGT) has asserted its powers to enforce environmental rights, clarifying that it has "the complete trappings of a civil court" and that its power of judicial review is "implicit and essential for expeditious and effective disposal of the cases"[9]. Moreover the Doctrine of Progressive Interpretation keeps the Indian judiciary sensitive to the needs and circumstances of the current times while making their observations.

Indian Legislature, Executive and Environment

Independent India has shown keen interest in protection of environment. The constitutional provisions are backed by a number of laws, acts, rules, and notifications that are being passed by the legislature. Even before India's independence in 1947, several environmental legislations existed but the real impetus for bringing about a well-developed framework came only after the UN Conference on the Human Environment (Stockholm, 1972). In pursuance to the constitutional obligations to protect and improve the environment, the Department of Environment was established in India in 1980 to ensure a healthy environment for the country. This later became the Ministry of Environment and Forests in 1985.

Although the articles 48-A and 51-A (g) may not be legally justiciable in the Indian courts of law, they have become the basis of several legally binding opinions expressed by the courts [10]. The 42nd Amendment Act made further amendments that inserted three new provisions under the Seventh Schedule, by virtue of Article 24639 & seventh schedule of the constitution the subject of legislations to the respective centre & state governments have been allotted. Item 56 of the list I empowers the union govt. to legislate in matters relating to regulation & development of inter-state rivers river valleys to the extent to which such regulation development under the control of union is declared by parliament by law to be expedient in public interest.

By virtue of list II subject like public health, sanitation, agriculture water supplies irrigation, drainage, fisheries is vested in state govt. Under concurrent powers list III both parliament & state government have shared jurisdiction over subjects like forests, protection of wildlife, mines and mineral development, minor ports, factories etc. Parliament is empowered to legislate on residual subject not covered

---

[39]Article 246 related with the subject matter of laws made by Parliament and by the Legislatures of States

in any list. When central laws are in conflict with state laws, the former prevail. Parliament is empowered to legislate in national interest on matters enumerated in state list also parliament is empowered to legislate to give effect to international treaty and conventions.

The 73rd and the 74th Amendment Acts (1992) that made grassroot administrative bodies a reality for Indian governance also made provisions for the protection of the environment and the ecology.

The Eleventh Schedule along with other matters contains following maters which are directly or indirectly related to environment like, agriculture, soil conservation, water management and watershed development, fisheries, social forestry and farm forestry, minor forest produce, drinking water, health and sanitation and maintenance of community assets.

Likewise the twelfth Schedule also gives powers in the matters of urban planning including town planning regulation of land use water supply, public health, sanitation, conservancy and solid waste management, urban forestry, protection of the environment and promotion of ecological aspects, provision of urban amenities such as park grounds, cremation grounds and electric crematoriums; prevention of cruelty to animals, regulation of slaughter houses and tanneries. It is evident that the Constitution imposes the duty to protect and preserve the environment in all the three tiers of the Government i.e. Central, state and local.

Although Indian legislature and executive tried hard to cope with the dynamic environment of policy making and implementation but somewhat failed to replicate the policies on ground level because of resource constraints. Yet actively participated in several multilateral treaties and has been active in admitting its commitments to the environment in accordance with the general principles of International Law while incorporating them into its national laws.

The country currently has several laws in place to extend protection to the environmental resources. Wildlife Protection Act (1972), Water (Prevention and Control of Pollution) Act (1974), Forest (Conservation) Act (1980), Air (Prevention and Control of Pollution) Act (1981), Environment (Protection) Act (1986), The Biological Diversity Act (2002), The Scheduled Tribes and Other Traditional

Forest Dwellers (Recognition of Forest Rights) Act (2006) are some of the major legislations pertaining to environmental protection that are available in the country.

Before the national Environment Policy 2006, the guidelines for policy making were followed by the policy statements of the National Forest Policy, 1988; the National Conservation Strategy and Policy Statement on Environment and Development, 1992; and the Policy Statement on Abatement of Pollution, 1992. Some sectoral policies such as the National Agriculture Policy, 2000; National Population Policy, 2000; and National Water Policy, 2002. The National Environment Policy 2006 seeks to extend the coverage, and fill in gaps that still exist, in light of present knowledge and accumulated experience. It does not displace, but builds on the earlier policies [11]. This policy is a reaction to our assurance to a clean environment mandated in the Constitution in Articles 48 A and 51 A (g), strengthened by judicial interpretation of Article 21. Policy statement talks about key challenges that are being faced by the nation today that includes nexus of environmental degradation with poverty in its many dimensions, and economic growth. Another major set of challenges arises from emerging global environmental concerns such as climate change and biodiversity loss.

The Need to Educate India about Environment Sustainability

India's mega diversity of natural resources, populace, traditions and indigenous knowledge is what which makes imbibing values of sustainability all the more important. Being a part of the oriental world, the ethos of protecting and preserving the natural wealth and keeping human civilization attuned to the natural environment have always been a part of the country's traditions and culture. However in its endeavours to achieve western standards of development without adequate finance, infrastructure and technological innovations, the country is rapidly pushing its resources towards jeopardy. Under these circumstances making sustainable values and practices a part of the education curriculum becomes important as the education system is responsible for preparing the quality of the future stakeholders and nation builders.

The following paragraphs are regarding the contributions by various communities and population groups towards popularizing ideas that have helped to take forward the objectives envisioned for environmental conservation and restoration.

Youth and Sustainable Environment

Promoting awareness and empowerment amongst the youth about sustainable development can help create a brigade of stakeholders with resources and expertise at their disposal that can be utilized to reverse the unsustainable practices and the consequent environmental dilemmas. Armed with this knowledge the youth can then further contribute to the cause of sustainability by disseminating the idea of cutting down on wasteful consumption, promoting equity, and preserving the ecological milieu.

Gender Equity for Sustainable Environment

For major part of the nation's history, gender issues have been among the most contentious. However it is now a known fact that encouraging education, improving nutrition and health, empowering with rights not only improves the status of the women in society but improves the livability aspect of the society itself. Similarly for achieving sustainability and for reducing the pressure on the environment and the natural resources, empowerment of women cannot be delayed primarily because climate change is unlikely to be gender neutral and almost 70% of the world's poor are women. According to UN Women's Executive Director Michelle Bachelet "Sustainable development in South Asia, including India, will not be possible without a holistic approach to women's empowerment and livelihood."

The reason why the women need to be included in attempts to achieve sustainability is that a large section of the womenfolk are still engaged in their traditional roles as caregivers, feeders and child bearers. Consequently most of the time the womenfolk deal directly with natural resources like water, energy, agriculture and forests before they are consumed by the other members of the family [12].Therefore if the women are sensitized about the need for sustainability and the methods of achieving it, then they will not only ensure that the knowledge is passed on to her children but also those in her immediate surroundings.

The concern that a woman has for her environment can be gauged from the fact that womenfolk were the leading participants of the Chipko Andolan in the Garhwal Himalayas in Uttarakhand.

Indigenous Communities for Education for Sustainable Environment

Having lived close to nature, the indigenous communities[40] have accumulated vast pools of knowledge over the years about the sustainable way of living. However with the advent of modern ideas and popularization of formal education, the traditional knowledge generally passed down orally or through cultural rituals are being forgotten and hence lost. The importance of safeguarding the 'folk knowledge' or the 'traditional wisdom' have been realized because "they encompass the sophisticated arrays of information, understandings and interpretations that guide human societies around the globe in their innumerable interactions with the natural milieu: in agriculture and animal husbandry; hunting, fishing and gathering; struggles against disease and injury; naming and explanation of natural phenomena; and strategies to cope with fluctuating environments"[12].

Within the geographical boundaries of India there are living innumerable numbers of indigenous groups. One among them is the Solinga tribals inhabiting the Biligirirangan Hills ecosystem of Mysore district of Karnataka. The Solingas practice community farming and harvest sharing. Their education begins at the forest and they learn from a very early age the sustainable utilization of the forest resources for fulfilling the needs of their day-to-day life and their overall well being. The interesting fact about this community is that it has never experienced severe scarcity of food and they share strong family and filial bonds.

---

[40] The working definition was given by Jose R. Martinez Cobo, the Special Rapporteur of the Sub-Commission on Prevention of Discrimination and Protection of Minorities, in his famous Study on the Problem of Discrimination against Indigenous Populations. "Indigenous communities, peoples and nations are those which, having a historical continuity with pre-invasion and pre-colonial societies that developed on their territories, consider themselves distinct from other sectors of the societies now prevailing on those territories, or parts of them. They form at present non-dominant sectors of society and are determined to preserve, develop and transmit to future generations their ancestral territories, and their ethnic identity, as the basis of their continued existence as peoples, in accordance with their own cultural patterns, social institutions and legal system."

Tapping into their traditional knowledge-base can serve as an inspiration for the sustainable use of the natural resources and take more people out of poverty and isolation. Bringing indigenous knowledge into the ambit of formal education has become necessary not only to protect the local knowledge-base but also to preserve and protect the natural ecological balance.

But are all the efforts making a difference ...

The question that needs to be answered is whether all the efforts taken to have a better environmental quality are going in the right direction. A critical examination will show that, more often than not, the situations are that of a paradox. In spite of having a plethora of environmental laws, constitutional directives and setting up of pollution control boards all over the country, the success in curbing environmental degradation has been quite negligible. For instance if we take the example of pollution rates in the country there seems to be overwhelming agreement over the fact that pollution levels in the nation's air, water, soil, rivers have worsened to almost the point of no return.

The puniest link in country's regulatory mechanisms is the loose administrative arrangements for monitoring and enforcing environmental standards that with lack of commitment and enthusiasm of governments to achieve better standards has left enactments virtually toothless.

One reason for this may be because ours is a country that is in a hurry to attain financial status as the likes of the First World Countries. With such a perspective envisaged for the long run, sacrificing the environmental assets at the altar of development looks like a small collateral to pay. Further complicating the situation are the complexities that are inherent part of Indian legislation. Sometimes the laws are so vague and complicated that it becomes difficult for the experts to decipher the complexities [13]. As an extension to this problem, according to Kuldeep Mathur (2004) [14], another widely prevalent problem in India is that the laws instead of getting implemented continue to languish in books. Therefore laws in India are "symbols of intention and not action"[14].

The mechanism or the will to bridge the gap between policy formulation and policy implementation continues to be a major impediment towards remedial action. Particularly in cases where the environment is involved it can be seen that the political leadership gives consent in the enactment of laws but puts up obstacles when time comes for their implementation.

Judicial activisim has played a positive role in an attempt to save the environment. However some actions taken in the name of environmental protection can be termed to be nothing short of anti-poor. For instance the order of the Delhi High Court to have all the polluting industries to be moved away from the city was a step that put into jeopardy the livelihoods of many poor people in the city who draw their sustenance from such industrial endeavours. In the process of cleansing Delhi's air a number of people were rendered not only jobless but also homeless.

Another point to be noted is that the nation has had a technocratic leaning since the time the country became independent. As a consequence the voices of the general people, who may often be also the stakeholders, often get lost in the technical aspects of rapid industrialisation and modernization. However a lot has changed over the years. But still more efforts need to be made to increase participation rates in matters that determine community's access to its environment.

Conclusion

With so much said and done, it can safely be said that the global community has travelled a long way on the path towards environmental protection and legal remedies have been one of the vehicles that have made the journey smoother. In the Indian context too several positive changes have come about as a consequence of legislations pertaining to environment. However there are certain problems that remain to be major obstacles towards the perceived goal of clean and healthy environment--- failures in arresting the population growth with attendant pressures on land and scarce natural resources, over-urbanization, haphazard industrialization and growth in rapacious consumption.

Development and environment are not necessarily incompatible. In a country like India where dichotomy exists in everyday life, pollution and environment hazards chiefly emanate from 'poverty related risks' and 'growth related risks'. As P.V.N. Rao, the former Indian Prime Minister would say at the National Environment Council meeting, the country needs to strike a balance between development and the preservation of the environment in the interest of both of environment as well as development... the race for development should not be a race for destruction".

We need a development process that needs to be in harmony with the environment that demands a new culture--- a culture where voluntary agencies has emerged as the harbingers of change. The non-governmental organizations have given the environment its dynamism and vigor. In fact, the growth of people's movements on environmental issues has been a marked feature in recent years. The agencies especially those working at the grassroot level, have taken over the responsibility of bringing about an eco-consciousness and have been playing a pioneering role in developing alternate models of equitable and sustainable use of natural resources built around people's participation and control. Twelfth Plan is also putting stress on more public participation in the decision making process in environmental concerns and expects to give more power to grass root agencies.

Financing of environmental issues is a major problem for developing country like India. Government must consider separate budgetary allocation for environment restoration and protection, either through existing resources or levying an environmental cess on industry and citizens. The government should encourage tax benefits for environment conscious initiatives and endeavors. Taking a cue from such incentives the industries should incorporate sustainable solutions to industrial issues as a part of their Corporate Social Responsibility (CSR) [15]

Hopefully the above-mentioned measures will help to further the cause of environment conservation. But however much is done shall continue to be a miniscule drop in the ocean of destructive activities that humanity continues to indulge in. It is time to realize where humanity stands vis-à-vis the environment. More remains to be done because of the sole reason:

"Man is both creature and moulder of his environment, which gives him physical substance and affords him the opportunity for intellectual, moral, social and spiritual growth. Both aspects of man's environment, the natural and the man-made, are essential to his well-being and to the enjoyment of basic human rights the right to life itself." [41]

---

[41]The preamble of the United Nations Declaration on Human Environment (1972)

References

1. Tarlock, A. Dan, Environmental Law: Then and Now. Washington University Journal of Law & Policy, 32, 2010, 1-31
2. Tarlock, A. Dan. "History of Environmental Law." UNESCO-EOLSS. http://www.eolss.net/Sample-Chapters/C04/E4-21-01.pdf
3. Verma, Nandita. "Religion: A Saviour for Environment with Particular Emphasis On Hinduism." 2008.http://www.iitk.ac.in/infocell/announce/convent ion/papers/Context%20and%20Human%20Resource-04-Nandita%20Verma.pdf
4. Karan Singh. "Declaration on Nature." Accessed on July 19, 2014, http://www.karansingh.com/index.php?action=enviro nment&subaction=env_nature
5. Bakshi, Pradeep and Madhur Yadav, "New Judicial Roles and Green Courts in India." In International Conference on Environmental Compliance and Enforcement Conference proceedings, June 2011. British Columbia, Canada: INECE Secretariat
6. NNLRJ INDIA. "Judicial Activism And The Role Of Green Benches In India." Law Resource India.July 22, 2014. http://indialawyers.wordpress.com/2009/05/24/ judicial-activism-and-the-role-of-green-benches-in-india/
7. Bhandari, Dalveer. "Public Interest Litigation: Definition, Origin & Evolution: Supreme Court." The Legal Blog. July 5, 2014. http://www.legalblog.in/2011/02/public-interest-litigation-definition.html
8. Yadav, Nivit Kumar and P K BharathKesav. "National Green Tribunal: A new beginning for environmental cases?" Centre for Science and Environment.http://cseindia.org/node/2900
9. National Green Tribunal asserts independence, is Environment Minister listening? http://www.firstpost.com/india/national-green-tribunal-asserts-independence-environment-minister-listening-1625527.html accessed on 24th July, 2014

10. Gupta, Shailendra Kumar, Principles of International Law and Judicial Response in India. Banaras Law Journal, 37 & 38, 1 & 2, Jan 2008 & Dec 2009, 132-145

11. National Environment Policy, 2006 http://envfor.nic.in/sites/default/files/introduction-nep2006e.pdf

12. Gangwar, Rashmi. "Empowering Self-Help Groups to Address Gender Inequity." In Education for a Sustainable Future International Conference, January 2005. Ahmedabad: Centre for Environment Education, 2005.

13. Nakashima, D., Prott, L. and Bridgewater, P. (2000) Tapping into the world's wisdom, UNESCO Sources, 125, July-August, p. 12

14. Battling for clean environment: Supreme Court, Technocrats and Populist Politics in Delhi by KuldeepMathur-http://www.jnu.ac.in/cslg/workingPaper/01-Battling%20for%20Clean%20(Kuldeep%20Mathur).pdf

15. Corporate Social Responsibility by SanjivAgarwal-http://www.taxmanagementindia.com/visitor/detail_article.asp?ArticleID=1119 Last Visited on 25th July, 2014

Chapter-XVII

Sustainable use of medicinal plants to control Meloidogyne incognita - A strategy to fight root knot disease of crops in Rajasthan, India.

Lily Trivedi, Soumana Datta & P.C.Trivedi*

Abstract

Medicinal plants acts as a source of drugs for rural areas in Rajasthan and the local healers use them for disease cure and prevention in humans, plants and livestock. Local communities and tribes play a great role in conserving medicinal plants since generations. Variable temperature and rainfall patterns often cause pathogens to thrive in various climatic regimes. Soil nematodes like the root knot nematode, Meloidogyne incognita, found in arid and semi arid soils of Rajasthan in India, attack roots and cause great loss to crops and other plants of economic value.

Farmers use indigenous methods as well as chemical means to control various plant pathogens. In the present study plant leaves of trees and shrubs growing abundantly in Rajasthan, were evaluated in vitro in the form of aqueous extract and in vivo as dry leaf powder against nematode M. incognita. The inhibition of egg hatching of M. incognita by different plant leaf extracts in decreasing order was as follows: Aegle marmelos >Prosopis cineraria >Nerium oleander > Clerodendron aculeatum > Bougainvillea spectabilis> Lantana camara > Withania somnifera >Thevetia peruviana > Cassia fistula > Nemacon > Vircon > Control at both lower and higher concentrations and was nemostatic in nature. Minimum gall formation was observed in Aegle marmelos and Prosopis cinerarea treated plants. Use of Aegle marmelos and Prosopis cinerarea (both as aqueous extracts and dry powder) is recommended for the management of root knot disease both in vitro and in vivo. Sustained ecofriendly strategies like use of leaf powders can help farmers in controlling root knot diseases in plants as well as retaining soil nutrition and health and should therefore be encouraged.

Keywords: Medicinal plants, leaf extracts, nematostatic, egg hatching, Meloidogyne incognita

Department of Botany, University of Rajasthan, Jaipur-302004

Introduction

Medicinal plants as botanical pesticides are readily available in many places, often cheaper than their synthetic counter parts and their crude extracts are easy to prepare even by farmers. These are also less likely or slow down the development of resistance or resurgence in pests. Leaves, root and valuable constituents of the plants have been used by most of the researchers for nematicidal activities [1], [2]. The use of botanical pesticides is now emerging as one of the prime means to protect crops. In India, botanical pesticides are available in many plants for which deep search and testing is required as many of them are still unexplored. As they are available in bulk, they are expected to be cheaper in comparison to synthetic chemicals. Hence, to make their use more meaningful, economical, feasible and environmentally safe, research efforts are needed to find out the toxic components present in them and their mode of action. Plant-parasitic nematodes are causing great damage to agricultural and horticultural crops. Hence, biopesticides of botanical origin have become focus of attention today for facing the nematode problems in an eco-friendly manner [3]. Soil nematodes like the root knot nematode, Meloidogyne incognita, found in arid and semi arid soils of Rajasthan in India, attack roots and cause great loss to crops and other plants of economic value. Therefore, a need was felt to explore the indigeneous plants of Rajasthan state to control root knot nematode disease of coleus.

Previous researchers have also worked extensively in utilization of plant extracts in various forms in disease control. Fresh leaf extracts of Datura stramonium, Calotropis procera, Verbesena enceloides, Parthenium hysterophorus, Morus alba, Phyllanthus amarus, Eichhornea crassipes, Ricinus communis, Jatropha curcas, Azadirachta indica, Tinospora cordifolia, Clerodendron multiflorum, Catharanthus roseus and Adhatoda vesica were tested against root-knot nematode, Meloidogyne incognita and wilt fungus, Fusarium oxysporum f.sp. cumini infesting cumin [4]. Chopped leaves of P. juliflora have shown a great effect in suppressing populations of the nematode Meloidogyne incognita [5]. The allelopathic effect of P. juliflora may be due to the presence of phenolic compounds in the leaves [6]. Crude extracts from Prosopis species caused mortality of another nematode, Meloidogyne javanica, causal agent of root knot disease in okra. Use of leaves as a soil amendment significantly reduced knot galls on okra roots [7]. Mixtures of P. juliflora plant extracts with those from Paecilomyces lilacinus were found to increase effectiveness against some nematodes and also against root infecting fungi [7], [8]. Fresh leaf extracts of Lawsonia inermis and Prosopis juliflora have also been tested against this pathogen [9].

Natural products with nematicidal potential have been identified by testing the effect of plant extracts (from leaves, stems, fruits and seeds), oil extracts, plant exudates and plant volatiles on nematodes that infect plants [10], [11].The toxicity of Moringa oleifera, Cassia fistula, Anethum sowa, Annona squamosa and Azadirachta indica was tested against root-knot and reniform nematode [12]. Leaf extracts of two latex-bearing plants such as Calotropis procera and Thevetia peruviana were used as bare-root dip treatment for the management of phytonematodes, Meloidogyne incognita [13]. The influence of organic additives on root-knot disease in roots of tomato plants has also been evaluated [14].

The effectiveness of some indigenous plant extracts like Azadirachta indica (Neem); Cannabis sativa (Hemp/Akotaba); Calotropis procera (Bomubomu); Carica papaya (Pawpaw/Ibepe); Cassia alata (Asunwon); Chromolaena odorata (Siam weed/Akintola); Jatropha gossypiifolia (Lapalapa); Ficus exasperate (Ipin); Mitracarpum verticillatum (Irawo ile); Nicotiana tabacum (Taba); Ocimum gratissimum (Efinrin); Parkia biglobosa (Irugba-oso) and Vernonia amygdalina (Bitter leaf/Ewuroas) as inhibitors of egg hatching in root knot nematode (Meloidogyne incognita race 2) [15].

Piper longum, Adhatoda vasica, Withania somnifera, Cymbopogon jwarancusa and Carica papaya have been evaluated for their hatching inhibitory potentials to egg masses of root knot nematode Meloidogyne incognita [16]. Similiarily, the effect of bark extract of different plant species viz., Azadirachta indica, Acacia nilotica, Emblica officinalis, Eucalyptus citriodora, Mangifera indica and Terminalia arjuna at varying concentration levels on the hatching of Meloidogyne incognita has been studied [17]. Some herbal powders and their aqueous extracts were evaluated for increased plant growth, caused mortality of Meloidogyne javanica second-stage juveniles (J2s), egg hatch inhibition, and reduction in the infection rate [18]. Different concentrations of leaf extract of Persian lilac, Melia azedarach were studied to control the root knot nematode, Meloidogyne incognita on chickpea, Cicer arietinum L. var. "Avarodhi" [19]. Egg-masses and 2nd stage juveniles of Meloidogyne incognita when exposed to aqueous extracts from fresh leaves of Calotropis procera, Azadirachta indica, Clerodendrum inerme and Lantana camara reduced the hatching of egg-masses whereas the most reduction occurred in Calotropis procera and the least in Lantana camara .Most mortality of 2nd stage juveniles was observed in leaf extracts of Azadirachta indica and least in Calotropis procera [20].

The effect of two organic amendments viz:-Bitter leaf (BL) and Cashew seed kernel (CSK) was seen in the control of Meloidogyne incognita on soybean and CSK amendment was more effective on nematodes than BL. The results further showed that both amendments could be used in nematode control and therefore recommended in soybean fields to control nematodes [21].

The potentials of organic soil amendments (OSA) to control plant parasitic nematodes (PPN) infection in yam production in Ghana were investigated. The ability of organic soil amendments; neem (Azadirachta indica A. Juss) seed powder, cocoa (Theobroma cacao L.) bean testa powder and cowitch (Mucuna pruriens L.) seed powder to suppress PPN in yam were compared to Fulan (a synthetic pesticide) and a non-treated control [22].

Present study was undertaken to see the effects of plants growing in arid and semi arid regions of Rajasthan and nearby states on Meloidogyne incognita infested Coleus forskohlii plants

Material and Methods

Test plant was Coleus forskohlii Briq. [syn: Coleus barbatus (Andr.) Benth.] Singh et. al. which is a plant of Indian origin belonging to mint family Lamiaceae and is an important medicinal crop containing forskolin in their roots. It is used in glaucoma, cardiac problems, eczema, asthma, etc. The present study was conducted to evaluate organic amendments in the form of dry leaf powder of various trees and shrubs abundantly present locally in arid and semi arid regions of Rajasthan and nearby states. Two sets of experiments were conducted in all:

In vitro evaluation of locally available plant leaves against M. incognita egg hatching:

The method followed for obtaining qualities of clean M. incognita eggs was that of Mc Clure [25]. Fresh leaves of the plants (Thevetia peruviana, Withania somnifera, Lantana camara, Clerodendron aculeatum, Bougainvillea spectabilis, Aegle marmelos, Prosopis cinerarea, Nerium oleander and Cassia fistula) were collected and washed in sterile water. Two commercial formulations Vircon and Nemacon were also used. Leaf extract was prepared by grinding 2g each of leaves in 5ml distilled water passed through a four- ply muslin cloth and centrifuged for 5 minutes at 4000 rpm and filtered through Whatman's filter paper no.-1. The stock solution, thus obtained was used for evaluating their nematicidal activity and designated as hundred per cent. From this Standard / Stock Solution (S.S.) (100%), required concentrations (25%, 50%, 75%) were prepared by adding distilled water. Distilled water alone served as control. For the hatching experiment special polyvinyl chloride (PVC) tubing (4cm dia; 0.5 mm high) were cut and 26μm stainless steel screen was sealed to ring. Four P.V.C. legs were attached to elevate each ring.

Effect on hatching was evaluated on two mature egg masses of uniform size suspended in the extracts and water (check) replicated three times in cavity blocks. The cavity blocks were kept at 26±1°C. The number of hatched juveniles was counted after 24, 48 and 72 hours of treatments. After every 24 hrs, test solution was discarded after counting the number of hatched larvae and the unhatched eggs in the sieve were placed in freshly made test solution. This was done to eliminate the effect of bacterial action on the unhatched eggs. Now, the unhatched eggs were placed in distilled water for another 24 hrs. to record further hatching, if any.

Efficacy of dry leaf Powders Against M. incognita

The leaves were used in pot trials in form of dry powder against Meloidogyne management. The leaves used were of 6 trees and 7 shrubs Thevetia peruviana, Withania somnifera, Lantana camara, Clerodendron aculeatum, Lawsonia inermis Bougainvillea spectabilis, Aegle marmelos, Prosopis cinerarea, Nerium oleander, Ficus bengalensis, Ficus religiosa, Cassia fistula and Anthocephalous kadamba in the first experiment. In the second experiment, dry leaf powders of Aegle marmelos, Clerodendron aculeatum, Lantana camara, Lawsonia inermis, Prosopis cinerarea, Thevetia peruviana, Withania somnifera,, were mixed with the soil in the pots at the two inoculum levels were used of 10gm and 20gm (15 days before the transplanting of Coleus) along with two commercial formulations Vircon and Nemacon were also used along with frequent watering, this gave sufficient time for decomposition of leaf powders. After establishment of the cutting of coleus, nematode inoculation was done (approx.1000 J2/pot). 30 days later, the organic amendment (leaf dry powder) was repeated. Nematode alone and uninoculated served as control parameters.

Observations were taken after 160 days for shoot and root length, shoot and root weight, tuber length and no. of tubers, no. of galls and their root knot index. All data were statistically analyzed and found significant.

Results

In our study best results were obtained by Aegle marmelos and Prosopis cineraria treated plants at maximum dose in reducing root knot infection.

There was an increase in hatching of juveniles with increasing time and dilution with maximum hatching was in control (D.W.) after 72 hrs. There was a linear relationship between egg hatch and concentration of the plant extracts. All the extracts showed inhibition in hatching, with Aegle marmelos treatment as the best followed by Prosopis cinerarea treatment at both lower and higher concentrations thus indicating their inhibitory action on egg hatching. However, there was a toxic effect observed on J2 larvae. (TABLE 1)

It appears that the egg shells of M. incognita are permeable to the toxic materials contained in the plant extracts used in this investigation, consequently, inhibiting the developing juveniles. In all cases, at lower concentrations, the nematicidal activity started diminishing, implying that leaf extracts, when used at higher concentrations was successful in inhibiting egg hatch and survival of juveniles in vitro.

The dry leaves powder improved plant growth characters of Coleus forskohlii over control. There was marked increase in shoot length, root length, shoot weight, root weight, tuber length, though they produced thick but less in no. tubers in comparision to control. (TABLE 2). The addition of these organic amendments was very effective in reducing number of galls. The disease was reduced with the treatment of Aegle marmelos and Prosopis cinerarea.

There was an improvement in tuber quality and could be due to some principles are absorbed by coleus roots, bring about acquired resistance and changes in biochemical composition of plant and such roots exert a broad spectrum influence on pathogens of Meloidogyne incognita and increased root tuber yield.

All plant extracts, when tried at higher doses were found to be controlling root knot nematode and Aegle marmelos and Prosopis cinerarea were highly effective in reducing root knot disease. (TABLE 3). Our results indicate that farmers can use leaf powders of medicinal plants to control root knot disease of crops of agricultural and medicinal value. Such results have also been found when the nematicidal and fungicidal effect of plant materials of two Iranian native plant species, Ferulago angulata and Zataria multiflora was evaluated [23]. In another investigation the efficacy of Trichoderma harzianum and Moringa oleifera at various concentrations (S, S/2, S/4) and in combinations on the reproduction, egg hatching and juvenile mortality of Meloidogyne javanica on eggplant was also evaluated both in vitro as well as in vivo [24].

Tables

Table 1: In vitro evaluation of leaf extract of different locally available plants on hatching of Meloidogyne incognita

Treatments	Botanicals	Duration in hrs.	% of Juveniles hatched				
			100.00 (SS)	75.00 (SS)	50.00 (SS)	25.00 (SS)	Control (DW)
A	Thevetia peruviana	24.0	12.3	21.3	28.6	33.0	65.3
		48.0	14.6	23.0	35.6	40.6	74.3
		72.0	20.6	32.0	38.0	43.3	86.5
B	Withania somnifera	24.0	10.6	21.0	43.0	45.0	65.3
		48.0	17.0	32.3	39.0	51.0	74.3
		72.0	38.6	43.0	49.0	56.3	86.5
C	Lantana camara	24.0	10.3	15.0	19.0	30.6	65.3
		48.0	12.6	14.3	24.0	32.3	74.3
		72.0	17.3	15.6	26.0	41.3	86.5
D	Clerodendron aculeatum	24.0	5.0	6.3	8.3	11.3	65.3
		48.0	5.6	7.0	10.0	14.3	74.3
		72.0	6.0	13.3	16.0	18.3	86.5
E	Bougainvillea spectabilis	24.0	9.6	21.3	25.0	33.0	65.3
		48.0	15.3	29.0	33.3	37.6	74.3
		72.0	30.6	35.6	41.0	44.6	86.5
F	Aegle marmelos	24.0	3.6	5.6	7.0	11.3	65.3
		48.0	4.33	6.3	9.6	12.0	74.3
		72.0	6.33	7.6	11.3	13.3	86.5
G	Prosopis cineraria	24.0	4.33	7.0	13.0	21.0	65.3
		48.0	6.67	10.0	17.3	25.6	74.3
		72.0	8.67	14.3	25.3	26.0	86.5
H	Nerium oleander	24.0	4.33	7.6	13.6	19.3	65.3
		48.0	6.33	9.3	15.0	20.6	74.3
		72.0	7.33	11.3	18.0	25.0	86.5
I	Cassia fistula	24.0	15.3	33.6	39.00	42.0	65.3
		48.0	21.0	38.0	45.6	45.3	74.3
		72.0	25.6	41.3	46.3	50.0	86.5
J	Vircon	24.0	46.0	52.0	56.0	64.0	65.3
		48.0	52.3	54.0	66.0	73.3	74.3
		72.0	64.6	71.0	75.6	84.3	86.5
K	Nemacon	24.0	21.0	25.3	31.0	45.0	65.3
		48.0	24.6	30.6	54.3	50.4	74.3
		72.0	32.3	36.0	40.3	53.2	86.5
CD at 5%			0.2	0.2	0.2	0.2	0.26

*Values are mean of three replicates SS-stock solution, DW-distilled water.
*Two mature egg masses were used (each with approx 200 eggs)

Table 2: effect of dry leaf powders in the biomanagement of root knot disease (meloidogyne incognita) in Coleus forskohlii Briq.

Treatments	Botanicals	Length (cm)		Weight gm)		Tuber Length cm)	No. of tubers	No. of galls	R.K.I
		Shoot	root	Shoot	root				
A	Bougainvillea spectabilis	31.6	29.3	100.0	24.0	14.6	8.3	110.0	5.0
B	Withania somnifera	41.6	31.3	106.6	24.6	16.6	9.3	85.0	4.3
C	Clerodendron aculeatum	53.3	45.0	183.3	28.3	26.0	10.6	93.3	4.3
D	Lantana camara	42.0	35.6	156.6	26.6	19.0	8.0	85.0	4.3
E	Nerium oleander	45.0	33.3	130.0	28.3	15.0	9.0	82.6	4.0
F	Lawsonia inermis	43.3	46.6	165.0	26.6	18.3	8.6	106.6	5.0
G	Prosopis cinerarea	51.3	26.3	176.6	32.6	24.0	9.6	10.0	2.3
H	Aegle marmelos	44.0	24.6	140.0	27.6	22.3	9.6	9.6	2.3
I	Cassia fistula	44.6	39.0	118.3	23.0	22.0	9.0	91.6	4.6
J	Ficus religiosa	60.0	36.6	80.0	20.0	18.3	8.3	110.0	5.0
K	Anthocephalous kadamba	34.0	35.3	135.0	20.3	18.6	10.3	116.6	5.0
L	Ficus bengalensis	32.3	29.0	120.0	24.3	20.0	9.0	100.0	4.6
M	Thevetia peruviana	34.0	34.0	105.0	23.3	21.6	9.0	20.0	3.0
	Nematode alone	26.6	23.3	46.6	13.0	7.3	7.6	130.0	5.0
	Control	43.3	27.0	105.0	25.6	20.6	14.6	0.0	0.0
	CD at 5%	4.1	3.5	13.1	2.7	2.1	0.9	3.8	0.1

Table 3: effect of diff doses of dry leaf powders in the biomanagement of root knot disease (Meloidogyne incognita) in Coleus forskohlii Briq.

Treatments	Botanicals	Doses (gms)	Length (cm)		Weight (gms)		Tuber length (cm)	No. of Tubers	No. of galls	R. K.I
			shoot	Root	Shoot	Root				
1	Aegle marmelos	10	58.3	12.3	30.0	18.3	10.6	9.6	20.6	3.0
		20	61.6	23.6	90.0	28.3	18.3	10.0	9.6	2.3
2	Clerodendron aculeatum	10	64.0	16.3	100.0	18.3	10.6	11.0	93.3	4.3
		20	71.6	20.6	116.6	26.3	33.3	10.6	85.0	4.6
3	Lantana camara	10	62.6	21.0	56.6	17.6	19.6	10.6	85.0	4.0
		20	71.6	26.6	106.6	24.6	20.6	14.0	21.6	3.0
4	Lawsonia inermis	10	58.3	18.0	101.6	19.0	11.6	10.6	110.0	5.0
		20	73.3	38.3	105.0	26.6	23.3	11.6	101.6	4.6
5	Prosopis cinerarea	10	65.6	13.3	96.6	18.0	9.3	8.0	12.3	2.6
		20	66.6	30.0	116.6	30.0	16.6	9.6	10.0	2.3
6	Thevetia peruviana	10	68.3	21.0	51.6	16.0	11.6	10.3	30.6	3.0
		20	74.3	24.0	76.6	23.3	17.0	12.6	20.0	2.6
7	Withania somnifera	10	56.6	18.3	91.6	18.6	11.6	10.0	103.3	4.6
		20	65.3	22.6	93.3	22.6	12.3	11.6	91.6	4.6
8	Vircon	10	58.3	23.0	43.3	14.0	14.6	10.6	116.6	5.0
		20	64.6	28.6	80.0	23.3	24.6	16.6	100.0	4.6
9	Nemacon	10	65.3	21.0	90.0	20.0	11.6	12.3	110.0	5.0
		20	70.0	23.6	98.3	20.0	14.0	13.0	110.0	5.0
8	Mixture	10	64.3	14.3	90.0	15.6	13.0	13.6	116.6	5.0
		20	70.0	16.3	110.0	20.0	16.3	15.0	100.0	4.6
	nematode alone		26.6	21.3	46.6	13.0	7.3	7.6	150.0	5.0
	Control		42.3	27.0	103.3	25.6	20.6	14.6	0.0	0.0
	cd at 5%		2.2	2.5	9.6	1.7	3.0	0.9	3.2	0.1

Conclusion

Amongst the plants tested, leaf extracts of almost all the plants exhibited a gradual increase in hatching of eggs from their higher concentration to lower concentration treatments. All the plant extracts significantly inhibited hatching but of minimum no. hatched larvae was observed in Aegle marmelos. From our investigations, the best results were from use Aegle marmelos and Prosopis cinerarea (both as water extracts and dry powder) and therefore, they are highly recommended for the management of root knot disease both in vitro and in vivo. This method of controlling the root-knot nematode is promising. These results are supported by previous researchers also support the use of medicinal plants as a measure of disease management through their investigations and found Aegle marmelos and Prosopis sp as very effective in nematode management. Other researchers have also found supportive results and use of plant extracts as organic amendments is highly effective in increasing plant growth and reducing the incidence of root knot disease.

Sustained ecofriendly strategies like use of leaf powders can help farmers in controlling root knot diseases in plants as well as retaining soil nutrition and health and should therefore be encouraged. Their availability in huge amount naturally is a beneficial factors for the farmers. However, for commercial use in vast amounts the active chemical constituent needs to be elucidated and commercialized.

References

1. Muhammad Murslain, Nazir Javed, Sajid Aleem Khan, Hafiz Ullah Khan,Huma Abbas and Muhammad Kamran, Combined Efficacy of Moringa oleifera Leaves and a Fungus, Trichoderma harzianum Against Meloidogyne javanica on Eggplant ,Pakistan J. Zool., 46 (3), 2014, 827-832.
2. Haseeb, A., Viquar, A. and Shukla, P.K., Comparative efficacy of pesticides, bio-control agents and botanicals against Meloidogyne – Fusarium oxysporum disease complex of Vigna mungo, Ann. Pl. Protec.Sci., 13 (2), 2005, 434-437.
3. Archana U Singh and Prasad D, Management of Plant-parasitic Nematodes by the Use of Botanicals, J Plant Physiol Pathol, 2 (1), 2014
4. Sharma, N. and Trivedi, P.C. , Screening of leaf extracts of some plants for their nematicidal and fungicidal properties against Meloidogyne incognita and Fusarium oxysporum, Asian J. Exp. Sci., 16(1&2) , 2002, 21-28.
5. Sundarababu, R., sankarnarayana, C. and Vedivelu, S, Nematode management with plant products, Indian J. Nematol., 23(2), 1993, 177-178.
6. Chellamuthu, V., Balasusbramanian, T.N., Rajarajanand, A. and Palaniappan, S.N., Allelopathic influence of Prosopis juliflora (Swartz) DC. on field crops, Allelopathy Journal, 4 , 1997, 291-302.
7. Ehteshamul-Haque, S., Abid, M., Sultana, V., Ara, J. and Ghaffar, A., Use of organic amendments on the efficacy of biocontrol agents in the control of root-rot and root-knot disease complex of okra, Nematol. Medit., 24, 1996a, 13-16.
8. Ehteshamul-Haque, S., Abid, M., Sultana, V., Ara, J., Sattar, A. and Ghaffar, A. ,Use of Prosopis spp., in the control of root-knot disease of okra, Pak. J. Nematol., 14, 1996b,101-106.
9. Chandrasekharan, A. and Rajappan, K., Effect of plant extracts, antagonists and chemicals (individual and combined) on foliar anthracnose and pod blight of soyabean, J. Mycol. Pl. Patho. 32(1,) 2002, 25-27.
10. Qamar, F., Begum, S., Raza, S.M., Wahab, A. and Siddiqui, B.S., Nematicidal natural products from the aerial parts of Lantana camara Linn. Natural Product Res., 19, 2005, 609–613.
11. Pandey, S. and Trivedi, P. C., Comparative efficacy of deoiled cakes and leaf powders of indigenous plants on population dynamics of Heterodera cajani on cowpea, J. Indian Bot. Soc., 82, 2002,119-122.

12. Prasad, A. and Tomar, S., Toxicity of plant extracts against Root knot nematode and Reniform nematodes, Ann. Pl. Protec Sci., 2, 2007, 469-539.

13. Tiyagi, S.A., Mahmood, I. and Rizvi, R., Application of some latex-bearing plants for the management of phytonematodes infecting tomato and eggplant. Thai J. Agricult. Sci., 42 (4), 2009, 183-189.

14. Ahmad, F., Rather, M.A. and Siddiqui, M.A., Nematicidal Activity of leaf extracts from Lantana camara L. against Meloidogyne incognita (Kofoid and White) Chitwood and its use to manage root infection of Solanum melongena L. , Brazilian Archives Biol and Technol.,53 (3), 2010, 543-548.

15. Adegbite, A.A., Effects of Some Indigenous plant extracts as inhibitors of egg hatch in root-knot nematode Meloidogyne incognita race 2, American J. Exp Agri, 1(3), 2011, 96-100.

16. Usman, A., Rehman, B. and Siddiqui, M.A., Effect of some botanical extracts for the management of Meloidogyne incognita infecting on Eggplant, Biosciences International, 1(1), 2012, 12-15.

17. Abbasia, H., Ambreen A. and Rushda S., Effect of bark extract of different plant species on the hatching of Meloidogyne incognita. Archives of Phytopathology and Plant Protection, 45 (10), 2012, 1201-1203.

18. Moosavi, M.R., Nematicidal effect of some herbal powders and their aqueous extracts against Meloidogyne javanica. Nematropica, 42, 2012, 48-56.

19. Rehman, B., Parihar, K., Ganai, M.A. and Siddiqui, M.A., Management of root knot nematode Meloidogyne incognita affecting chickpea, Cicer arietinum for sustainable production, Biosciences International, 1(1) 2012,1-5.

20. Abdul Nazir Chedekal, Effect of four leaf extracts on egg hatching and juvenile mortalityof root knot nematode Meloidogyne incognita ,IJALS, , 6(1) 2013.

21. Umar, I. and Aji, M.B., Effect of Botanicals in the Control of Meloidogyne incognita (Kofoid and White) Chitwood on Soybean [Glycine max (L) Merr.], IOSR Journal of Agriculture and Veterinary Science, 2319-2372 (4), 2013, 43-45.

22. Osei, K, E. Otoo, Y, Danso, J. Adomako, A. Agyeman and J. S. Asante, Organic soil amendments in nematode management in yam production, Nematropica ,43, 2013,78-82.
23. N. Ghazalbash and M. Abdollahi , Effect of medicinal plant extracts on physiological changes in tomato, inoculated with Meloidogyne javanica and Fusarium oxysporum f. sp. lycopersici , Pakistan Journal of Nematology, 31 (1), 2013, 21-37.
24. Muhammad Murslain, Nazir Javed, Sajid Aleem Khan, Hafiz Ullah Khan, Huma Abbas and Muhammad Kamran, Combined Efficacy of Moringa oleifera Leaves and a Fungus, Trichoderma harzianum Against Meloidogyne javanica on Eggplant, Pakistan J. Zool., 46(3), 2014, 827-832
25. McClure, M.A., Trunk, T.H. and Misaghi,I., A method for obtaining quantities of clean Meloidogyne eggs, J. Nematol., 5, 1973, 230.

Chaptee-XVIII

Flora and Forest Ecosystems in Morocco: Diversity, Threat and Conservation

Mohammed Sghir Taleb*

Abstract

Located at the northwest corner of the African continent between 21 ° and 36 ° north latitude and between the 1st and the 17th degree of west longitude, Morocco with a total area of 715,000 km2 enjoys a privileged position with a coastline of 3 446 km long opening to the Mediterranean and the Atlantic Ocean. Its privileged location with a double coastline and its diverse mountain with four major mountain ranges: the Rif, Middle Atlas, High Atlas and Anti Atlas with altitudes exceeding 2000 m in the Rif, 3000 m in the Middle Atlas and 4000 m in the High Atlas.

The Moroccan mountains are characterized by an important forest genetic diversity represented by a rich and varied flora and many ecosystems: forest, preforest, presteppe, steppe, Sahara that spans a range of bioclimatic zones: arid, semiarid, subhumid and humid. The vascular flora of Morocco has 3913 species and subspecies in 1298 (including 426 sub-species types), distributed among 155 families and 981 genera. The number of endemic species amounted to 640 (16%) and 280 subspecies (32%). The rare or endangered flora species is estimated to be 463 and 1284 subspecies.

However, this diversity is subjected to many natural pressures (climate change, parasitic attacks...) and antropic pressures (clearing, overgrazing etc.).
Conscious of the risks that weigh on biodiversity, Morocco set a strategy of biodiversity management that focus on programs of in-situ conservation and more 154 protected areas in Morocco are proposed for a management of their natural resources.

This chapter focuses on ecological diversity, flora, ecosystem of Moroccan mountains while focusing on the major threats and conservation strategies developed by Morocco.

Keywords: Flora, ecosystem, diversity, threat, conservation, Morocco.

Institut Scientifique, Université Mohammed V-Agdal, Avenue Ibn Battouta, B.P. 703, Rabat, Morocco

Introduction

Located at the northwest corner of the African continent between 21 ° and 36 ° north latitude and between the 1st and the 17th degree of west longitude, Morocco enjoys a privileged position with a coastline of 3446 km long opening of the Mediterranean and the Atlantic Ocean.

With a total area of 715,000 km2, is located at the intersection of large very distinct sets between the Mediterranean Sea to the north, the Atlantic Ocean to the west and northwest and the Sahara desert southeast. Its privileged location with a double coastline and its diverse mountain with four major mountain ranges: the Rif, the Middle Atlas, High Atlas and Anti-Atlas with altitudes respectively exceed 2000 m, 3000 m and 4000 m and 3000 m.

The climate of Morocco, Mediterranean, undergoes ocean, mountains and Saharan influences. It is essentially characterized by two distinct seasons: a hot, dry summer and a short winter with brutal and concentrated precipitation. Variable depending on the region, the climate of Morocco is also marked by a strong annual and interannual irregularity. Thus, average annual temperatures are around 10 ° C, while the average maximum temperature can reach 45 ° C in the center of the country and 50 ° C within the Saharan regions. The average annual minimum temperatures range from 5 ° C to 15 ° C depending on the region with the absolute minimum of about 0 ° C (may even reach -3 to - 10 ° C) in the mountains and surrounding areas.

Precipitation, in general, decreases from north to south and are only more important in the mountains where they reach 2000 mm in the Rif. They are less than 150 mm in the pre-Saharan and Saharan regions. Morocco is characterized by high genetic diversity represented by a rich and varied flora and highly diverse ecosystems: forest, steppe, grassland which extend over different types of climates: arid, semi-arid, sub-humid, humid and high mountain climate.

In this article we give a brief description and caracterization of Morocco views flora and vegetation. We also focus on threats and and the measures proposed by Morocco to reverse the trends of degradation.

Methodology

The methodology is mainly based on a literature review of principal theses and projects for the conservation of flora and vegetation.

Results

Overview of Plant Genetic Resources

This diversity of topography and climate generates high ecosystem diversity with a very significant range of different natural environments: forest formations, pre-Saharan and Saharan formations, steppe formations and important plant diversity.

Forest ecosystems diversity

The main natural forest ecosystems of Morocco [4] are organized by the Fir (Abies maroccana Trabut), the Atlas cedar (Cedrus libani A. Richard subsp. atlantica (Endl.) Batt. & Trabut), the holm oak (Quercus rotundifolia Lam.), the cork oak (Quercus suber L.), red juniper (Juniperus phoenicea L.), Cade juniper (Juniperus thurifera L.), the pines (Pinus halepensis Miller and Pinus pinaster Aiton), Thuja (Tetraclinis articulata (Vahl) Masters), the Atlas Cypress (Cupressus atlantica Gaussen), the argan tree (Argania spinosa (L.) Skeels).

Steppe ecosystems [1] are organized by Juniperus communis L., Ceratonia siliqua L., Pistacia atlantica Desf., Stipa tenacissima, Artemisia spp., spiny xerophytics (Alyssum spinosum L., Bupleurum spinosum Gouan, Erinacea anthyllis Link., Vella mairei Humbert and Cytisus balansae (Boiss.) Ball) and Saharan Acacias (Acacia raddiana Savi, Acacia seyal Delile and Acacia ehrenbergiana Hayne).

Table 1: Area of the main mountain ecosystems in Morocco

Ecosystems	Area (ha)
Quercus rotundifolia	1 415 201
Cedrus atlantica	133 653
Argania spinose	871 210
Quercus suber	377 482
Juniperus spp. (J. thurifera, J. phoenicea and J. oxycedrus)	244 837
Reforestation	490 518
Others	102 207
Tetraclinis articulate	565 798
Pinus spp. (P. halepensis, P. maritima…)	82 115
Quergus faginea	9 091
Abies maroccana	3 174
Others	5 764
Total	4 301 050

Flora Diversity

The vascular flora of Morocco [2] has 3913 species and subspecies in 1298 (including 426 sub-species types), distributed among 155 families and 981 genera. The number of endemic species amounted to 640 (16%) and 280 subspecies (32%). The rare or endangered flora species is estimated to be 463 and 1284 subspecies. This species richness is heavily represented in the forest ecosystem, where nearly two-thirds of the species, and the remaining third is divided mainly between the steppe formations and wetland habitats. The mountainous regions of the Rif and Atlas are the most important sectors in terms of endemism.

Mushrooms and lichens are also relatively well represented with respectively around 820 and 700 species. Multicellular algae have nearly 700 species with 489 macro-algae and nearly 200 species of phytoplankton. However, this exceptional natural wealth has for decades been subject to increasing pressure by human and climatic conditions characterized by a succession of droughts.

Major Threats to Forest Ecosystems

The main threats to the Moroccan forest ecosystems (Fig.1) are overgrazing and deforestation. Climate change, including increased drought, urbanization and forest fire is a threat that seems to materialize and may increase in the future. Degradation of vegetation cover is accompanied by the rarefaction of species up sometimes at risk of extinction and also soil erosion.

Figure Showing Major threats to Forest Ecosystems

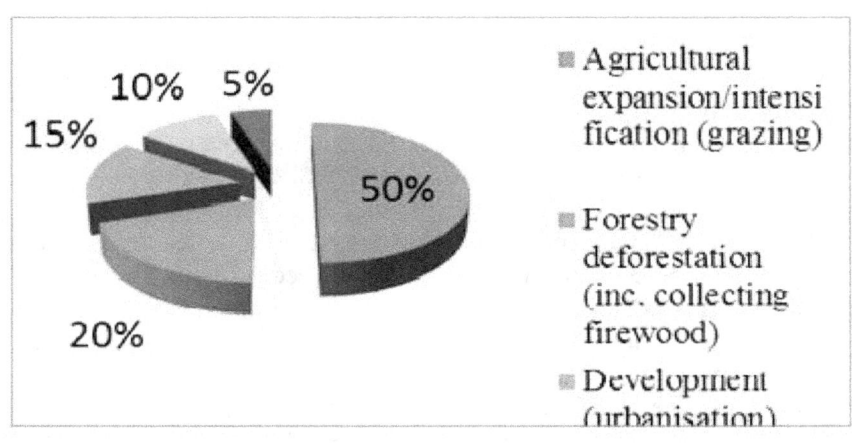

Conscious of threats to biodiversity, Morocco has implemented a strategy of in situ conservation based on a network of protected areas.

In Situ Conservation

The conservation of forest genetic resources is based primarily on in situ conservation (National Parks, Nature Reserves, Biosphere Reserves), in its natural condition, in protected areas. In the case of genetic resources of forest trees, this method of preservation is associated with the ex situ conservation (Botanical Gardens, arboretas etc.). The main objective of this network of protected areas has focuses on the following outcomes:

Secure the conservation of a representative sample of biodiversity, ecosystems and the most remarkable natural landscapes;

- Manage and develop these protected areas so as to harmonize conservation and local development.;
- Make these important protected areas planning for economic and social development tool;
- Promote participatory and partnership approach to co-management of protected areas;

Morocco currently has a large number of Protected Areas, including 10 national parks and 146 Sites of Biological and Ecological Interest classified as Nature Reserves, 138 in continental domain (including 29 wetlands) and 38 reserves in coastal area. 21% of SBEI receive support for facilities and management and 91% are subject to restrictions necessary for sustainable management of natural resources such as the prohibition of hunting, fishing, opening careers or massive exploitation.

Biological and Ecological Interest Sites in Biosphere Reserves

The geographical distribution of protected areas covers all regions of the country with a very satisfactory representation of major ecosystems and major habitat types. Protected Areas are distributed throughout Morocco and cover the majority of natural ecosystems. A significant number of Protected Areas are located in mountainous areas and are created for the conservation of biodiversity and some remarkable ecosystems as Cedrus atlantica, Cupressus atlantica, Dracena draco subsp. ajgal and Abies maroccana. Talassemtane National Park, National Park of Tazekka, National Park of Ifrane, Easter High Atlas National Park and Toubkal National Park are the most important protected areas in mountains. In addition to these National Parks, other interesting sites like Bou Hachem, Bou Naceur, Bou Iblane, Tichoukt, Ayachi, Maasker, Mgoun, Tamga,

Krouz, Kest and Aghbar mountains and Mamora forest have identified by Morocco as Sites of Biological and Ecological Interest and as Important Plant Areas (IPAs) due to the presence of remarkable ecosystems and flora with a high degree of endemism.

Table 2: Main Mountain Protected Areas

Protected Areas	Remarkable ecosystems	Flora diversity
Bouhachem mountain	Quercus faginea, Quercus pyrenaica, Quercus suber, Pinus pinaster ssp maghrebiana, Cedrus atlantica.	16 endemic taxa; 14 rare taxa; 20 very rare taxa [3]
Parc National de Talassemtane	Abien maroccana, Cedrus atlantica, Quercus ilex, Quercus suber, Pinus halepensis, Pinus nigra, Pinus pinaster, Teraclinis articulata.	47 endemic taxa; 19 rare taxa ; 26 very rare taxa [3]
Bou-Naceur mountain	Cedrus atlantica, Quercus rotundifolia, Juniperus thurifera, Juniperus phenicea, Pinus halepensis, spiny xerophytics.	556 taxa ; 92 endemic taxa; 5 rare taxa; 10 very rare taxa [10]
Bou Iblane mountain	Cedrus atlantica, Quercus rotundifolia, Juniperus thurifera, Juniperus phenicea, spiny xerophytics.	500 taxa ; 25 endemic taxa; 9 rare taxa ; 8 very rare taxa . [3]
National Park of Tazekka	Cedrus atlantica, Quercus rotundifolia, Quercus suber.	500 taxa ; 31 endemic taxa; 18 rare taxa ; 31 very rare taxa [3]
Tichoukt mountain	Cedrus atlantica, Quercus rotundifolia, Juniperus thurifera, Juniperus phenicea, Juniperus communis, spiny xerophytics.	300 taxa ; 22 endemic taxa; 7 rare taxa ; 9 very rare taxa [3]
National Park of Ifrane	Cedrus atlantica, Quercus rotundifolia, Juniperus thurifera, spiny xerophytics.	1015 taxa ; 1/4 endemic taxa (25% are special to the Park) ; 13 rare taxa ; 24 very rare taxa [3]
Easter High Atlas National Park	Cedrus atlantica, Quercus rotundifolia, Juniperus thurifera, Juniperus phenicea, Pinus halepensis,	More than 400 taxa ; 66 endemic taxa ; 13 rare taxa ; 6 very rare taxa [5]

	spiny xerophytics.	
Ayachi mountain	Cedrus atlantica, Quercus rotundifolia, Juniperus thurifera, Juniperus communis, spiny xerophytics.	260 taxa ; 75 endemic taxa; 9 rare taxa ; 4 very rare taxa [5]
Maâsker mountain	Cedrus atlantica, Quercus rotundifolia, Juniperus thurifera, Juniperus phenicea, Juniperus communis, spiny xerophytics.	150 taxa ; 34 endemic taxa ; 7 rare taxa ; 3 very rare taxa [5]
Krouz mountain	Juniperus phoenicea, Pistacia atlantica.	261 taxa ; 2 endemic taxa ; 7 rare taxa ; 7 very rare taxa [8]
Mgoun mountain	Quercus rotundifolia, Juniperus thurifera, Pinus halepensis, Pinus maritima, Tetraclinis articulata, Xérophytes épineux.	500 taxons ; 54 endemic taxa; 7 rare taxa ; 10 very rare taxa [3]
Tamga forest	Pinus halepensis, Quercus rotundifolia, Tetraclinis articulata, Juniperus phoenicea	366 taxa ; 33 endemic taxa [7]
National Park of Toubkal	Quercus rotundifolia, Juniperus thurifera, spiny xerophytics.	536 taxa ; 164 endemic taxa [9]
Aghbar forest	Cupressus atlantica, Quercus rotundifolia, Juniperus phoenicea, Tetraclinis articulata.	45 endemic taxa; 7 rare taxa ; 13 very rare taxa [3]
Kest, Anezi and Imzi mountains	Dracaena draco ssp. ajgal, Quercus rotundifolia, Tetraclinis articulata.	17 endemic taxa; 2 taxons rares ; 5 very rare taxa [3]
Maamora forest	Quercus suber.	408 taxa ; 26 endemic taxa; 29 rare taxa ; 35 very rare taxa [6]

In addition to national parks, Morocco has four Biosphere Reserves, which are promoting solutions reconciling biodiversity conservation and sustainable use. These are:

- The Biosphere Reserve of Argania spinosa, with an area of 2.5 million hectares in the South West.

- The Biosphere Reserve of Southern Oasis Morocco, declared in 2000, to the oases of southern Morocco, an area of about 7.2 million ha.

- The Intercontinental Biosphere Reserve of the Mediterranean, extending over an area of nearly one million ha, divided almost equally between both Moroccan and Spanish banks. The relevant part of Morocco is located at the Tingitane Peninsula.

- The Biosphere Reserve of cedar ecosystem this Biosphere Reserve, is seen in the Middle and High Atlas. It will include three national parks: National Park of Ifrane, Eastern High Atlas National Park and National Parc of Khénifra created over an area of about 500,000 ha and will declare "Cedrus atlantica ecosystem of the Atlas" World Heritage.

Conclusion

Morocco has a great geographical diversity (plains, low, medium and high mountains, valleys, cliffs etc.) accompanied by climate variability has led to the installation and development of several natural ecosystems occupying large areas of the mountains and a rich and varied flora. The flora of the mountainous areas is characterized by a high degree of endemism and rarity especially on the high peaks that are refuges for rare and endemic flora. This richness is increasingly subject to natural disturbances (drought, parasites, etc.) and anthropogenic pressures (agricultural land clearing, timber harvesting, harvesting of aromatic and medicinal plants, grazing etc.). To reverse these trends, Morocco has developed a strategy for biodiversity conservation based on a network of Protected Areas covering major ecosystems. These Protected Areas are an effective means for the conservation and sustainable management of biodiversity and also for the development of local populations. Despite the achievements in biodiversity conservation, much remains to be done to relieve the pressures of degradation of ecosystems and the flora of mountainous areas for the development of local populations and ensure the availability of natural resources for future generations.

References

1. Taleb M S, El Oualidi J. Steppes and grasslands in Morocco: Diversity, functional ecology and socio-economic role. pp. 1682-1684. Proceedings 22nd International Grassland Congress. Revitalising Grasslands to sustain our communities. 2013

2. Fennane M, Ibn Tattou M. Statistiques et commentaires sur l'inventaire actuel de la flore vasculaire du Maroc. Bulletin de l'Institut Scientifique, Rabat, section Sciences de la Vie, 2012, n°34 (1), p. 1-9.

3. Taleb M S, Fennane M. Zones Importantes pour les Plantes au Maroc dans Zones Importantes pour les Plantes en Méditerranée méridionale et. orientale: Sites prioritaires pour la conservation. Rapport national. 2010.

4. Taleb M S, Fennane M. Forests, steppes and grasslands in Morocco: Diversity, ecological importance and socio-economic role. XXI International Grassland Congress, VIII International Rangeland Congress. Multifunctional Grasslands in a changing World. Vol. 1. Edited by organizing committee of 2008 IGC/IRC Conference 2008.

5. Taleb M S, Fennane M. Diversité floristique du Parc National du Haut Atlas Oriental et des massifs Ayachi et Maâsker (Maroc). Acta Botanica Malacitana 2008; 33: 125-145.

6. Aafi A. Etude de la diversité floristique de l'écosystème de chêne-liège de la forêt de la Maora. Thèse de doctorat es sciences. Institut Agronomique et Vétérinaire Hassan II, Rabat. Maroc. 2007.

7. Ibn Tattou M. Projet de gestion des Aires Protégées (GEF – TF 023494 – MOR). Elaboration des plans de gestion. Etude de Diagnostic. Sibe de TAMGA. Volet Botanique. Rapport final. 2006.

8. Ibn Tattou M. Projet de gestion des Aires Protégées (GEF – TF 023494 – MOR). Elaboration des plans de gestion. Etude de Diagnostic. Jbel Krouz. Volet Botanique. Rapport final. 2006.

9. Ouhammou A. Flore et végétation du Parc National de Toubkal (Haut-Atlas de Marrakech, Maroc): typologie, écologie et conservation. Thèse de doctorat d'état es-sciences. Faculté des Sciences Semlalia, Université Cadi Ayyad. Marrakech. Maroc. 2005.

10. Rahou A. Contribution à une étude floristique et biogéographique du Massif du Bou-Naceur (Moyen Atlas Oriental, Maroc). Thèse de troisième cycle. Facultdes Sciences. Université Mohammed premier. Oujda. Maroc. 1992.

Chapter XIX

Securitization of Climate Change: Issues, Concerns and Implications

Sachna*

Abstract

If twentieth century was the century marked by fears of wars and struggle to get supremacy over power then twenty first century is the century marked by fears of climate change and struggles to get as much energy resources as one can. The concept of security is undergoing change with the emergence of new kind of threats out of which climate change and environmental pollution come at first place. These new threats are posing new kind of risks and dangers to a nation's sovereignty and stability. Sometimes climate change has turned out to be a threat multiplier in politically unstable countries. Because of its potential of disrupting the security of a country, the issue of securitization of climate change has come into limelight. This paper will highlight the various issues, concerns surrounding the debate on 'securitization of climate change' keeping India and China in focus as these countries are at the forefront to oppose the move to securitize climate change.

Keywords: Climate Change, Securitization, Developed and Developing countries, India, China.

*Research Scholar, Panjab University, Chandigarh, India

Introduction

The traditional concept of risk and danger is undergoing a change due to the emergence of new kinds of risks. Now it's not only the nation states poking into each other affairs and posing threat to the other nations. Now the new sub regional and local level actors are emerging which are posing new kind of risks and dangers to a nation's sovereignty and stability. This risk can be from NGOs, local governments, business sector, civil society lobby and any other actor having political motives. Then there are some soft risks which have the equal potential to disrupt the political stability of the country

These include new threats of poverty, human rights, environmental rights, labor issues etc. The most recent example of these threats leading to political violence is the Arab spring. This movement was not the result of direct government's intervention but it started as a result of high food prices. The rising food prices were the driving force behind this movement which raised the anger and frustration level of the people and they decided to resort to protests and violence. Now the competition for the finite natural resources and their changing pattern of their availability due to climate change is increasing and this will have an impact on the future conflicts among the nations and within the nations thus impacting the geopolitical landscape of the world. Climate change is also another 'soft risk' which can often ignite the spark of protest imbedded deep inside the people (Andrew, 2014)

This paper will highlight the fact that how climate change is being securitized by many especially the developed world for their own selfish interests without giving a thought to the consequences it will have. No doubt climate change have many security implications but completely securitizing it and involving military into this issue has become a topic of discussion at the highest levels of decision making in almost all the countries specially India and China as it will have major repercussions for these countries.

Securitization of Climate Change: Issues, Concerns and Implications

Now-days securitization of climate change has becomes a hot topic for debate at the highest echo leans of the governments so it becomes important to understand how countries are reacting to this new dynamics of linking climate change with security. Even after 60 years of adoption of UN declaration of human rights on 10th December, 1948, human rights are being violated in one form or the other. Now besides the traditional threats of war, nuclear bombs, state intervention, armed conflicts, human beings are facing new types of threats out of which threat of environmental pollution and climate change comes at the first place. This crisis of environmental degradation besides impacting the environment infringes the basic human right of the individuals which is right to non threatening environment. So it becomes important to understand the linkage between environment and the human rights in the face of degrading environmental condition in the present times. A degraded environment does not go well with the fullest enjoyment of other socio-economic rights. (Postiglione, 2010)

Even the IPCC report clearly mentioned that climate change impacts will lead to displacement of millions of people especially among those people with high exposure to extreme weather events and lacking resources to deal with it. This is more so in the case of developing countries where people are highly exposed to the dangers of climate change because of that region's higher vulnerability and their government's less capacity to handle such crisis. Along with poverty and economic crisis the situation may become worse leading to violent conflicts. (IPCC, 2014a)

The executive director of the United Nations Environmental Programme (UNEP) once reported that "as many as 50 million people could become environmental refugees" if the world did not act to support sustainable development. (Bates, 2002)

Then in 2006, British Defense Secretary John Reid warned, "Global climate change and dwindling natural resources are combining to increase the likelihood of violent conflict over land, water and energy. Climate change will make scarce resources, clean water, viable agricultural land even scarcer—and this will make the emergence of violent conflict more, rather than less, likely." This statement is a clear reflection of what should be expected in the future due to the impacts of climate change. Now the world leaders are rising to the fact that environmental factors along with resource scarcity will add to the stress posed by climate change thus leading towards instability and violent conflict in the near future. The European Security Strategy noted, "Climate change will aggravate competition for natural resources, and likely increase conflict and migratory movements in various regions". (Drexhage, 2007)

So the Defense and Political authorities around the world have started looking at climate change as posing serious threat to the national and international security. It is believed that armed forces being the respectable wing of the government, their active involvement will make the people take interest in this issue thus raising the awareness level of the people. Though China has openly accepted the security implications of climate change but it is totally against placing climate change under the UN Security Council for discussion. China along with India has totally opposed this view. India is strictly against linking climate change with security as for both these countries it is developmental issue rather that security issue. (Lobe, 2013)

So climate change has become a security issue for many countries of the world. This has led some countries to involve those actors in the climate change debate who are involved in the national security of the country- the top most being the armed forces. They believe that climate change will have serious policy implications so in public concern it becomes important to include climate change in the national security issues. Though at present we don't have much knowledge regarding the impact of climate change on role of armed forces, but there is a need for planning for the future in this regard. There are few countries where military has openly taken interest on the climate change issues and its security implications but there are many countries where climate change and military are kept separate. In these countries army is discouraged from taking active part in the climate change discussions at least publicly. (Brzoska, 2012)

China provides a perfect example of those countries where climate change has not reached the army. There is no denying fact that Chinese army is well aware of security implication of climate change on its role, operational demands, logistics and other installations but the public discussions are prohibited and army's role is limited to relief operations and tree planting. These limits have been set by political authorities of China who want army to toe the official line which is that climate change is a development issue not a security issue. The active participation of army in security challenges of climate change debates may undermine the official position. (Ibid)

So the fears of "militarization of climate change" for the time being have not come true in all the cases. The IDSA Working Group on Security Implications of Climate Change for India also felt that while it would be in India's interest to oppose the securitization of climate change, but at the same time it should not ignore its likely security dimensions. It highlighted the point that it that climate change, energy security and economic growth cannot be studied in isolation. So India should work towards those strategies which will help in energy efficiency as well as help in climate change mitigation too. Like energy efficiency in transport, household and industrial sector will not only save energy but also improve air quality, reducing green house gases in the atmosphere in a way working in the direction of climate change mitigation.

This study made a point that not only the climate change impacts on army should be studied but also the armed forces activities impact on climate change. (IDSA, 2009). There are many ways climate change will impact working of armed forces. As we will face the problem of environmental refugees[42], the navy will be called upon to have a check on the influx of migrants through the sea route.

Then the increase in tropical cyclones storms and other extreme activities will increase the search and rescue activities of the navy. Influx of migrants will have many latent implications like sanitation, hygiene and spread of infectious diseases. Rise in sea level can have significant impact on the navy establishments on the sea shore which may lead relocating the establishments. This becomes even tougher because armed forces installations are always situated at strategic and sensitive areas requiring large mass of land so relocation is likely to be a big problem. This will be a big problem for Chinese and Indian military establishments as these are located on the shores of densely populated cities. (Ghosh, 2013)

Melting of Himalayan glaciers and erratic pattern of rainfall may lead to change in the army deployment pattern too in the Himalayas thus affecting the army establishments near Indo-Pak and Indo-China border especially in the disputed region of Siachen glacier where the glaciers have been melting. These excessive melting of glaciers and excessive rainfall may increase the difficulty level of troop movements to a great extent as arranging helipads and logistics becomes a herculean task. So all this calls for change in tactical and strategically approaches.

Besides this weapons and their platforms also face increase in tear and wear due to changing weather conditions. In order to reduce the impact of armed forces on climate change, in case of the Navy, ships with reduced carbon footprint and in case of army and air force all installations and weapons with carbon efficiency need to be designed and constructed without compromising with their ability to strike. Besides this ships also require to have greater sea-keeping ability for higher sea states and

---

[42] UNEP researcher Essam El-Hinnawi first defined environmental refugees as: those people who have been forced to leave their traditional habitat, temporarily or permanently, because of a marked environmental disruption (natural and/or triggered by people) that jeopardized their existence and/or seriously affected the quality of their life. By 'environmental disruption' in this definition is meant any physical, chemical, and/or biological changes in the ecosystem (or resource base) that render it, temporarily or permanently. (Bates, D.C, 2002)

prolonged extreme weather operations. As mentioned in above points regarding the climate change effects on health of its citizens, this may require more and more involvement of army relief operations, with medical help from the army topping the list. (Ibid)

The entire Indian Ocean Region, especially South Asia, has witnessed extreme weather events in great numbers during the last few decades which in turn has affected many people's lives and livelihood in this region. World Bank has reported human causalities of around 230,000 and economic damage of around US$ 45 billion. Because of climate change the intensity and frequency of natural disasters will increase thus demanding the deployment of armed forces personnel for humanitarian assistance on a large scale. The whole doctrine of warfighting will be changed as weather support is critical for various kind of operations like aerial operations, reconnaissance, para-dropping missions, transport operations, search and rescue and combating but with climate change increase in extreme weather events will affect the implementation and operationlizing all these tactics. (Ibid)

Another interesting thing is melting of snow in Arctic Ocean will be beneficial for China as it will give China access to pacific ocean and warm ports. Then in the ocean region navy is also concerned about how changed climate will shape the Indian Ocean in the context of maritime boundaries issue, exclusive economic zone, port operations, shallow water operations for submarines and naval tactics. The Indian and Chinese already in the race of accessing more and more energy resources will try to outdo each other to increase their influence in the Indian Ocean Region (IOR), which is of utmost strategic importance to them for security of energy supplies. Climate change will also change the dynamics of the IOR. (Sharma, 2009).

Food has been and it still works as a trigger to any kind of protests and revolution. From the times of French and Russian revolution to the Arab spring of recent times, it is a fact that unless and until food is affordable people can tolerate even the worst of regimes but when food prices cross the redline, it means it goes beyond the toleration level then they get together and rise against the government very soon. If we can't say that climate change was the dominant factor leading to the rise of people in 2010 and 2011 but we can't ignore the fact that even if not a dominant factor, it worked as a threat multiplier. Another reason was the cross country effects of globalization as one event happened in one corner of the world can have impact on the nation on the other corner of the world. Same goes with climate change as Climate change impacts know no boundaries.

A regional climate change event can have global impacts and globalization has made the whole world even more integrated. For example drought in China and Russia had an impact on the wheat supply of the whole world. This wheat shortage in turn increased the prices by leaps and bounds in Egypt, the world's largest wheat importer. Even the effects of tsunami were not confined just to the epicenter but were truly cross border. (Ibid)

Then another reason fueling political instability can be the use and dependence on fossil fuels. The debiting effects of excessive use of fossil fuels are a well known fact now as energy resources have always been a dominant reason for political instability for such a long time. For example oil politics of the middle east in 1970's and 1980's, attack on Iraq for oil, New Great Game going on among various nations in the Central Asia, disputes over South China sea, Arctic and Antarctic resources all are examples of energy being the central point of conflict between various countries. With the increase in population, situation will get worse as demands for these energy resources will increase but supply will not be enough to satisfy everybody's needs. When people's basic needs are not fulfilled it creates a perfect storm triggering civil unrest. So we can say that climatic factors are not the decisive factors but they obviously add to the already complex and burdened socio economic and political system. (Ibid)

These food and fossil fuel problem will be quite prominent in the case of India and China as both will be facing shortage of food and fuel supply as a result of increase in demand and the increasing growth rates of their economy. This has been explained by points mentioned above under the topic impact of climate change on agriculture.

Then the other issue of importance is the kind of government i.e. type of political system in a country because that also determines the environmental condition and environmental rights provided to the people. A special focus now days have been shifted towards relationship between environmental concerns and the democracy. This becomes all the more important in the case of India and China as both are having different kind of political system. One is working democracy with multi party and secret ballot system and the other is an authoritarian government with one party in control for quite a long time. The linkage between democracy and environmentalism has been established strongly as both are mutually reinforcing.

According to Mason (1999), "A democratic determination of collective choices requires necessary ecological preconditions, while only a socially inclusive environmentalism justifies long term public support." This idea has been implemented in the present day concept of Green State. The basic question that arises is that when faced with the situation of extreme pressure because of environmental problems, what kind of actions will be taken by the government of that day? So out of these two possible strategies may be adopted. One will of course be by a benign and considerate government thinking of some hopeful antidote to the present day environmental concerns and the other one being an authoritarian government leading a very strict control over the ecology and environment and maintaining a strict rationing system. (Mason, 1999).

These two represent the case study of India and China. India is the country with great commercial prospects, has a population of 1.2 billion with middle class growing at a significant rate and will continue to do so in the future with more and more increase in their buying power. But this growth has come at a great cost of environmental degradation, conspicuous consumption with no waste disposal and treatment facilities, pollution and now days increase in e-pollution. Then there is another problem looming large on the future of India which is the threat of climate change. India is covered with a thick layer of green house gases which are raising the temperature to a great extent and bringing along extreme weather events. According to western countries democracy is the solution of all the problems but then why India is stumbling in the environmental context? Giving voting rights is not enough when people are least bothered to use. In India middle class hardly makes use of their voting rights. In India democracy is the result of a strange confluence of affluent and the impoverished Indians, but without the support of middle class. So, it's not the disenfrenchment but rather political dysfunction that is at the root of India's problems (W.U., 2012).

Indian political system is fraught with so many problems. Then the problems like inequality, environmental degradation, and climate change weak governance and infrastructure worsening the problem beyond contestation. It's high time to bring a change in the system. If India will continue on this path of economic growth without taking any preventive measures then the degradation and exploitation of nature will outweigh the economic growth achieved leading to civil and political unrest. (Ibid)

Now the question is what does China wants to do in the context of climate change?

It's an obvious yes that China is serious in this matter as it cannot afford to put at risk its political stability and legitimacy of the communist party to be in power. Besides this one cannot forget the domestic and international incentives it will get by acting on climate change. Acting on climate change will help in improving the air quality which is most pressing problem China confronts now-days. This is most serious domestic challenge China has to deal with. As the Chinese progress has come by over exploitation of coal which has left its air quality deteriorate over time. This was also one of the reason that China was blamed for human rights violation as non threatening environment is a human right issue so it is a good progress on the crucial issue of human rights. Then the other issue is that the growing pollution levels have started threatening political stability of the communist party. China in the past many years has witnessed lot many mass incidents of protests, demonstrations, unofficial gatherings on the issue of environmental degradation and pollution. So the message is clear that its high time government should do something in this regard otherwise this environmental crisis will turn into an political crisis (West, 2014).

China political structure has been beautifully explained in the work of Jonathan Watts:

"China's political system is neither dictatorship nor democracy. For the environment it contains the worst elements of both. At the top, the state lacks the authority to impose pollution regulations and wildlife conservation laws, while at the bottom citizens lack the democratic tools of a free press, independent courts and elections to defend their land, air and water. The gap in between is filled by local governments, township enterprises, migrant workers and foreign corporations, many of which are focused on economic growth at the expanse of all else. The result is neither red nor green; it is black or gray. Money is concentrated in this bulging middle belt, which is also the main source of corruption and pollution."(Watts, 2010).

Then the issue of sharing water across nations is already very problematic and climate change will further complicate the situation. Melting Himalayan glaciers and erratic rainfall could aggravate tensions between emerging powers of India and China. Then the extreme weather events like draught, heavy rainfalls could place a huge burden on the economy of India, China and Pakistan. The feeling of distrust between India and China is already very high due to clashes of the last five decades and they are already in a race to tap as much water of Himalayas as they can with plans to build more than 400 hydropower projects in the region which will cut the flow of the Himalayan rivers to a great extent without taking into account the impacts of climate change. Other security implications can be due to sea level rise and resultant submergence of land leading to mass scale migration, conflict over economic zones, sea routes, damage to marine biodiversity, reduction in food yields, and rise in temperature as a result rise in infectious diseases leading to civic unrest and sometimes migration. But inspite of all this we all are moving very slow in the direction of climate change mitigation waiting for UN negotiating body to do something in this regard. (Ed King, 2014).

According to Lukas Ruttinger, an author of the report from Adelphi, a German policy think tank stated that it is high time that efforts should be made to reduce as much pressure as we can from climate change having the potential to disturb stability of a nation because "we are already at the limit of what we can manage" (Goering, 2015).

Conclusion

Climate change is essentially a consequence of the industrialization process of the developed countries at the development cost of developing countries. But it is basically these developing countries only which will be hit hard by the changes taking place in the climatic conditions. They are also least capable of dealing with the climate change crisis which makes them more vulnerable as well as more dependent on developed countries. It can be said that developed countries made progress at the expanse of developing countries and today when it's their turn to develop, developed countries by moving away from their responsibility are thus denying the developing countries the right to develop. Huge technological gap between developed and developing countries also make developing countries heavily dependent on the developed countries for the transfer of technology and finances. Now by making climate change a security issue, developed countries want to bring developing countries under the ambit of legally binding emissions cuts. By showing to the world the security of the world is in danger, developed world wants to pressurize developing community to accept legally binding cuts. But this is acceptable to the developing countries and they are bent upon keeping the firewall between the developed and the developing intact as they do not want to compromise with their development.

References

1. Andrew Van Den Born (2014). Adapting to Climate Change: Political Instability, WillisWire, http://blog.willis.com/2014/04/adapting-to-climate-change-political-instability/ Accessed on 9th July, 2015.
2. Bates, D.C. (2002). Environmental Refugees? Analyzing Human Migrations caused by Environmental Change, Population and Environment, 23 (5): 465-477.
3. Brzoska, M. (2012). Climate Change and Military, E- International Relations, http://www.e-ir.info/2012/03/16/climate-change-and-the-military/ Accessed on 14th October, 2013.
4. Drexhage, J. et al. (2007). Climate Change and Foreign Policy- An Exploration of Options for Greater Integration, International Institute for Sustainable Development and Chatham House, https://www.iisd.org/pdf/2007/climate_foreign_policy.pdf. Accessed on 12th January, 2012.
5. Ed King. (2014). Climate Change could lead to China-India conflict, Responding to Climate Change, http://www.rtcc.org/2014/06/11/climate-change-could-lead-to-China-India-water-conflict/ Accessed on 9th March, 2015.
6. Ghosh P.K. (2013). How Prepared is our Military for Climate Change?, Observers Research Foundation,http://www.orfonline.org/cms/sites/orfonline/modules/analysis/AnalysisDetail.html?cmaid=57983&mmacmaid=57984 Accessed on 21st January, 2014.
7. Goering, L. (2015). Climate Pressures threaten Political Stability- Security Experts, Thomson Reuters, U.K. Edition, 24th June, 2015, http://uk.reuters.com/article/2015/06/24/climatechange-security-politics-idUKL8N0ZA2H 220150624Accessed on 18th July, 2015
8. IDSA (2009). Security Implications of Climate Change, Report of the IDSA Working Group, Academic Foundation, http://www.idsa.in/book/SecurityImplicationsofClimateChangeforIndia.html Accessed on 19th February, 2012.
9. IPCC (2014a). Climate Change 2014: Impacts, Adaptation and Vulnerability, Summary for Policy Makers, https://ipcc-wg2.gov/AR5/images/uploads/WG2AR5_SPM_FINAL.pdf. Accessed on 14th December, 2014).

10. Lobe, J. (2013). Climate Change now seen as a Security Threat Worldwide, Inter Press Service, http://www.ipsnews.net/2013/03/climate-change-now-seen-as-security-threat-worldwide/ .Accessed on 25th November, 2014.

11. Mason, M. (1999). Environmental Democracy, UK: Earth Scan Publications, http://samples.sainsburysebooks.co.uk/9781136548253_sample_824235.pdf Accessed on 7th April, 2013.

12. Postiglione, A. (2010). Human Rights and the Environment, International Journal of Human Rights, 14(4): 524-541.

13. Sharma, R. (2009). Changing Climate New Adversary of Indian Armed Forces, India Strategic, http://www.Indiastrategic.in/topstories376.htm

14. W.U. (2012). How Climate Change affects Indian Political Stability.Washington University- Political Review, http://www.wupr.org/2012/12/11/how-climate-change-affects-Indian-political-stability/ Accessed on 8th August, 2013.

15. Watts, J. (2010). When a Billion Chinese Jump, New York: Scribner Publications.

16. West, J. (2014). Here's Why China care more about Climate Change than Congress does? Mother Jones, Environment, http://www.motherjones.com/environment/2014/11/China-obama-climate-deal-pollution-crisis-politics Accessed on 17th March, 2015.

Chapter- XX

Resettlement and Rehabilitation Policy: Issues and Challenges faced by Executors in Context of Climate Change

Kewal Krishan*

Abstract

Environmental problems resulting from human displacement and resettlement and rehabilitation are considered to be secondary impacts of hydro projects. There is a significant gap in knowledge concerning the environmental consequences of resettlement and rehabilitation of the HEP's of Himachal Pradesh Power Corporation Limited. This study examines environmental problems associated with the HEP's resettlement and rehabilitation. On the positive side, countermeasures that are discussed include: engineering works for farmland protection, developing eco-agriculture, reforestation and constructing a green belt in the peripheral zone of the project area, and adjustments to resettlement and rehabilitation policy. During the last few years back, hydroelectric projects in hilly areas have attracted attention concerning the social and environmental impacts that have arisen from such hydroelectric power projects. Construction and operation of dams have always been associated with changes in the social, physical and biological environment. Some of the negative impacts of hydroelectric projects include loss of vegetations, topographical disturbances, changes in rivers flow patterns, involuntary resettlement, health problems, loss of cultural values and marginalization of local people. The impacts due to hydropower development, especially of reservoir and dams are always extensive in term of space. It covers upstream, on site, and downstream areas and surrounding of hydropower plants. The R&R Policy of HPPCL is playing a vital role to mitigate the environmental impacts.

Key words: Environment, Hydro Electric Project, Change, Resettlement and Rehabilitation

---

* Assistant Professor, Department of Sociology, PSR Govt College, Baijnath, Kangra, Himachal Pradesh India

Introduction

Hydropower is using water to power machinery or make electricity. Water constantly moves through a vast global cycle, evaporating from lakes and oceans, forming clouds, precipitating as rain or snow, and then flowing back down to the ocean. The energy of this water cycle, which is driven by the sun, can be tapped to produce electricity or for mechanical tasks like grinding grain. Hydropower uses a fuel-water-that is not reduced or used up in the process. Because the water cycle is an endless, constantly recharging system, hydropower is considered a renewable energy. It is found that water is gold for Himachal Pradesh and Himachal Pradesh is harnessing this for the economic and social development of the state. Himachal Pradesh has more hydro power potential, because of five rivers flowing through it, namely Satluj, Ravi, Beas, Chenab, and Yamuna. Hydro power potential of the order of 23000 MW has identified for the development of Himachal Pradesh and, as Govt. of India has envisaged in its mission power to all, so achievement of this mission it require development of power projects and Himachal Pradesh has planned to harness the vast hydro electric potential in the state with mission to development and prosperity in Himachal Pradesh through power generation, Himachal Pradesh has also committed to harness the water potential with environmental friendly manner.

State has approved Rehabilitation and Resettlement plan for all its projects with its different welfare schemes as a part of the corporate social responsibility, which assists in better livelihood and better welfare of the people in the State. Himachal Pradesh is a mountainous State, located in the North of the country. The State has a diverse topography-high mountain ranges interspersed with deep gorges and valleys to fertile Gangetic plains in its south East. The attitude ranges from 350 meters to 6975 meters bove mean sea level. Himachal Pradesh is blessed with abundant water resources in its five ajor rivers i.e. Chenab, Ravi, Beas, Satluj and Yamuna, which emanate from the western Himalayas and flow through the State. These snow fed rivers and their tributaries carry copious discharge all the year round which can be exploited for power generation. All the rivers basins and its valleys are connected by roads, other communication network and strong base of other social infrastructure like health & education etc. Hydro Electric Power is a critical for the socio-economic development, and efforts at accelerating the rate of economic growth in the new globalised economy. Development of hydro Electric power is essential for the sustainable development of the country. Large untapped hydro potential exists in the Himalayas, which can make a substantial contribution to the total power generation in the country.

The Government of Himachal Pradesh is committed to this onerous task and is doing its best to develop the total hydro power potential of the State, which is to the tune of 23,000MW. Hydropower is the most effective source of energy and has played a major role in the development of modern civilization. This technology has a lot of benefits; it is a renewable source of energy with limited or no emissions of carbon dioxide in comparison to other forms of energy. In addition, hydropower projects can be used for multipurpose use, such as irrigation, fishery, flood control and water supply. All the above mentioned benefits can with appropriate management improve the socio- economic state of local, regional as well as the national level welfare or livelihood condition. Over the past decade or so, hydropower projects around the world have attracted much attention concerning the environmental and social impacts that have arisen from such developments. Construction and operation of dams have always been associated with changes in the physical and biological environment. Adverse effects have more often than not, out-numbered the positive effect. Some of the negative impacts of hydropower include loss of vegetations, changes in river flow patterns and regimes, involuntary resettlement, health problems, loss of cultural values, marginalization of local people, inundating of valuable agricultural land, and drought and severe reduction of flow downstream.

Most hydropower projects in the past have been given much attention regarding the technical design and economic issues of the project rather than their environmental and social impacts. In view of this, there are several issues of environmental impacts, which have not been considered under mitigation measures as should have been done in a proper environmental impact assessment (EIA). However, today, the hydropower industry is in quest for improved project performance. Enhancing the level of energy consumption, particularly in less developed and developing countries, is a global challenge. 20% of world population living in industrialised countries consume 60% of energy and remaining 80% of population have to manage within 40% of total energy. This has obviously resulted in wide disparities between the standard of living and quality of life of high energy consuming countries on the one hand and those who do not have the opportunities of adequate access to energy on the other. It is precisely for this reason that development of different sources of energy and increase in its consumption has become a priority agenda of all the developing countries.

Hydro Power Potential in India

India has a vast untapped resource of HEP. The total hydro potential assessed by CEA is approximately 1, 48,701 MW, of which Economic Potential works out to 84,044 MW at a PLF of 60%. The above Hydro power potential has been assessed by CEA from 845 economically feasible schemes in different river basins with likely annual generation of 600 billion units including seasonal energy variation. As on October 2014, about 49 schemes having an aggregate potential of about 14287MW are under execution for 12th Plan. All India Generating Installed Capacity (MW) (As on October 2014) is (Thermal-70%, Hydro- 15%, Nuclear- 2%, RE Sources- 13%) The percentage of Hydro has come down from 42% in 1970 to 17.49% in 2014-15. With planned addition of 10,897 MW & 12,000 MW by the end of 12th and 13th five year plan respectively, the share of hydro is expected to increase to 25.14%. The long-term goal is to increase the share of hydropower capacity from the present level of 20% to 40% of total Installed Capacity.

Power Shortage in India

In India, though over 100,000 MW of capacity has been added in last 50 years, there is a huge gap between the demand and supply of power. While in the last few years it has marginally reduced, the peaking shortage continues to be over 12% to 13% and the average energy shortage at about 8.8%. Indian power system has an installed capacity of 108,207 MW in May 2003, with hydroelectric accounting for 25%.

Challenges in Hydro Electric Power Development

Hydro Power Projects are Site specific and location disadvantage- Projects are located in far flung areas having very little infrastructure and communication facilities. So it takes at-least 2 days for a normal passenger to reach project sites& if there are multiple landslides, hundreds of vehicles could easily get stuck for days together without access to basic amenities such as food & water. In such conditions, one could easily imagine how difficult it would be to transport project equipment, machinery, etc via such routes. And if by chance there aren't much of landslides, locals / student bodies of neighboring districts and states normally calls Bandhs and block the roads. Lengthy process of preparation of DPR and clearances having uncertainty of time line and shortage of people with clearing agencies. e. g. Land Acquisition, Environment, Forest &Wildlife clearances& Forest Rights Settlement, Project features, layout plan, land requirement and certain environment management plans are required for forest clearance.

Details for a Hydro Electric Project are known after investigations and preparation of DPR and EIA/EMP reports. The biggest problem with such clearances is the dynamic nature of changing requirements for obtaining these clearances. Improper circulation of such dynamic changes to the Project Proponents & general public. Improper circulation/notification of Intermittent changes in law and new notifications. Non adherence to a fixed Guideline/Checklist by Govt. personnel at the lower levels due to their overconfidence of knowledge of clearance process & document requirements, which causes rework in the clearance process.

Thrust on Hydro Power

In the recent years, the Govt. of India has committed quantum jump, in the financial allocation and also by way of other supports so that Hydroelectric projects not only get right priorities but also contribute in an increased way to the future capacity addition programmes of the country. Accordingly, in the 10th Five-Year Plan (year 2002-2007), the target for hydroelectric capacity has been placed 14,393 MW, which is more than the total installed capacity (13,666 MW) created in the last 20 years. The thrust on hydroelectric development is based on the following considerations:

1. Hydroelectric involves a clean process of power generation. Once the projects are constructed, there is no pollution ramification unlike many other power generation technologies and processes.
2. Since it does not suffer from the limitation of inflation on account of fuel consumption, in the long run, it is the most cost-effective option for power supply.
3. In Indian context, where more than 45% of Indian population has yet to have access to electricity at an affordable price, this is an important consideration.
4. Indian power supply system has a peculiar limitation of huge variation between peak and off peak requirements. Management of peak load in an effective manner could be conveniently handled through availability of hydroelectric support.
5. The system at present does suffer from large frequency variations. Better hydro support could address this problem better.
6. Locations of Hydroelectric projects in India are also in areas which need substantial support for their economic development.
7. These areas are North-east, Uttaranchal, Himachal Pradesh and Jammu & Kashmir where more than 80% of potential exists. Developing projects in these areas will spur economic activities and will lead to overall economic development.

In an integrated hydroelectric project – there are many such projects – the schemes involve not only supply of electricity but also provision of drinking water and irrigation. These are important issues in many parts of India. Hydroelectric projects, in many cases, do have the ability to mitigate these problems.

In view of complexity in development of Hydroelectric projects, particularly large ones, emanating from dam height, submergence, ramification of submergence, dam safety, drinking water schemes, irrigation, infrastructure etc., the process of clearances obviously gets linked with multiple agencies and authorities. Short cuts could create problems. Inordinate delays could entail huge cost and therefore unaffordable tariff. Harmonious balance has, therefore, to be struck. Here again, experience of last many decades has brought about a reasonable consensus on how to address this situation.

The process of improvement on this front also continues. Procedures have been streamlined, and they would continue to be streamlined, to see that project development process, prior to commencement of main plant construction, by way of permission and clearances is made faster. Ministry of Environment and Forest, Ministry of Power and other authorities continue to search for better solutions. Construction time is another area of concern, which needs to be compressed. Large projects have taken inordinately long time. There are two major aspects which could make a difference – one is relating to construction management techniques starting from planning to monitoring and another relates to construction technology. Here again, there are recent examples of making substantial improvement on both the fronts. Some of the projects which have been sanctioned in the recent months are being targeted to be completed within 4-5 years. Based on the benchmarks which have been established, the techniques and technologies would be further improved. Choice of technology will have to be given serious consideration. For the next few years, project development agencies are being advised to target 4 years for completion of small projects, 4 ½ years for medium size projects and 5 years for large projects. These schedules are significant improvement over the past performance. After these results are achieved, the norms would be further improved.

Challenges faced by the Hydro Electric Power Projects

Identification of Land for Compensatory Afforestation (CA)

In accordance with Forest Conservation Act, 1980, CA shall be done over double the area for diversion on Degraded or non-forest land. Thus, finding a large non-forest area or degraded forest area for CA in the State is very difficult & time consuming for the developer. Problems of non-availability of Grid Power during Construction phase of Project, Creation of new sanctuaries and national parks by Forest Department without consulting the Hydro Power Department of State. Security concerns – Vast hydro potential of the country is available in the areas affected by insurgency and militant problems. The law and order problem in such areas lead to delay in execution of the project as well as cost over runs.

Inadequate Infrastructure

As Hydro Projects are located in interior far flung areas, hilly terrain, landslides, hill slope collapses, road blocks particularly during monsoon season because of heavy rains and unprecedented floods cause severe setbacks in construction leading to time and cost over-runs. Non-availability of access road to Project site – The cost of access road, if included within the Project infrastructure, results in increase in overall project cost. Apart from poor road connectivity, the region has extremely poor or no mobile connectivity.

No Objection Certificate

Under Indian Constitution, water is a state subject. No Objection Certificate is required from each downstream state for getting sanction even for run-of-the-river projects which is a time consuming job. If all major rivers are made National resources and its water is distributed by Centre keeping requirement of States in mind, the time could be saved. Inter-state issues are not limited to State Govt. but also the local populous.

Public Awareness

There is inadequate public involvement during the project planning stage conducted by the Government Agencies and limited or no effort is taken to gain public acceptance through public involvement and transparency. Geological surprises: The features of the hydro electric projects, being site specific, depend on the geology, topography and hydrology at the site. The construction time of a hydro project is greatly influenced by the geology of the area and its accessibility. It is, therefore, essential that state-of-the-art investigation and construction techniques are adopted to minimize geological risks as well as the overall gestation period of hydro projects. Even if, extensive investigation using new techniques of investigations are undertaken, an element of uncertainty remains in the sub-surface geology and the geological surprises during actual construction cannot be ruled out.

Hydrological Challenges

River discharge observations are made available to the developers on pretext of confidentiality to the concerned government department only after the approval of the Ministry of Water Resources, GoI. Considerable time is lost in getting the approvals and the data. Storage Vs ROR Projects – There is a lot of controversy in the development of Hydro Projects as Storage vs R-O-R. Most of the distress caused by storage schemes occurs in the hill states whereas the benefits are largely in the states in the plains which are perceived to be more prosperous. Therefore, hill states prefer R-O-R schemes. For the maximization of benefits in a basin, the judicious blend of both type of schemes (Storage/ROR) needs to be considered.

Land Acquisition by Projects

The guidelines of LA Act, 1984 were applied in its nature and practice in all irrigation projects. After independence the needs of resettlement and rehabilitation policy were diverted toward compensation issues. Though, this act made the provision of compensation for the loss of land, standing crops and house structures but neglects the policy guidelines for resettlement and rehabilitation. All these projects acquired lands from the people in the name of public purpose. It is also true that the natural disaster due to recurrent floods brings huge economic loss and disruption in human habitations during rainy seasons in the state. The people living in the downstream suffer a lot. The major dam projects could check these problems to a large extent. Thus, these projects protect the state from huge economic loss and damages every year. These projects also provide irrigation facilities to the downstream people. It also generates low cost electricity through hydroelectricity projects. Thus, no doubt the state as a whole and the people from the downstream were largely benefitted. But to what extent the people who lost their lands, lived in the upstream of the dam projects and resettled in faraway places from the projects are benefitted is a matter of question.

The purpose of projects and the purpose of the people those who lost the lands for the projects are not similar. Was there any mechanism to address the issues as what happened to the people because of whom the dam projects came into being in the state? In fact, none of the irrigation projects had adequate social impact assessment (SIA) and environmental impact assessment (EIA) before actual land acquisition took place in the affected villages. It was a deliberate strategy adopted by the irrigation department while acquiring lands throughout the state in the past. In the name of five year plans, economic development and funding agency like WB the state succumbed to the capitalistic path of development over the years. Since none of the projects could ever expose the legal guidelines to the land oustees as how land acquisition would take place almost the land oustees hardly aware of land acquisition process in the past (Pandey,1998). Further, the displaced people hardly have had prior informed consent on whether they would like to support or oppose the land acquisition. The processes of land acquisition under LA Act, 1894 such as notification, objections and evacuations are immaterialized for the large section of oustees than what it was supposed to be there. There are cases where the oustee knew that it was pro-project and anti-people but they could not help except surrendering to the repression of LA Act guidelines operationalized by the government authority. Thus, a win-win prospect between projects and the affected people were not visualized at the time of land acquisition for projects. Land Acquisition Act compulsory acquisition under section 17 (4).

The New Land Acquisition Act

There is 'The Right to Fair Compensation and Transparency in Land Acquisition, Rehabilitation and Resettlement Act, 2013'. The Act, which replaces the century-old Land Acquisition Act, 1894, proposes a unified legislation for acquisition of land and adequate rehabilitation mechanisms for all affected persons.

Key Features of this Act are as under:-

1. Consent of 80 per cent of landowners required in case of land acquired by private companies and 70 per cent for land acquired under Public Private Partnership (PPP) model for public purpose.
2. Compensation up to four times the market value in rural areas and twice in urban areas.
3. Mandatory Social Impact Analysis (SIA) to assess nature of public interest and estimation of socio-economic impact prior to acquisition for all projects except irrigation projects.
4. Land cannot be vacated until the entire compensation is awarded to the affected parties.
5. No irrigated multi-cropped land shall be acquired under this Act.
6. Companies can lease the land instead of purchasing it.
7. If the acquired land has been unused for 5 years from the date of the possession, then it shall be returned to the original owner or owners or their legal heirs or to the Land Bank. If any unused acquired land is transferred to another individual within five years of it being acquired, 40% of the appreciated land value shall have to be shared amongst the original land owners or their legal heirs.
8. The award or agreement made under this Act shall be exempt from stamp duty and Income Tax and fees.
9. The Act had a retrospective clause saying compensation must be paid in line with the proposed law for ongoing projects (except irrigation projects) where the money has not been disbursed or possession of land has not been taken up.
10. In every project those losing land and belonging to the SC or ST will be provided land equivalent to land acquired or two and a one-half

acres, whichever is lower (this is higher than in the case of non-SC/ST affected families).The land for land clause has been relaxed for irrigation projects, where land is not available.
11. Government also moved the amendment to specify that either compensation or Rehabilitation and Resettlement (R&R) will be given to farmers whose land is acquired for irrigation projects

Resettlement and Rehabilitation (R&R)

Following are some provisions in R&R plan of Himachal Pradesh:

- Plot of 250 Square
- Built up house 150 squares
- Colony with basic amenities
- Land for cultivation to needy
- Loss of benefit from forest land
- 100 unit of free power
- Transitional Subsistence Allowance 25x12 days to those who shift house or livelihood
- Employment to each landless family subject to suitability and availability or 1000 days minimum wages
- Annuity policy to vulnerable Rs. 1000 PM for 10 years
- Secondary employment
- Medical fund
- LADA and LADF 1.5% of total project cost
- For infrastructural development 80% to Panchayats based on number of PAF
- Land acquired and extent of underground works, 20% for common works
- Direct benefits like Scholarships
- ITI sponsorship
- Medicine
- Books
- Agriculture and related inputs
- Tours and exposure visits
- Sports and cultural activities

These provisions relating to R&R under this Act shall apply when (a) Private companies acquire/purchases land through private negotiations which is equal to or more than such limits in rural & urban areas, as may be prescribed by the appropriate government in accordance with provisions of Section 46 & (b)

Private companies requests appropriate Govt. for acquisition of a part of an area so prescribed for a public purpose. Affected families include land owner, farm labour, tenants, sharecroppers and workers on the piece of land for three years prior to the acquisition.

Compensation includes

- House
- Land for Land
- Choice of Annuity/ Employment
- Subsistence grant for one year
- Transportation grant
- Grant against Cattle shed/Petty shops
- One time grant to Artisans/Small traders/others
- Fishing Rights and One time Resettlement allowance

Rehabilitation & Resettlement

Rehabilitation & Resettlement (R&R) of Project Affected People (PAP) is another major issue affecting the smooth execution of Hydro electric projects particularly where in submergence areas, the number of project affected people are large. Experience of last several years has brought about sufficient amount of understanding on the subject. The expectations of people, local authorities and project development agencies are being synthesized so that there is greater degree of acceptability of the system of R&R. Govt. of India is contemplating a national policy on R&R for Project Affected People. In the meantime, Ministry of Power of Govt. of India and its public sector undertakings are coordinating their efforts with the State Govts. So that R&R issues are adequately addressed and project implementation is smooth. In cases, where large projects are involved, specific monitoring mechanism has been put in place at senior most level in the Govt. so that proper implementation of R&R plans by project agencies is done in letter and spirit. Having capacity to generate the HEP from the rivers and its tributaries, large number of hydropower projects are undergoing in whole state of H.P. Hydropower development in the district is a big source of economy for the state and its help in the growth of economic conditions of the state. Development of HEPs in the area needs sustainable development by maintaining balance between the quantity of development and quality of environment. Sincere efforts are required to ensure that the developments do not disturb the delicate equilibrium of the fragile area. The deforestation rate is decreasing and hydropower projects development in the study area achieves the target of renewable energy and growth of power and the construction works are carried out in sustainable manner maintaining balance with the environment and natural resources of the area and if the degradation of environment is there, this is negligible. Loss of vegetation, flora and fauna is being disturbed in limited spheres, soil erosion and deforestation has been increased after initiation of HEPs. The sustainable development of the area is not possible, without keeping balance between development and preservation of natural resources.

Conclusion

No doubt hydropower projects have made an important contribution to the human development and the benefits derived from them have been considerable, but along with this such developments had altered and diverted the natural river flows, affecting existing rights and access of the locals to water and resulting in significant impacts on livelihood and the environment. The researcher is not against the installation of power projects but these must be eco-friendly and sustainable in nature and there must be sustainable improvement of human welfare. This means a significant advancement of human development, which is economically viable, socially equitable and environmentally sustainable. If the dams are the best way to achieve this goal, then deserve the full support of the researcher. The local issues must be taken into consideration properly and with true spirit, not in paper and must not be engulfed by the red tapism of the Indian bureaucracy. The policies should be framed in such a way by visiting local sites so that environment can be maintained and the potential capacity of water can be utilized properly.

Before sanctioning any other power project the World Commission on Dams recommendations must be taken into consideration, which has stressed four fundamental values regarding the dam building, these are; equity, efficiency, participatory decision-making, sustainability and accountability. Everything can be generated but water cannot. Once it is lost it will be lost forever, it cannot be generated. So the need of the hour is to use this wonderful gift of god to meet our need not to greed. We must keep ourselves away from the natural cycle of the water and should not disturb it in the name of so called development. We must keep in mind that Nature can live without man but man cannot live without nature.

It can be conclude that the LA Act and R&R policy are arbitrarily should be used by government and project authorities for the construction of dam projects in country. Unfortunately, many displaced families in the country have been suffering in the resettlement sites due to inappropriate compensation, resettlement and rehabilitation guidelines as and when developed by the government. It is because of the impact of colonial legacy of land acquisition Act in State. However, each and every case of development induced displacement is unique and needs separate strategy for the rehabilitation and resettlement of the displaced people. In this regard, the R&R policy in the state over the decades though has been progressive but the history of its application has been not up to the mark. Thus, the actual history of compensation, rehabilitation and resettlement needs to be addressed for a better future. It is an open secret that the replacement cost of displacement cannot be entertained by the government authority as because they tend to compensate against displacement in order to actualize the project but not to develop the affected people. This bureaucratic mindset has to be changed for the betterment of all stakeholders of the projects. Unfortunately, though past experiences help improving the next policy but could not help it to be applied for the victimized displaced and affected people for all the time to come.

References

1. Environmental Impact Assessment Report of Tidong Hydroelectric power project in Himachal Pradesh, Unpublished Report.
2. Bose, P., Pattnaik, B. K., and Mittal, M. (2001) Development of socio-economic impact assessment methodology applicable to large water resource projects in India. International Journal of Sustainable Development & World Ecology
3. Central Electricity Authority, Ministry of Power (2006). Baseline Database for the Indian Power Sector User Guide.
4. Government of Himachal Pradesh, 11th five year plan 2007-2012, Himachal Pradesh Development Report, Planning Commission.
5. B.Terminski, Development-Induced Displacement and Resettlement: Theoretical Frameworks and Current Challenges (Geneva, 2013)
6. W. Fernandes and V. Paranjpye (eds.) Rehabilitation Policy and Law in India: A Right to Livelihood. (New Delhi: Indian Social Institute, 1997)
7. Government of India, Right to Fair Compensation and Transparency in Land Acquisition, Rehabilitation and Resettlement Act, (Government of India, Lok Sabha, 2013)
8. S. K. Mishra, Development, Displacement and Rehabilitation of Tribal
9. Development, Displacement and Rehabilitation of Tribal People: A Case Study of Odisha, (Journal of Social Sciences, 6 (3), 2002)
10. Ramesh Chandra., Bottlenecks in Hydro Power Development.
11. Srivastava A.B.L., Hydro Power in India: The bottlenecks, NHPC Ltd.
12. CEA website
13. BBMB website

www.ingramcontent.com/pod-product-compliance
Lightning Source LLC
Chambersburg PA
CBHW071149290526
45788CB00001BA/69